P9-CFJ-888

MAKING GROUPS EFFECTIVE

Alvin Zander

MAKING
GROUPS
EFFECTIVE

Second Edition

Jossey-Bass Publishers • San Francisco

Substantial discounts on bulk quantities of Jossey-Bass books are available to corporations, professional associations, and other organizations. For details and discount information, contact the special sales department at Jossey-Bass Inc., Publishers. (415) 433-1740; Fax (415) 433-0499.

For international orders, please contact your local Paramount Publishing International office.

Manufactured in the United States of America. Nearly all Jossey-Bass books and jackets are printed on recycled paper that contains at least 50 percent recycled waste, including 10 percent postconsumer waste. Many of our materials are also printed with either soy- or vegetable-based ink; during the printing process these inks emit fewer volatile organic compounds (VOCs) than petroleum-based inks. VOCs contribute to the formation of smog.

Library of Congress Cataloging-in-Publication Data

Zander, Alvin Frederick, date.
    Making groups effective / Alvin Zander. — 2nd ed.
        p.   cm. — (The Jossey-Bass management series)
    Includes bibliographical references and index.
    ISBN 0-7879-0009-5
    1. Nonprofit organizations—Management. 2. Directors of corporations. 3. Corporate governance. I. Title. II. Series.
HD62.6.Z36 1994
658'.048—dc20   94-18129
                                                         CIP

FIRST EDITION
HB Printing   10 9 8 7 6 5 4 3 2 1   *Code 9487*

The Jossey-Bass
Management Series

CONTENTS

ix

Part Two: Effective Group Members

**Part Three:
Working Effectively with Other Groups**

PREFACE

Every group has special qualities — some desirable, others unwanted. Examples of desired group properties include sensible agreements about group procedures, effective methods of making decisions, sound strategies for resolving conflicts, easy flow of communication among members, realistic group goals, pride in the group's achievements, harmony among members, and strong cohesiveness. *Making Groups Effective* is about the steps members take to create such characteristics in their unit.

   Research in group dynamics has been conducted for over fifty years, yet little effort has been made to say how its results can be put to practical use. Researchers' reports on their work usually do not address everyday group problems, and most writers on improving groups pay little attention to research findings. Textbook writers are more interested in results than in the application of research. The writings of some social scientists can be valuable to members of a group because these persons, like the practitioners, try to determine the causes of certain group conditions and the effects of these conditions on an organization. Where reliable explanations of such issues exist, it is possible to deduce which procedures will create what kinds of effects in natural settings.

In this book I consider important qualities of groups and describe how students of groups explain the sources of these qualities on the basis of their research. I use the explanations offered by scientists to describe how responsible members can generate favorable conditions or avoid unfavorable conditions in their groups. I attempt, in brief, to summarize research on what gives rise to causes and conditions within groups and to show members how they can use such explanations to understand events within their own groups.

Notes on the Second Edition

An earlier edition of *Making Groups Effective* was published in 1982. During the intervening years, research on group psychology has steadily progressed. New problems have been investigated, new techniques of research have been invented, and new explanations of these events have been developed. Initially, this work was done almost entirely by social psychologists. Nowadays, studies of groups are also conducted in settings where the scholars are interested in problems of management, government, public health, social work, psychotherapy, education, or behavior within large organizations.

In preparing this second edition, I have attempted to create a book that reflects these changes. Although the original approach is basically unaltered, I have made many changes to accommodate new findings or to round out particular topics. As before, I used only those results from scientific writings that help in the creation of desirable conditions within social units. I did not aspire to a complete coverage of knowledge about group dynamics, because I believed it was necessary to omit work that has no practical value in active group life or does not suggest useful behaviors by members. I chose main topics for which a reasonable amount of research has been done on group behavior. I did not begin with a list of problems members meet in making their groups effective and then hunt for results of research that would help members deal with such issues. The central subjects are ones on which students of groups have conducted research and on which we have some integrated knowledge.

A good theory suggests sound practices. I tried to summarize such practical suggestions in these pages. To complete discussion of a topic or to fill a hiatus between theory and application where it was necessary, I drew on my own experience. But even there I stayed closer to issues discussed by researchers than to problems raised by practitioners.

I wrote these chapters for persons responsible for the fate of their unit and required to plan and act on its behalf. These people work in responsible positions and want their groups to do well, whether the group be active in business, government, education, the military, social welfare, professional life, or leisure time activities. These are innovative men and women who are ready to consider ways of improving their group and of adopting practices that promise to help their organization.

Making Groups Effective does not offer readers step-by-step methods for doing their jobs better. Instead, it describes why certain conditions arise in groups and how participants can create particular ones in their unit if they wish to do so.

Overview of the Contents

The opening chapter considers the characteristics of a strong group. Chapters Two and Three discuss several basic problems: choosing realistic goals for a group and strengthening members' desires that their group be successful. Chapter Four examines how members make decisions most effectively, followed by a review, in Chapter Five, of the ways communication among members can be helped to flow smoothly in informal relationships and group discussions. Chapter Six examines how members establish rules and standards for their group and keep these alive. Chapter Seven discusses how harmony among members can be fostered and how a conflict among those in a group is settled. Chapters Eight and Nine consider how a member becomes influential within a unit and how one's social power can be strengthened. In Chapter Ten I describe how members cope with the greater power of persons in their social body. In Chapter Eleven I look into the origin of conflicts between groups and into the conditions that cause such events to worsen; in Chapter Twelve I note a variety of ways to resolve intergroup conflicts. In the final chapter I suggest ways members can evaluate their group's performance and decide how to improve its operations.

An in-text citation of a published article or book refers to the appropriate item in the References at the end of the book. I used such citations only where I believed readers might like to learn more about a given topic and where the reference is worth perusal for that purpose. I did not cite references to show published sources for what I say — that would have required too many distracting citations. Useful suggestions for additional reading are at the end of each chapter.

Walnut Creek, California   ALVIN ZANDER
June 1994

THE AUTHOR

ALVIN ZANDER has been a student of group behavior for many years. From 1948 to 1980, he was program director in the Research Center for Group Dynamics at the University of Michigan. For twenty of those years he served as director of that center. As professor of psychology and of educational psychology, he has taught courses in the social psychology of groups. During his last seven years at Michigan, he served as the associate vice president for research. Zander is now retired from academic duties.

Zander earned his B.S. degree (1936) in general science, his M.S. degree (1937) in public health, and his Ph.D. degree (1942) in psychology—all at the University of Michigan. He developed an interest in group behavior while employed as a graduate student during the Great Depression, helping small towns develop social services that they could not afford to obtain from professional consultants. After a postdoctoral year with Kurt Lewin at the University of Iowa (1942) and nearly three years as a clinical psychologist and a commissioned officer in the U.S. Public Health Service during World War II, Zander returned to the University of Michigan.

Zander has done research on the relations among people who differ in their ability to influence others, on the impact of group membership on a person's self-regard, on the nature of identification between people, on the sources of members' motivation to help their group succeed, and on the origins of a group's goals. He is coauthor of *Group Dynamics Research and Theory* (1968). He is author of *Motives and Goals in Groups* (1971), a presentation of results of a program of investigations; *Groups at Work* (1977), a discussion of needed research in group dynamics; *Making Groups Effective* (first edition, 1982), a guide to fostering the development of well-functioning groups; *The Purposes of Groups and Organizations* (1985), an essay on the origins and objectives of social entities; *Effective Social Action by Community Groups* (1990), an examination of how citizens generate changes in their towns through group effort; and *Making Boards Effective: The Dynamics of Nonprofit Governing Boards* (1993).

MAKING GROUPS EFFECTIVE

1

INTRODUCTION: WHAT MAKES A GROUP EFFECTIVE?

A group is a set of persons who interact with and depend on each other — who collaborate and behave in ways that suit mutual expectations. A number of individuals engaged in the same activity — walking down Fifth Avenue, traveling on a sightseeing tour, picking apples in an orchard, working in a personnel department, or attending a lecture — are not necessarily a group. They can become one if they talk with one another and do things where each can count on the help of colleagues.

A collection of persons is a weak group if members are primarily interested in their own accomplishments within that assembly, are not concerned with the activities of fellow members, see others as rivals, and are often absent from meetings. How can conditions be arranged so that collected individuals become a strong group? What qualities must a group have so that it will be strong enough to move effectively toward the body's goals? First, they must be brought together and organized.

The Formation of Groups

Individuals create a group, with the help of organizers, when they develop a mission that collaboration can help them meet.

1

Groups have different purposes, but all are alike in one respect: they intend to be beneficial to members, nonmembers, or both.

At least four circumstances exist before organizers and persons they recruit become interested in developing a new unit. When any of these states are not present, developers are less likely to create a group (Zander, 1985).

1. *Conditions in the environment or in the lives of potential joiners are unsatisfactory or suggest an opportunity for desirable change.* Organizers realize that a situation is not what it might be and that something could be done to improve things. Examples of such conditions are fear among would-be members, displeasure with activities of larger organizations, personal problems, a too-heavy physical task, boredom, opportunities for starting a business, need for formalizing an informal body, or services needed by society or individuals.

An unfavorable situation often encourages organizers to bring people together so they can respond to that circumstance. Examples of such gatherings are familiar. College students feel that teaching on their campus is not "relevant" and should be modified to deal more closely with problems of the day, so they organize to pressure the faculty toward changes in the curriculum. Citizens create groups to address air pollution, unpaved streets, nuclear fallout, unsafe automobiles, dishonest pharmaceutical firms, or research in genetic engineering. Workers join hands to protest distressful aspects of their jobs (Zander, 1990).

Some groups come about because persons in the community need counseling, food, clothing, fun, or housing. Other groups are created to provide a service: repairing computers, selling homemade cookies, guiding tourists, marketing a cure for poison ivy, or caring for gardens. Organizers create groups to solve problems: a manager appoints a committee because the firm needs new products or a better policy on family care; parents convene because their adolescent children need clear rules all parents will enforce alike.

A group is developed, in some instances, because a task is too big for one worker and can only be completed, or done better, if taken up by several colleagues. Teams created for such reasons are assembly lines, construction crews, restaurant staffs, battle parties, or orchestras. A group is more willing to tackle an unpleasant assignment, moreover, if several persons approach the task together. We see examples of such joint support in meetings of self-help groups whose members assist one another to reduce their consumption of alcohol or food. Joggers last longer if they trot as a crowd. Sets of college students help one another in preparing for an examination.

2.   *Organizers conceive of a more satisfactory state of affairs.* Recognition that something should be changed is not enough to inspire persons toward organizing. Developers must also have ideas about what could be done and how conditions could be different and beneficial. The group purposes we just noted were conceived by their initiators as a more satisfactory state than had existed. The invention of a purpose, as we shall see in later pages, is an intellectual procedure influenced by social problem solving, personal preferences, and the desires members have for their unit.

The goal they choose must have several qualities if they are to convince others that it is appropriate for the new body. First, the objective must provide an incentive for members. An incentive is a state or end that, once achieved, provides satisfaction to those who value it. Second, the objective of the group, when attained, must furnish a true change from the state of affairs that led to formation of that body. Third, the chosen mission must appear to be attainable because members have necessary resources, ability, and experience for the group's activities as well as sound procedures to follow. Fourth, the group's goal must specify who will benefit from the unit's activities: members exclusively, members and nonmembers alike, or parts of the group's environment. The focus of a group's programs has to be defined so that an appropriate objective, method, and group structure can be selected.

3.   *Members believe they can achieve a more satisfactory state of affairs through activities of a group.* In order to give recruits confidence that their unit can accomplish its aims, responsible persons make sure that participants know the group's purpose and elaborate on this knowledge over time through speeches, mottoes,

memoranda, conferences, discussion groups, demonstrations, or displays. They make sure that movement toward those ends is visible to all and publicly praise those who take steps toward attainment of joint goals. They identify forces that could prevent achievement of desired ends and describe what needs to be done to counter these pressures.

　　4.　*Conditions surrounding the unit encourage persons to establish a group and to take part in its activities.* Developers and members are more likely to form a group, or find it easier to do so, if circumstances in their surroundings help rather than hinder its creation. The way of life among likely recruits makes them more or less likely to join a new group. For example, people more often help create an entity if they have frequent and easy contact with one another, belong to the same social network, live in the same neighborhood, share the same sidewalk, work in the same office, or belong to the same church, pub, or club. Potential recruits are also more willing to join a body if they are similar to other members in such matters as age, aspirations, hopes, socioeconomic status, interests, or values. Recruits are best sought among people who like to work in a group; many people avoid joining any organization. It also helps to find members among persons who are interested in trying something new, not among those who avoid doing things outside their usual routine.

Attributes of a Strong Group

When a group is strong, it is better able to move toward its objectives. Such a body has four main qualities. The first two, as already noted, identify it as a group: (1) members interact freely and (2) depend on the actions of each other. The second two help make it a stronger body: (3) members want to remain as members because the group is attractive to them, and (4) the body has the power to influence those whom it is supposed to guide and to deal with pressures or restraints arising outside its boundaries.

　　Responsible members make their group stronger by increasing the effects of these four attributes within their unit. They make such characteristics salient by introducing conditions in their body that help strengthen them.

Members Interact Freely

In most groups, members exchange ideas or collaborate on group tasks in order to accomplish what they should. Such interaction is necessary for members to define and understand their unit's mission, set immediate goals, develop and assign roles to members, make decisions, plan implementation of the group's decisions, support the group's officers, foster harmony among members, react to external pressures on their unit, settle conflicts with other groups, evaluate their unit's performance, or devise better procedures.

Members can create conditions within their group that foster better involvement among them. If they keep the group small, as an example, more members are likely to talk with one another. By small, I mean a body not larger than twenty — better if closer to seven or eight. When a small number share activities of the group, each person is likely to have more responsibilities, which heightens their interest in the programs of the unit. Smaller groups, compared to larger ones, are less inhibiting to members because the listeners are fewer, closer at hand, and easier to know well.

A simple way to increase intermember interaction during a meeting is to leave time on the agenda for discussion and to call for and welcome it. Interaction is further enhanced by giving members a chance to gather ideas in subgroups where the main issue is discussed, assigning several persons to be question askers, displaying films, engaging in role playing, or hearing brief talks in which questions are posed for the board to consider. We examine such methods more closely in Chapter Five.

Members Depend on Each Other

In order for members to count on one another's actions, they need to understand what each is saying or doing within the group and why. Such understandings are fostered by creating a cooperative relationship among participants.

Members cooperate when many of their goals are similar and few are contradictory. Individual members may be alike, for example, in wanting to find friends, learn skills, win approval, exercise influence, develop confidence, or have fun. Or they may share a desire for the group to win its games, grow in influence, serve disadvantaged persons, provide good products, or develop sound policies.

When members are in a cooperative relationship because their aims for themselves and the group are alike, they trust one another's actions because they understand what each is trying to accomplish and recognize that the moves of one person help all because their goals are alike. Members who work to benefit themselves in a cooperative group benefit others as well. Colleagues welcome actions of colleagues as they are for the good of each and the group as a whole. No person gains more than others from the efforts of anyone. Each depends on what others intend and do (Deutsch, 1973, 1990).

Groups differ in their degree of cooperativeness — that is, in the visible similarity of members' goals. Where cooperation is strong, a number of useful consequences follow: members try to develop good procedures for the group's work so that the gains of each person, and of the group, are likely to be achieved; they press each other to do well because each has a vested interest in what others accomplish; they are friendly because they understand and welcome others' actions; they provide accurate information so they can help others; they are pleased by contributions of associates (rather than envious) because they are not rivals; they welcome success by the group because this leads to more cooperation; and they try to understand roles assigned to members so they can collaborate smoothly. These qualities develop in a group simply because members depend on, and trust the aims of, one another (Deutsch, 1973).

Members Want to Remain as Members

If a group provides a reasonable amount of satisfaction to members, they are attracted to that body and want to remain within it. If membership is not satisfying, they leave (unless they are compelled to participate). The more members wish to remain because they are attracted to the group, the greater the cohesiveness of their unit. Cohesiveness increases among associates when needs they hope to satisfy together become more valuable to them and they believe that the chances of fulfilling them are good. If, as a case in point, they join a governing board in order to make friends, advance the work of that group locally, or gain prestige from being part of an active body in their community, they will be more attracted to the group when these desires are stronger, better met, and likely to be satisfied in the future. Members develop new sources of satisfaction as experiences within a body teach them to have such desires. They may newly learn, as instances, to like approval or acceptance by others, unselfish work, success as a member, protection from external agents (which the group provides), collaboration with others, or social power. They stay in the group in order to satisfy such wishes.

A group can heighten its appeal for a member by (1) increasing the number of personal needs the member can satisfy by belonging to the group, (2) increasing the importance of these needs to the member, (3) improving the group's ability to fill the needs, (4) convincing members that the group will be able to fill them, (5) measuring the degree to which the group actually does meet the member's needs, and (6) giving the results of this measurement to the member.

One who accepts membership in a group may have to forgo a part in other bodies or activities. Thus, a joiner decides whether the entity at hand or another unit or program is more attractive or a better place to spend time. A person will stay in a group if it is more attractive than comparable opportunities and will resign if competing memberships or duties become more appealing. An individual is more likely to join a group, moreover, and prize that membership, if the values of other members are similar to the recruit's (Scott, 1965). As a result of belonging, members come to be more alike in their values and aspirations; they share the same hopes and feelings about what is right or wrong in that body's plans, programs, or procedures. Members conform more closely to the rules and plans of their group as that entity grows in cohesiveness (Cartwright and Zander, 1968). In a group with high cohesiveness, members work with and for each other in ways that help that unit.

They talk more, listen to others more closely, are more influenced by them, have greater impact on them, attend meetings more regularly, and more faithfully complete tasks for that body. Because they value the qualities of their group, however, members in a highly cohesive group tend to resist changes in that body and may be rigid in their thinking and deciding (Janis, 1972).

The Group Has Necessary Social Power

Members of some groups must monitor and guide the actions of specified persons. Examples of such governing bodies are boards, councils, committees, executive staffs, or legislatures. Those in other kinds of entities want to influence certain target persons. Such units are devoted to social action, dissemination of propaganda, protection of citizen's rights, or support of political issues. Still other groups exist to provide education, advice, therapy, food, or other specific services for persons who are in need. And most groups, whether they serve the good of members or nonmembers, are subject to social pressures exerted by external agents or to restraints created by superiors or lawmakers. All in all, if an active group is to be effective, it must have sufficient social power to influence others or to respond appropriately to others' demands (Zander, 1985).

When members of a group attempt to change the behavior of outsiders, they are more likely to have their proposal accepted by target persons if it is based on a sound decision and valued by both members and nonmembers. A good decision, as will be seen in Chapter Four, is more often achieved if a group uses good procedures in making it. A decision is more acceptable to listeners, moreover, if it is true to that body's mission and moves them toward ends the group hopes to achieve.

When persons in a group make a decision, they will better persuade others to abide by it if they do not generate resistance among those to whom it is addressed. By resistance, I mean an emotional response (anger, fear, dismay) among those hearing the group's message, which is aroused by the style that agents of change use in delivering their instructions. Opposition, in contrast, refers to rejection of the content of the message.

Members make an action more acceptable to listeners by arousing a given motive in them such as a desire for achievement, acceptance by the community, or better service to clients, and by helping them recognize that the change being proposed will satisfy the motive. A group is more able to win a favorable response among those it wishes to influence if it is legitimate — it has the right to make requests, even demands, that listeners have the duty to obey. A group may win legitimacy through the following: legislation passed by a government entity or association of which the unit is a part, group support of values that are important to those who are asked to accept its mandates, or election of group members by those who are to hear its decisions. The actions of a legitimate group are respected by persons who receive the messages of that body and recognize it as a legitimate source of influence.

When a group is pressured by nonmembers to behave in a certain way, its members must be able to implement the requested behaviors. If the group is pressed to make changes that they cannot accept, a dispute may arise. A conflict develops when two parties disagree about what they ought or ought not do. Such a difference is more likely to develop under special conditions and worsen under others, as described in Chapter Eleven. A group that has much traffic with influential others needs to establish plans for settling disagreements with those external agents.

Summary

A group is a set of persons who interact with and depend on each other — who collaborate in the activities of their unit and behave in ways that suit mutual expectations.

Four circumstances cause organizers and recruits to become interested in developing a social unit:

1. Conditions in the environment or in the lives of potential joiners are unsatisfactory or suggest an opportunity for desirable change.
2. Organizers conceive of a more satisfactory state of affairs.

3.   Members believe they can achieve a more satisfactory state of affairs through activities of a group.
4.   Conditions surrounding the unit encourage persons to establish a group and to take part in its activities.

   A strong group is one that is better able to move toward its objectives. Such a body has four main qualities. The first two, as already noted, identify it as a group: (1) members interact freely and (2) depend on the actions of each other. The second two help make it a stronger body: (3) members want to remain as members because the group is satisfying for them, and (4) the body has the power to influence those whom it is supposed to guide and to deal with pressures or restraints arising outside its boundaries. Increasing the effects of all four attributes makes a group stronger.

Recommended Readings

Cartwright, D. "The Nature of Group Cohesiveness." In D. Cartwright and A. Zander (eds.), *Group Dynamics Research and Theory*. New York: HarperCollins, 1968.
   This chapter treats the origins and effects of group cohesiveness.

Carver, J. *Boards That Make a Difference: A New Design for Leadership in Nonprofit and Public Organizations*. San Francisco: Jossey-Bass, 1990.
   The author is a consultant for governing boards. This book is based on the problems he sees in such bodies and on the no-nonsense advice he gives them for improving their performance.

Kanter, R. *Commitment and Community, Communes and Utopias in Perspective*. Cambridge, Mass.: Harvard University Press, 1972.
   This study of communes colorfully describes the means organizations may use to generate commitment to a group.

Larson, C., and LaFasto, F. *Teamwork: What Must Go Right, What Can Go Wrong*. Newbury Park, Calif.: Sage, 1989.
   Reports on a study of successful teams to determine why they perform so well.

Napier, R., and Gershenfeld, M. *Groups, Theory and Experience.*
Boston: Houghton Mifflin, 1993.
A college textbook on the social psychology of groups. It contains many exercises group members can use to understand
events in group life.

Part One

EFFECTIVE GROUPS

2

CHOOSING CLEAR, CHALLENGING, MEASURABLE GOALS

While an American expedition was ascending Mount Everest, Richard Emerson, who is interested in group motivation, made private, preplanned comments to his colleagues early in each day and recorded their responses on a tape recorder he lugged along through the snow (Emerson, 1966). He predicted that the responses by team members would emphasize and seek to increase their motivation to succeed. Because they were roped together, the success of one was affected by the success of all.

Emerson made either a pessimistic prediction about the day's climb to come, or an optimistic one. As he expected, replies to discouraging remarks were cheerful assurances that the team would do well, and replies to enthusiastic statements calmly sought to dampen that ardor. Both kinds of conversations fostered uncertainty about what might occur during that day. That is, the climbers would not say that the coming climb would be either very hard or easy. The day was seen to be a challenge, in the moderate range of difficulty, with a fifty-fifty chance of success. In many groups, like these climbers, members fashion a stronger desire for success by choosing a challenging, but not too difficult, objective for their unit.

A group's goal is a desirable state of affairs members intend to bring about through combined efforts. Because attainment of this goal requires collaboration among members, it is usually chosen by common agreement. An important value of such a group decision is that it causes participants to promise publicly that they will prize the chosen objective and work together to attain it. The goal becomes the unit's criterion of excellence and, often, its prime reason for existing.

Many social bodies have useful purposes, such as to protect members from harm, make resources available to nonmembers, accomplish heavy or arduous tasks, make routine work more tolerable, set rules for nonmembers to follow, guide the work of another body, worship a deity, be reverent toward ideas or objects, heal members and nonmembers, teach information or skills to scholars, make things for consumers, seek and integrate the truth, enrich leisure time, decide on the guilt of peers, entertain observers, or capture lawbreakers (Zander, 1985).

In their study of the qualities that characterize successful versus unsuccessful teams in government, business, and sports, Larson and LaFasto found that "in every case, without exception, when an effectively functioning team was identified, it was described by the respondent as having a clear understanding of its objective. . . . the explanation for the team's ineffectiveness involved, in one sense or another, the goal" (1989, p. 27). Team members ignored their group's goal, these writers say, only when they disagreed on the objective or tried to satisfy self-oriented aims.

What does a goal do for a group? It may provide any or all of the following six functions:

1. A standard of excellence to be used in evaluating the performance of the group
2. A source of stimulation for arousing involvement in a group's task or for stopping action when it is attained
3. A guide for directing members' actions and integrating their moves
4. A criterion for making group actions appear to be justified because these moves are headed toward the objectives
5. A basis for relations with sources outside the group, as in cooperating or competing with other units

6. A means for determining if members deserve rewards or penalties

Some goals are broad and vague, others are narrow and precise. The most general ones describe a group's grandest and highest *mission,* or what the group wants to do and for whose benefit. A general purpose or mission is a value-loaded statement because it describes the good things the body intends to accomplish or the benefits members wish to generate for themselves or other persons. It also guides the selecting of other, smaller, more exactly defined objectives.

The mission of the Athena Club in a midwestern town is to "improve the culture of the community." The object of Rotary "is to encourage and foster the ideal of service as a basis of worthy enterprise. . . . " The purpose of the Community Club in Rossmoor, a village of elderly citizens, is "to promote civic knowledge and appreciation of Rossmoor, and understanding of its plan of operation; and to promote and support measures affecting its continuing success as an outstanding attractive community." The aim of the Ryan Pure Liquid Company is "to provide a reasonable financial return to our shareholders by offering filtering equipment that removes impurities from a gas or liquid."

A statement of a body's mission, as in the above illustrations, says nothing about how the purpose is to be fulfilled, what procedures among an endless variety of possibilities will be used in doing so. The statement of a body's objective helps decision makers to be sure that its programs and activities are in accord with the general purpose.

A group goal, to be useful, must be true to the mission members agreed upon. This *objective,* in contrast to its mission, is stated in more concrete language. It names accomplishments to be achieved within a given period of time, such as the number of dollars to be solicited, animals to be rescued, souls to be saved, books to be loaned, games to be won, products to be sold, or homeless to be fed. A *subgoal* is a level of achievement which, if attained, helps toward the accomplishment of a larger objective. A church congregation can build a new building (a broad

objective) only if it gathers a given number of dollars (a subgoal). A company can stop polluting a local stream (broad goal)
only if it determines what wastes its factory exudes and how
to make these harmless (subgoal).

A larger goal lends value to a smaller one; that is, the
more members of a group prize a main goal, the more they value
a subgoal that must be reached on the way to the important
end. As an illustration, the need to find a president for a college (main goal) makes the work of interviewing these persons
(subgoal) into an important task. If the prime objective is not
valued, subgoals on the path to that end will not have significance
(Thomas and Zander, 1959).

Some groups make minor activities into main goals because their missions are so ambiguous, unmeasurable, or un-
attainable that members cannot know if they are reaching them.
Participants may be unable to determine, for instance, if their
activities are helping to attain such missions as improving the
local culture, helping students to find higher meanings in their
lives, promoting greater civic knowledge, or better understanding the brotherhood of mankind. In order to determine what
they have accomplished, they create goals for the group whose
attainment (or failure) can be measured accurately but which
have little relevance to the group's broader goals. Instead of assessing the salvation of churchgoers, for instance, those on the
board of a church put their prime interest in, and judge the organization's success by the amount of income in the collection
plate each Sunday, the number of new members each year, or
the approval of the congregation by higher officials of their
denomination. Instead of speaking in favor of planks in their
party's political platform, supporters of a candidate during an
election campaign propose whatever goals will win votes in a
given region. These simpler goals cause responsible members
to concentrate on aims that are concrete, easy to achieve, and
clearly indicative of the board's performance, regardless of
whether they suit the body's mission (Zander, 1985).

Properties of Group Objectives

Each group goal has characteristics that affect how well members
can live up to it and how much satisfaction they will derive

from attaining it. Examples of such properties include *impor-tance* (the amount of change its accomplishment will create in a group), *power* (the degree of influence the objective has on the behavior of members), *flexibility* (the ease with which the goal will yield to change in its content), and *consonance* (how well it fits with other goals of the group's board) (Zander, 1985). Three characteristics of a board's intentions are noteworthy for our present purposes. They are accessibility, measurability, and difficulty.

The *accessibility* of a board's objective indicates whether members know of methods they can use in moving toward their goal. A goal's accessibility is determined by the probability, as members see it, that identified paths will move them toward that target. The extent of a goal's accessibility is determined by ob-serving whether a group's programs, projects, procedures, or policies bring them closer to its goal. This movement may be through psychological space, as in the solution of an intellec-tual problem, or a change in belief. It may also be through phys-ical space, as in completing an overland journey or a construc-tion job, or affixing address labels to a number of newsletters. The notion of accessibility implies that not all activities by group members are relevant for reaching its larger goals. The more a group's effort makes it possible to attain its purpose, the more that objective has accessibility. Members cannot improve their unit's treasury by merely wishing for more money; they must take steps toward finding more funds.

The *measurability* of a group's goal indicates how reliably the actual achievement of an objective can be determined. The description of a measurable objective explains what events or signs should change and how much, under what conditions the end is to be considered achieved, and what data are to be taken as evidence that the goal has actually been attained. To illus-trate, if a board of trustees wants their college to be more widely known, how can they be assured this has occurred? Shall they judge movement toward this goal by the number of requests for school catalogs, the number of news stories in area news-papers, the speeches made about the college by board and faculty, the success of their basketball team, the number of stu-dents transferring from other schools, or the results of a public opinion survey in their market area? Because a measurable goal describes what changes are to be accepted as evidence that the goal has been reached, a goal is more measurable as the evidence for its accomplishment is more precisely defined.

The *difficulty* of a group's goal is determined by the amount of energy, skill, time, or resources required to achieve that end. The potential goals that members of a group consider when choosing an objective may be arrayed along a scale of difficulty from easy to hard. While colleagues are deciding what goal their board ought to have, they recognize, of course, that there is less chance of achieving a harder goal than an easier one. Even so, a more difficult goal almost always has greater appeal, because members believe they will get greater satisfaction from achieving a higher aspiration than from attaining a lower one: they will get more done, receive more approval, and feel prouder of their group. Members sense as well that they will not be proud of earning a score that their group has regularly achieved in the past. And they will not be embarrassed if the body falls short of an objective the group has never been able to reach. They will be ashamed, however, if they fail on a task they have previously attained with ease.

The anticipated consequences of a group's activities, then, are almost always better when the group is striving toward a difficult goal: members will develop more pride if they succeed and less embarrassment if they fail. Thus they tend to aim high. Anyone who has been involved with groups that set a level of aspiration will have observed that most of them aspire to reach high, often unrealistically difficult ones. As a consequence, they tend to fail more often than they succeed.

How do they respond to their group's failure? They may have either of two reactions. On the one hand, they may plan how the group can improve its chances of success in the future by setting a lower goal or by trying to improve the group's procedures, equipment, tools, supplies, or skills. On the other hand, they may attempt to reduce the embarrassment that follows a poor performance by changing its meaning, distorting its size, or doing other things that reduce the shame they feel. If a group fails several times, members tend to place more weight on reducing their embarrassment than on figuring out how their group can perform better, because there is a greater need, given the group's recent failures, for overcoming embarrassment than for attaining pride that follows success. In their efforts to reduce shame, they may refuse to lower their group's goal, even though it is too hard to attain, because they will not be embarrassed if they fail a difficult one; indeed, they may be praised for attempting it, for "making a good try." They may even refuse to set any goal at all. They may deny that they are embarrassed by their unit's poor performance. They may blame procedures, tools, or methods of measuring the group's achievements rather than their own skill or effort — "it wasn't our fault." They may misrecall the group's score in its recent attempts (Zander, 1971, 1977a).

Such efforts to get rid of group-oriented embarrassment ordinarily do little toward ensuring that the group will later attain its goal; thus, a group that fails often and that primarily focuses on reducing embarrassment will most likely fail again. It develops a circular-causal system that is hard to stop. This cycle has three phases: (1) the group's failures cause members to feel embarrassed, (2) members act in ways that do not improve the group's effectiveness, (3) its subsequent failure generates further embarrassment (Zander, 1971, 1977a; Zander, Forward, and Albert, 1969). The interest in avoiding embarrassment rather than trying to improve the group's performance will be stronger, moreover, among members who have more important roles in the group, know that others expect their group to set and achieve high goals, are sure their personal performance as a member is of high quality, or are anxious when faced with a challenge (Zander, 1977a).

Choosing Goals for a Group

In most instances, members prefer a group goal that will provide as much satisfaction after a success or as little dissatisfaction after a failure as possible. The objective must be difficult enough to provide satisfaction when achieved, but not so hard that it cannot be reached. The goal, in short, ought to be a challenge, a moderate one that is a bit, but not too much, harder than the best so far accomplished. In effect, members set their goal by looking backward more than by looking forward. If their group succeeds, members choose a more difficult end for the future; if it fails, they typically do not change the goal, or they lower it slightly. As a result, over time, as I said, a group's average goals are above its average level of achievement.

Members' choice of a goal for their group may be influenced by external sources. Four of these are notable.

1. Nonmembers depend on the group's work, so they try to influence its goals. Customers or suppliers, for example, request a shop to set a particular goal, or heads of local agencies for social welfare try to influence the objectives of a community fund-collecting organization. Welfare agencies always can use more money and accordingly urge the money finders to raise the goal for the next financial campaign so agencies may get a larger share (Zander, Forward, and Albert, 1969; Zander and Newcomb, 1976).

2. Members know of other units like their own, such as similar companies, assembly lines, academic departments, or platoons. When they hear the "score" of such bodies, they compare their own record with that of the others. As a result of such comparisons, a group often modifies the level of its goals. Members raise their group's objectives if they learn that other units have done better than their body. They do not lower their group's goals, however, if others have done worse. Apparently, a rival group's success has a greater impact on a group's goal setting than does a failure. Comparisons commonly stimulate higher goals but seldom encourage lower ones.

3. External pressure on a group's goals comes also from onlookers who informally comment on the group's performance. Such a commentator may be a member of a relevant profession, a writer of editorials, a stockbroker, a spokesperson for a consumer's association, a member of a legislative body, or parents appearing before a school board. Members raise their aims for their group when outsiders expect the group to do well, but they do not lower them when commentators predict the group will do poorly.

4. A fourth kind of pressure on a group is a direct order from an individual who has the right to make such a demand. A familiar example is a superior who asks a group of workers to reach a given level of attainment. More often than not, such an officer wants an improved rather than a worsened output, and his harder demand is more influential than an easier one in affecting the unit's choice of a goal.

A group may choose an unrealistic goal when members lack accurate evidence about how well their entity is performing. They may be unable to get such information because their group's goal is too vague; thus, they cannot evaluate how well their unit is doing. When feedback on their group's productivity is not available or is untrustworthy, members' hopes for success typically determine their reaction, and they tend to believe that the output of their group has been good (no news is good news) and will continue to be so in the future (Zander, 1971, 1977a). Thus they choose a difficult group goal.

Members' Motives and Their Group's Goal

Persons who join a group bring personal motives with them. They want, as illustrations, to find friends, develop new skills, pick up specific knowledge, win approval, attain prestige, or engage in activities the group performs. A recruiter for a group tries to discover what kinds of interests are important to a potential member, tells which ones he can satisfy there, and identifies those he cannot hope to meet. Some group officers enhance a newcomer's satisfaction by providing him with experiences, successes, approvals, learnings, or opportunities that will satisfy needs the person is known to have. Common parts of a business meeting in many groups are the praising of members who have recently done things for the body and the offering of opportunities to volunteer "for tasks that interest them."

Not uncommonly, an individual develops new motives as a result of experiences while a member of a unit. Satisfying them often becomes more attractive than meeting ones he or she brought there. Examples of such discovered ambitions include a desire to be an influential participant, an officer of the group, a winner over colleagues, a provider of expert knowledge, a solver of problems faced by the group, or an advocate of the body in the surrounding community. Motives that were not important to a member before joining a group become attractive after being in that body for a while.

Members' personal motives affect the actions and beliefs they display within a group. One who joins with an eye toward finding new friends, for example, will emphasize socializing, interacting with likeable associates, agreeing with colleagues, fostering harmony, or suppressing disagreements. One who thinks the group may be a means to win personal prestige will try to get into a high-status group, run for office in that body, use the group as a means to become well known, or work hard on a public task so that his work is noticed. One who seeks membership in order to reform a group's goals or actions will look for allies, find fault with current leaders, disapprove of aims or methods of the body, or encourage like-minded outsiders to voice their complaints. They become more attracted to the group, incidentally, as they manage to gratify such needs within it.

Sometimes all members of a unit have the same individual motive, and it gains strength as they work together toward this single-minded aim. Such units are called *interest groups* because they work to change things and press persons on boards or councils to support their special interest. They try to achieve a desired end state, such as salvation for sinners, accreditation for their school system, greater beauty in the community, success for their candidate, guns for all, or more power for their union's local. Among the associations in our country, two-thirds exist to help members fulfill a common purpose; each association is in effect a large self-help group. One-third intend to help society or persons who are not members of their association (Zander, 1971, 1985).

Members of groups usually recognize that their unit will be more productive if it has a specific goal than if it has no objective or merely tries to do well (Larson and LaFasto, 1989; Locke and Latham, 1990). This recognition is strongest if the group's task is one the unit repeats from time to time so that members can compare their performances from one trial to another, as in setting a budget, running a financial campaign, conducting a year's programs, or preparing an annual report. When setting or resetting a group's aspiration, members' personal motives affect their choice of a group goal, which, in the long run, influences their individual desires, as follows: (1) In an early stage, a member privately considers what goals he personally wants to achieve, for his own good, while in that organization. (2) His decision on that issue affects the goal he wants the group to have for the task it is to take in hand, as he wants the group to work toward ends that will benefit him somewhat. (3) The goal he prefers the group to have, along with what other members propose, and the group's performance while working toward prior objectives, determine the members' shared group goal — the group's goal for the group. (4) This joint agreement influences what kind of goal the group sets for each member; that is, what the person should do for the good of the group.

Next, in light of the above experiences, a member decides what goal he now wants for himself; the above four-phase cycle starts again, and continues. The point is that a circular-causal system develops between a member's personal goals and a group's selection of its goal; each affects the other. Group members achieve satisfaction when a goal for the self, the unit, or both, is reached (Zander, 1971).

As an illustration of this cycle, suppose a member wants to become more widely known in the town (a personal goal), so he joins a service club. In order that he might improve his chances of becoming visible, he urges the club to build a swimming pool in the park (member's goal for the group). The club accepts his plan and asks the city fathers to approve the venture (the group's goal for the group). The group asks the initial sponsor to chair a committee of supporters for the pool (the group's goal for the member). The member now has a task and a goal, so he feels free to ask colleagues to set future goals in the campaign for the pool; thus the cycle continues.

Members typically decide, as a group, on what goals their group should have. If these are in accord with personal aims, they cooperate in working toward the objectives because each participant sees that his chances of achieving his own goals are improved as all members work toward the group's goals. The result is a supportive interaction among those in that unit: members trust one another's intentions, listen to what others have to say, and feel free to be persuasive when that is necessary. If, in contrast, members cannot agree on a common goal, and rivalry arises among them because their aims differ, the atmosphere within the body is different. Each person feels disadvantaged when others say useful things, is suspicious of their intentions, and talks seldom or in misleading ways. Such members are in a competitive relationship where each tries to perform better than any other.

Helping Members Choose
Realistic Goals for Their Group

Because groups often choose unreasonably difficult goals, it is helpful if leaders press participants to avoid unwise choices and assist colleagues in selecting sensible objectives. It is noteworthy, incidentally, that persons with more responsible positions in their organizations tend to prefer sounder goals for their unit (Medow and Zander, 1965; Zander, 1971). Given the consequences of failing to achieve their group's goal, responsible members usually want to prevent further failure. Ideally, as we noted earlier, they prefer a goal that is moderately challenging, neither too hard nor too easy. In practice this means that the goal is placed at a level just a bit higher than the body has ever attained. How do leaders encourage such a choice?

At the outset it is important for them to obtain an accurate account of the group's past performances on the given task or ones like it. This is to ensure that goal setters do not have false beliefs about the group's ability. Then they need to state the group's objective in measurable terms so that it is possible to determine exactly how close the group comes to achieving that valued end. A further step is to foster members' desire for group success by pointing out the attractiveness of things that follow a good performance and by emphasizing the importance of these with an eye toward promoting members' pride in their unit. Persons who have a stronger desire for group success develop a stronger preference for a moderately challenging group goal — one their group can attain, with some effort. Another action is to play down the fear of what might happen if the group fails, and to reduce members' fear about being embarrassed if the group does poorly. Also, they need to compare the group's performance to that of comparable bodies, because members take seriously any indication that they do better than others like themselves. Finally, they should encourage members to introduce changes in the group's methods that enable them to work effectively for their unit.

It is useful to make sure no member "is lost in the crowd," or feels his contribution is not needed because others are already doing what needs to be done. Such unwillingness to participate is called *social loafing* — a reduction in effort by a few when many are jointly completing a task. An individual may, for example, make a conscious decision not to take part in a group's actions on the assumption that a good performance by him or her will not be approved by others in the group, that working hard is futile, or that he might "choke" and perform below his usual skill (Mullen and Baumeister, 1987). A group's leader needs to give a social loafer an assignment that makes that person's actions visible within the group and important to that body. Otherwise, the submerged member develops a weak desire for success by the group and does little toward that end.

Summary

A group's goal is a desirable state of affairs members intend to bring about through their combined efforts. Some goals are broad and abstract, others are narrow and concrete. The most general ones describe a group's grandest and highest mission — what the group wants to do and for whose benefit. Such a purpose or mission is a value-loaded statement because it elucidates the good things the body intends to accomplish, or the benefits members wish to generate for themselves or others. A group's specific goals must be true to its mission.

The accessibility of an objective indicates whether members know methods they can use to move toward the goal. The

measurability of a goal relates to how reliably members can determine if their unit has actually achieved that end. The difficulty
of a goal is determined by the amount of energy, skill, time,
or resources required to achieve it. Groups tend to prefer a more
difficult objective; as a result, they may fail more often than succeed. Failing groups are more concerned with avoiding the embarrassment following failure than with doing the things that
ensure success.

　　Because a moderately challenging goal is more beneficial
than a difficult or easy one, members and officers should ensure that the group chooses and supports such a goal. A number of practices foster the selection of such an objective.

Encouraging Realistic Group Goals

- Report to members how well their group is doing over time.
- Clearly define the group's mission and goals.
- Make sure members understand the values of having a group
  goal.
- Encourage a desire for group success among members.
- Play down fear of failure among members.
- Encourage members to compare the group's score with that
  of other groups.
- Try to have outsiders place realistic demands on the group.
- Improve the group's procedures so they are as efficient as
  possible, and work to keep them that way.

Recommended Readings

Carver, J. *Boards That Make a Difference: A New Design for Leadership in Nonprofit and Public Organizations.* San Francisco: Jossey-
Bass, 1990.
　　The author emphasizes the practical significance of a board's
mission.

Christopher, W. *The Achieving Enterprise.* New York: American
Management Association, 1974.
　　Discusses how a business firm establishes its identity and
purpose.

Locke, E., and Latham, G. *A Theory of Goal Setting and Task Performance.* Englewood Cliffs, N.J.: Prentice-Hall, 1990.
This book presents the results of studies into the goals of individuals and groups and the influential role goals have in human attainments.

Mohr, L. "The Concept of Organizational Goal." *American Political Science Review,* 1973, *62,* 470–481.
This wide-ranging essay considers how social entities in various parts of the organizational world define their objectives.

Zander, A. *Motives and Goals in Groups.* San Diego, Calif.: Academic Press, 1971.
This book describes a program of studies I conducted into the goals of groups and their impact on members.

Zander, A. *The Purposes of Groups and Organizations.* San Francisco: Jossey-Bass, 1985.
A systematic account of why people form a group, why they choose particular purposes for that entity, and how they develop a desire for success by their unit.

3

STRENGTHENING THE DESIRE
FOR GROUP SUCCESS

Members may be more interested in their group's achievement than their own and may suppress efforts to satisfy personal needs so they can devote themselves to helping the unit do well. They work hard for the group's success, moreover, when there is not the slightest possibility of personal benefit from these efforts or, in the extreme case, when efforts in behalf of the group may eliminate the chances of individual satisfaction. Such individuals include the benchwarmers who never play in a game but faithfully work hard in practice sessions, the stage-scenery crew who help in each performance of a play but are never applauded, or a group of volunteers who run a food service for homeless people but are seldom thanked. Because we are interested in the behavior of groups with a defined purpose, we need to know the source of members' desire that their group be successful.

As we noted, a *motive* is a capacity to find satisfaction in the attainment of a specific state of affairs and a disposition to seek that satisfaction. We can understand the intentions of members who hope their group's actions will be successful by assuming they have a more or less selfless interest in the achievement of their group as a whole. When a member serves group needs rather than his own and takes more pride in the group's performance than his own, we say he has a *desire for group achievement*.

30

Most group participants have this desire to some degree. They feel proud of their group when it wins a game, does better than last year on an annual task, is praised by the local paper, becomes an influential entity in community affairs, or completes an arduous job.

For members to develop a group-oriented motivation, their unit has to have a goal that requires collaboration among them. The product of their joint effort may be a score, report, plan, record, construction, or other result that is not merely a summation of each member's output while working on a personal task in the presence of others. A group effort, in contrast, where members work together to satisfy the group's goals, makes members aware of the performance by the whole. No person can complete his job unless others do likewise. Each pays more attention to the quality of the group's accomplishment than his own. Several examples follow.

In a slipper factory with twenty-eight assembly lines of eight or ten women each, where the production of every line was posted for all workers on the floor to see, I asked the ladies on three occasions whether they placed more importance on personal success or on success by their group. In every one of the assembly lines, members said the group's outcome was more important. A study of the executive boards of forty-six community agencies that raise funds for social welfare revealed that members were prouder of the success of their fundraising organization than of their personal performance. And among fourteen student project groups, the excellence of each report was more important to members than the quality of their individual efforts.

The opposite also occurs. Think of the player on a basketball team who prefers to keep the ball and shoot for a high personal score rather than passing it to teammates, the member of a board who talks most of the time and insists on getting his way, or one who breaks a rule set by the group because he will benefit by doing so.

An important issue is implicit in these examples. A member has the choice of working for (1) himself alone, (2) his group as a unit, (3) both the group and himself, or (4) none of these options. Preferences 1 and 2 (for self or for group) may be directed toward similar ends, thus supplementing one another and creating a stronger effect than either preference alone. Or preferences 1 and 2 may be contradictory, in which case the effect of each is weakened (Forward, 1969).

When members are most interested in their group's product, they naturally begin to judge how well their unit performs. Their satisfaction when the group does well fosters a taste for more of the same. Their dissatisfaction when the group does poorly invokes a wish to avoid such an experience again. These affect-laden responses to a group's accomplishment lead to either of two tendencies in members: a *desire for group success,* so they will be proud of their group if it successfully completes a challenging task, or a *desire to avoid group failure,* so they will not be embarrassed if it fails. These desires, it should be noted, are not enduring characteristics of individuals, as hopes for personal achievement are, but are the products of a particular situation in a given group. The strongest tendency to work in behalf of a group exists when the desire for group success is greater than the desire to avoid group failure.

Sources of Group-Oriented Desires

Members become more interested in the fate of their group and develop more desire for it to succeed when conditions exist that make members feel involved in, or responsible for, how well their unit performs. A member who knows that his efforts, compared to those of colleagues, have a greater effect on the unit's movement toward its goal is more likely to want that body to do well. One example is a highly skilled or experienced member. Another is a leader of the organization. Central members of governing boards for forty-six fund-soliciting organizations, compared to peripheral persons in those bodies, had a stronger desire for their annual campaign to be successful, were more confident their body would do well, saw more value in working toward a difficult level of achievement, praised their chapter's performance more fully, rated their personal contribution higher, worked harder during campaigns, and intended to continue working hard (Medow and Zander, 1965; Zander, Forward, and Albert, 1969).

If a group faces a challenging task and members take time to discuss how they will approach it, they make more encouraging, praising, and help-giving remarks to one another than criticizing or blaming ones. Thus, their desire to have their group succeed is likely to be enhanced if they have a chance to talk about how their body might meet the coming situation. Members are more eager to do well, moreover, if their actions will affect the welfare of others.

Participants are less likely to engage in "social loafing," and more certain to work diligently for their group, if they have duties that are visible to others and if the quality of their output can be seen by those observers. Also, a member will try to do well if it appears that colleagues are doing likewise. He loses enthusiasm for helping his group, however, if he sees that others are not trying and he is being a "sucker" if he works hard (Kerr, 1983).

Effects of Group-Oriented Desires

Placing value on the consequences of a group's success or being repelled by the results of a group's failure influences the behavior of members. The goal members choose for their group is determined by how strongly they want the group to succeed. Members with a greater desire for group success are more attracted to goals of intermediate difficulty than to very hard or very easy ones; a very difficult goal might lead to group failure, while succeeding at an easy one cannot be satisfying (Zander, 1971, 1977a).

Members who have a great desire for group success (compared to those who strongly fear the consequences of group failure) try to ensure that their associates perform well by behaving in the following ways:

1. They more often make comments that reveal their eagerness to have colleagues work hard on the group's assignment. These comments encourage colleagues and suggest

ways of improving the group's procedures, as in a pep-rousing meeting that a CEO holds for his organization, or a discussion in which members of a team urge one another to do their best during the coming year.

2. They are more prepared to work hard for the group. Members express a deep interest in the group's activity, anticipate that their colleagues will exert effort in its behalf, want to do better than other teams engaged in the same work, and expect members to help one another (Zander, 1971).
3. They more frequently help their group perform better by working hard, developing needed skills, making fewer errors, helping colleagues, deciding how to improve quality, and rehearsing new methods (Zander, 1971).
4. They regularly want precise information about their group's quality of performance and about how rival groups are doing. They help their group compete ardently with other groups, set personal goals close to the group's goals, and are prouder of their group's output than of their individual contributions to the group's activity.

Consider now, in contrast, how members act when they desire to avoid group failure. This tendency makes it difficult for members to decide what their group's goal ought to be. Members who more strongly want their group to avoid failure prefer either an easy goal because the group is less likely to fail at that level or a very difficult goal because failing a hard task is not embarrassing. Which level do they choose? Ordinarily, they prefer to fail on a hard task than succeed on an easy one because doing so provides a better chance (given the group's prior record of failures) of preventing embarrassment for themselves (Zander, 1971, 1977a).

Group members who want to diminish unpleasant results of failure have many ways of doing so. They include declaring that attainment of the goal is not worth the effort (this enables them to reject a difficult goal that may lead to failure); believing that demands on the group by outsiders are easier than they really are (doing so encourages them to think they will not fail); denying that they are chagrined if their group fails; misrepresenting the group's score so that it looks better than it actually is; denying that members were the reason for a poor performance (lack of resources, equipment, or good procedures were the causes); or alleging that the group tried its best and should not be expected to do more (Zander, 1971, 1977a; Zander, Forward, and Albert, 1969).

We see that the effects of a desire to avoid group failure are not merely the obverse of ones caused by a desire for group success. Members who want to prevent embarrassment due to failure do very different things than members who want the pride generated by success. To prevent the effects of failure, participants try to evade such unpleasant results of it as anxiety, chagrin, loss of reward, public disapproval, and devaluation of their group. To acquire the consequences of success, however, members try to attain such features as pride, approval, or favorable evaluation of one another. Accordingly, these different desires for group output stimulate dissimilar intentions and activities by members.

Strengthening the Desire for Group Success

If members are to develop a desire for group success, they must know how well their group is doing and experience the satisfaction (pride in group) that accompanies success. A leader needs to have the group repeat a given assignment several times and then provide members with information about their score on each trial. Next, members, or a subset of them, need to estimate how well the group will do next time. Such an estimate is the group's goal. If the unit attains that goal, members derive satisfaction, which stimulates interest in further success. This satisfaction is increased and its effect heightened if members thereafter work to maintain pride in their group. A manager can encourage members to think of group pride as an asset by doing such things as the following:

- Explaining the sources of group pride, what causes it to develop among members, and what consequences pride has for the unit. One administrator I know makes his older em-

ployees responsible for supporting these ideas among newer
members and for keeping up everyone's interest in the body's
quality of work.

- Increasing members' desire for their group to be successful
  by arranging the group's goals, procedures, work plans, and
  resources so they help the group earn a good score. An ex-
  cellent outcome does not dull the taste for further success;
  as is often said, instead it makes good work more desirable
  to members.
- Helping the organization set clear goals. Members cannot
  feel successful if they are uncertain about whether they have
  reached their group's objective or what they must do to attain the objective.
- Selecting goals that are realistic challenges for the members,
  not unreasonably hard or easy ones. Because goals are standards of excellence, they should not be conducive to failure
  or an absence of pride.
- Making sure each member understands what his or her contribution is to the final product of the group and that this
  work is valued.
- Indicating to members how their membership in the group
  has been helpful to them so that each person views the group
  as an attractive entity and wants to remain in it.
- Making it clear to all that each member depends on the work
  of others. Their unit is a cooperative entity.
- Emphasizing the unity of the group, its output as a team
  effort, and that all members in the group are serving its
  needs.
- Changing goals that are too difficult. The warmest pride
  comes from living up to reasonable expectations, not from
  failing impossibly difficult ends.
- Encouraging talk in meetings about how performance can
  be improved and how boring parts of the job can be made
  more interesting.
- Avoiding fear of failure and the way it causes members to
  evade challenges.
- Helping members feel responsible for their group's fate, so
  that each knows the group depends on his or her efforts and

wants to improve the quality of his or her contribution. Feelings of responsibility to the group can be aroused by telling each member that he or she is needed, useful, and eligible for equal shares of earnings by the unit.

• Giving members assignments that suit their abilities and make it possible for them to feel competent. Confident members develop a stronger desire for group success. Those who think they are less competent develop more concern about failure. A manager can enhance a desire for group success by helping members perform well and by telling them they have done well when that is the case.

A Group Considers Taking Action

Even though a desire for group success is strong among members, it is not likely they will behave in accord with that motive unless they are confident that (1) they will be satisfied by accomplishing relevant aims and (2) the chances of achieving those ends are good.

Satisfaction from Achieving Aims

Incentives are states or outcomes that, when attained, provide satisfaction for a person with a given motive. The presence of an incentive serves to arouse the motive. Typical group-relevant incentives are a good score, financial gain, friends, food, fun, or approval by colleagues. Incentives vary in their value, that is, they differ in the amount of satisfaction they promise to provide. The amount of incentive value one anticipates in an upcoming action by a group is the result of that unit's past reactions to similar situations, or of other groups' reactions. The value of an incentive increases as members become more sure that achieving it will provide satisfaction. Leaders of a group therefore try to make members see that attainment of the objective will be gratifying. They point out that the amount of energy members exert toward attaining a goal results both from the strength of their motive and from their confidence that the group will be able to achieve its goal. Their intent is to modify members' sources of satisfaction and thus to change participants' behavior. A group's purpose or goal, it can be seen, is a special kind of incentive. Toward such ends, a group leader may ask members to develop a vision of how the group will benefit from accomplishing a given incentive. Responsible persons in some groups, when trying to increase the motivation of members, devote their attention to the value of attaining the group's goal and ask members to commit themselves to attain that end.

Achievable Goals

A member typically estimates what the chances are that the group can attain a state or outcome that promises to provide a feeling of success. One may have a strong motive for group success and place greater value on a pertinent incentive for the group, but these views will not arouse the person to take action in behalf of that body if he believes it cannot attain the state that would furnish this satisfaction. The member may be sure, as an illustration, that the group will benefit if it can take in one hundred thousand dollars in its next financial campaign, but the member will also recognize that less than one-quarter of that amount is a more feasible level of aspiration for the unit. Or a group may want to be highly influential in the community, provide housing for homeless people, or win a conference championship but recognizes that such an achievement, even though rewarding, is not achievable. Leaders typically try to increase members' confidence in attaining an objective they value by helping them believe they can accomplish the group's goal. The leaders help choose a realistic but challenging goal and provide necessary training, adequate time, appropriate personnel, or whatever else is needed in order for members of that unit to recognize they can be successful if they try.

Members are more aroused to act for the success of the whole if they believe the incentive is achievable (with some effort) and will provide pride in the group when attained. All in all, the total strength of a group's readiness to take action is the product of the three separate factors noted: members' desire for success by their group, the value of a relevant incentive, and how good the chances are (as members see it) that they can attain that incentive.

Arousing Members to Take Action

In order to help a group move toward its goal, decision makers decide on the programs and procedures members must follow. These are *group activities* and can be conceived as paths to the unit's goal because they help members move through physical or psychological space to reach the designated objective. A given group activity is created when participants choose, or are told, what they will do, how they will carry it out, who will do what, the steps they must take to overcome barriers along the way, and the resources they need to attain its completion. If these phases are followed, members maintain their desire for group success, and their group proceeds toward the end it values.

The effectiveness of such movement by a group depends on whether the unit had adequate resources and on the appropriateness of its activity. A *resource* is a state, person, or thing that can contribute to a group's movement and is appreciated by the persons involved. Five kinds of resources are useful. The first is people, especially ones who know what is expected of them in that situation and who can live up to those expectations. Next are necessary tools, supplies, or equipment. Third is space sufficient to accommodate activities performed there. Fourth is specific or general knowledge that bears on the group's operations. And finally come reserves of money, equipment, supplies, plans, or persons ready for use as needed (Weicker, 1987). The art of using available resources in order to achieve established objectives is called *strategy*. The deployment of resources is a fundamental commitment in planning for a group's action because once they are distributed they cannot easily be redeployed.

An *appropriate* activity in a group leads toward that unit's objective. An *inappropriate* activity leads elsewhere. Compared with its opposite, an appropriate activity requires members to complete fewer and simpler steps in order to reach a satisfactory state; thus it is more direct. It calls for less energy or fewer resources and therefore is less costly. It can also be completed more quickly. In sum, an appropriate activity tends to be a more efficient means for fulfilling a group's objectives. An appropriate activity generates interest in attaining the group's goal because it promises a greater probability of fulfilling that aim. Members who see that their group is making progress toward its objectives tend to maintain a strong desire for group success.

An *inappropriate* group activity asks members to move through more steps and more complicated ones than does an appropriate one. Thus, such an activity is a more indirect path to the group's objective. It demands more effort of members and more resources; therefore it is a more costly course. It requires more time to reach an end point and is characterized as well by a poor fit, redundancy, or conflict with other activities in the group. An inappropriate activity generates inefficiency (see Chapter Thirteen).

Given that participants in a group have an objective for their unit and wish to attain it, it seems reasonable that they would make sure they select suitable activities. Why then, do they become involved in inappropriate ones? One reason is that people who make decisions for a group are not able to judge the appropriateness of a potential plan because the group's purposes are not stated precisely enough to guide this appraisal. If a group's objectives provide little guidance, members' ideas about the group's activities will probably not fit together well, as each person favors a kind of activity that satisfies his or her own personal interests. Members may settle such disagreements by bargaining, and the final choice is often weighted with activities that meet members' private purposes; the group's needs are given less weight. Another cause for choosing inappropriate activities is that decision making by leaders and members when establishing the group's methods is ineffective. Critics outside the unit may pressure the group to follow a given procedure that turns out to be unwise. Some members advocate a procedure that gives them a role they prefer or a chance to have a valued position in the unit. A final reason for inappropriate activities is that members become defensive, angry, or suspicious about goals they are required to meet, and they act in accord with these emotions even though such moves take them along a path that leads away from the goal.

Summary

When a member serves his group's needs rather than his own and takes more pride in the group's performance than his own, he has a desire for group achievement. For members to develop such a group-oriented motivation, their unit has to have a goal that requires collaboration among them to produce a group product.

Members become more interested in the fate of their group and develop more desire for it to succeed when conditions exist that make them feel involved in, or responsible for, how well their group performs. Members' reactions to their group's accomplishments lead to either a desire for group success or a desire to avoid group failure. Members with greater desire for group success are more attracted to group goals of intermediate difficulty than to very easy or very hard ones.

Actions of Members Who Desire Group Success

- They encourage colleagues to work hard on the group's task.
- They reveal their readiness to aid the group.
- They help the group do well.
- They keep aware of how well their own and comparable units are doing.
- They compete ardently with rival bodies.
- They feel proud of the group when it achieves success.

Encouraging Group Success

- Stress pride in the group.
- Arrange group goals and work methods so that the group succeeds.
- Set clear and realistic goals.
- Make sure each member is aware that his contribution to the group is useful.
- Emphasize teamwork.
- Change unrealistic goals.
- Help the group overcome obstacles to success.
- Stress communication about improving performance and eliminating boredom.

- Avoid fear of failure.
- Instill in members a sense of responsibility for the group's fate.

Even though a desire for group success is strong among members, it is not likely they will behave in accord with that motive unless they are confident that (1) they will be satisfied by accomplishing relevant aims and (2) the chances of achieving those ends are good. They will tend to choose an inappropriate activity for their unit if the group's goals are not stated with enough precision to guide this choice.

Recommended Readings

Leary, M., and Forsyth, D. "Attributions of Responsibility for Collective Endeavors." In C. Hendrick, *Group Processes and Intergroup Relations.* Newbury Park, Calif.: Sage, 1978.
This review discusses how members come to feel responsible for their group's fate and how they react to this responsibility.

Mackie, D., and Goethals, G. "Individual and Group Goals." In C. Hendrick, *Group Processes and Intergroup Relations.* Newbury Park, Calif.: Sage, 1978.
Considers the consequences when individual and group goals are at cross purposes.

Zander, A. "Team Spirit and the Individual Achiever." *Psychology Today,* 1974, *8,* 64–69.
Describes how personal aspirations help a group to do well.

Zander, A. "Group Motivation and Performance" and "Group Embarrassment." In A. Zander, *Groups at Work.* San Francisco: Jossey-Bass, 1977.
These chapters treat more fully some of the ideas presented in this chapter.

Zander, A., Forward, J., and Albert, R. "Adaptation of Board Members to Repeated Success or Failure by Their Organization." *Organizational Behavior and Human Performance,* 1969, *4,* 56–76.
Examines the contrasting motives of central and peripheral members on the board of a fund-collecting agency.

4

IMPROVING THE
GROUP DECISION-MAKING
PROCESS

Anyone who has sat in meetings when decisions were being made knows that all such sessions are pretty much alike. A number of persons are at a table talking and listening. They ask questions, give answers, and make suggestions while seeking a view they can jointly accept. Their discussion moves through several stages: A problem is presented to them for their attention; they shape the problem to make it more discussable, propose alternative solutions for the problem, and eventually select one option as the answer. The participants decide on a course of action following this decision, designating who will do what and when.

But no meeting is exactly like another; each is different enough in important respects that it is not easy to generalize about decision-making groups. In many cases, a resolution is a product of talking past one another, offering conflicting ideas and evidence, ignoring each other's comments, saying the same things over and over, displaying one's biases, and deciding to agree on some plan, any plan, because time is running out.

Because a group's decisions can affect persons both inside and outside that unit, scholars have long been interested in how they are made. One purpose of this research is practical, as investigators try to identify how groups reach a conclusion most efficiently. Another purpose is scientific, as students try to understand what happens in the flow of discussion and explain what causes these events. The results of the practical and scientific approaches together suggest ways whereby groups or their leaders can improve methods for making decisions.

The simple fact that members have a part in discussing and deciding arouses a desire in them to develop sound plans and to collaborate in reaching the best answer they can. When they adopt a decision, moreover, those who helped to make it are committed to it, and want to make sure it is implemented — unless it is a weak solution that is poorly supported within the group. Participants derive benefits from being in a group that is seeking an answer which they are less likely to derive if they are working on that issue alone. They gain a better and shared understanding of the matter being discussed and of the varied viewpoints colleagues hold on the question. They have a greater quantity and variety of ideas to consider in the discussion. They create notions during their give and take that are unusual, ir-reverent, or even overdue challenges to the group's valued stan-dards. They invent plans that are better than those the most capable members can contrive. And they learn to trust and de-pend on one another. Such advantages are less likely to occur if the leader of a group, or an external agent, forces a decision on them which members have to accept (Napier and Gershen-feld, 1993).

Members of a group, or outsiders who have an interest in the work of that body, may see disadvantages in group deci-sion making. The deciders may be asked to settle an issue that has already been solved by higher authorities — thus, the meet-ing is merely a place to air dissatisfaction about the problem at hand, not to develop a new plan. The group leader may be unskilled in leading a problem-solving discussion, so members waste time in reaching a solution, develop disorder, and arouse little interest in implementing the final agreement. Some mem-bers may talk considerably more than their share, offer useless ideas, and thereby make it impossible for more helpful ones to have the floor. A group's decision may not be welcomed by non-members who believe that the results of collaborative thinking cannot be as useful as the product of one wise problem solver.

The Problem-Solving Process

The need for group members to work toward a decision arises while they are engaged in a larger activity called *problem solving*. The distinction between solving a problem and making a decision is not important in a natural setting because one seldom occurs without the other, but the two processes differ in their range of activities. Problem solving requires that members attend more closely to matters before and after a decision is made—a process of several steps. Group decision making is but a single step in problem solving. To trace the development of the problem-solving process, first let us define terms.

A *problem* for a group is a specific situation to which members must respond if the group is to function effectively. Members face a *dilemma* if they have no immediate effective response for the problem. In a group *problem-solving process,* members identify alternative ways of dealing with the situation and then select the most satisfactory course, the solution. A *solution* to a group's problem is therefore a response that alters the specific situation so that it no longer causes a dilemma. Thus, *group decision making* is the selection of a preferred solution from several alternative solutions. If there is no problem, no decision is needed, and things continue as they are, unless a need for a decision arises because members wish to make an improvement in their group or in their group's environment when an opportunity arises to do so.

Defining Problems

A problem-solving process begins when a problem is stated for the group and members respond to this presentation by considering whether the issue is worthy of discussion, whether they ought to work on it, and if so, how the discussion should begin.

How do members know a problem when they see it? Moreland and Levine suggest that "problems usually betray themselves by producing symptoms that attract the attention of group members. These symptoms involve unusual and often unpleasant events within the group. A problem is detected when group members notice its symptoms and realize that something is wrong. They may not understand the exact nature of the problem, but they do know that it exists" (1992, p. 19).

These authors go on to say that once a problem is detected, members try to understand the problem by giving it a label and then speculating about why the issue developed and what will happen if it is ignored. The more chances there are that a problem will create undesirable consequences if ignored, the more weight members attach to it.

Members are more likely to accept an issue as being worthy of study under certain circumstances. One of these conditions is the severity of the problem. When a problem is more serious, it is more noticeable, more arousing, and probably easier for discussants to understand. A second condition is the familiarity of the problem; discussants previously worked on issues like the current one and recognize it as one they know how to handle. Another is that the problem is not too complex; its causes and consequences are not so tangled that members cannot see how to attack it. A further condition is that norms in the group do not forbid discussion of the matter. As examples, they are not prohibited from discussing such topics as salaries of superior officers, discrimination against older members, poor food at their club's potluck dinners, failures by the group's leaders, domination of discussions by a few members, or religious or political issues (Moreland and Levine, 1992).

An additional condition is members' detection of poor group processes during an evaluation of the group. One more is that members notice problems in their unit as a result of comparing its procedures with ones used by bodies like their own. And last, members may be told about a problem within their group by outsiders who have an interest in the unit's functions and outcomes.

Suppose a member of a group recognizes that the unit faces a problem, but no colleague seems to see it. What might the former do? There are several available options. The member might deny (to himself) that the problem exists and say nothing about it to others if he feels it is too difficult for the unit to solve or if he is responsible for that undesirable state of affairs and hopes to conceal it. He might wait to see what happens if the group is already burdened with difficulties, the matter appears to be a minor one, or he fears being labeled as a complainer. He might try to solve the problem on his own if he is an expert in such matters and does not need or want others' help while working on it. Or he may seek help from nonmembers who are capable of solving such a problem. The point is that leaders of a group cannot be confident that a responsible member will always speak up when he or she recognizes a problem exists or is likely to arise. A chairperson, therefore, must generate an atmosphere in which insightful members feel free to share their beliefs without fear of retribution from colleagues or of generating discomfort among them (Moreland and Levine, 1992).

There has been no research on how a problem needing a solution should be presented to discussants, but experience suggests that the person raising the issue should not overlook certain practical matters. It is sensible, at the outset, for the presenter to explain the significance of the issue facing members without revealing her feelings about it or her preferred solution, because a slanted introduction stimulates biased comments from discussants. The problem poser ought to explain what information members need and where this may be obtained so that they can consider the matter in the light of relevant data. Finally, it helps if the one who presents the problem makes it clear what kind of action, if any, is needed and what the outcome of an appropriate decision eventually could be.

Although the point is obvious, it is important that the problem be stated clearly by the person presenting it. Members cannot easily clarify a muddy topic when a discussion is under way, and they usually feel compelled to begin discussing when asked to do so, even though they are not sure what kind of contribution they should offer; the discussion is accordingly disjointed. Members are embarrassed if they do not know what is relevant, and they do not like to ask the chairman what is supposed to be going on. Discussants need to understand the problem in the same terms so they can work on the same issue in light of the same facts. I have seen groups proceed directly to comparisons of potential solutions without defining the problem they are trying to solve, such as faculty members in a university department arguing about what changes should be made in the curriculum before they agreed on what is wrong with the current menu of courses. Such a discussion cannot be efficient, because no one is sure what topic is under consideration.

When members judge a problem worthy of attention, they nevertheless may feel it is unwise to discuss it because certain characteristics of the problem, such as too many parts, excessive differences among these parts, or vagueness in definition of the main issue, make it difficult to handle. Thus, members may decide to pass a problem along to a subgroup, to the leader, or to a consultant. It is clear that some matters are not suitable for group consideration, but little is known about what characteristics of issues make them more appropriate. Reasons why some problems are more fitting for a meeting are suggested by the results of early studies into the comparative effectiveness of group versus individual problem solving. The work revealed that a problem for which there is only one correct answer is better given to a group than an individual because when a number of people consider a topic, the probability is greater that one of them will come up with the solution and that inferior contributions will be discarded during the searching and evaluating of ideas that goes on during a discussion. A problem more appropriate for individual than group consideration is one whose solution requires careful, sustained, and logical thought without the distractions that occur during group members' give and take. Also, a group is not as quick as an individual when an answer is needed in a hurry.

Identifying Potential Solutions

Once members accept a problem as worthy of their effort, they begin to think up solutions. It is clear that the soundness of the final answer depends on the quality of the ideas developed during this searching stage and the willingness of discussants to find answers that meet the needs of the group rather than their personal desires. Because a better resolution is more likely to be found if deciders have more alternatives to compare, test, and choose from, the climate in the group and the methods members use in collecting these notions must be such that they feel free to say what they have in mind. It is often necessary that participants be encouraged to stretch their thinking and generate unfamiliar ways of approaching the issue at hand so that creative solutions are made possible, and that conferees not settle too quickly upon a likely looking proposal or start evaluating suggestions before that activity is appropriate. In order to encourage freestyle searching for alternative solutions, the leaders of a group may use idea-stimulating procedures like the following.

Brainstorming. In 1937, Osborn proposed a discussion method for increasing the number of ideas a group develops during deliberations. The four basic rules of this procedure are that criticisms of one another's suggestions is strictly prohibited, free thinking and wild notions are welcome, numerous ideas are sought, and combination or modification of notions already offered is in order. Osborn suggests that members be instructed at the outset on the four basic rules, be asked to practice their use before the discussion begins, and then be required to follow them closely. Each idea offered by a speaker is to be recorded on a blackboard or pad of newsprint, and the question for discussion should be as open-ended as possible.

Does brainstorming improve the quality of ideas? The results of research and experience (Camadena, 1984; Connolly, Routhieux, and Schneider, 1993; Fisher, Ury, and Patton, 1991) suggest that the method is more useful under certain circumstances. For instance, after members can think of nothing more to say, they are asked to invent improvements for the ideas on hand while criticism is permitted. Things also go better if the group is small (five to eight members), each participant is to speak in turn, the atmosphere is informal, and discussants are allowed a chance to think about the question privately before the contributing of suggestions begins. Among the four basic rules, the prohibition against criticism of others' ideas is the most important. Better-producing groups, in brainstorming sessions, contain persons who like the activity more and who tolerate ambiguous situations better, as measured on a standardized test of that personal characteristic.

The most important value in brainstorming is that members

who ordinarily might talk very little feel free to take part. Any group, when in need of new ideas during a regular meeting, can generate the good effects of brainstorming by temporarily imposing its four rules on interaction among members. As a result, participants will find that no one person dominates the group's flow of ideas, more members talk than usual, discussants feel free to offer unusual notions, they develop more suggestions than is typical in a brief period of time, no members are "lost in the crowd," and they are surprised at their creativity while having fun.

Electronic Support Systems. In years to come, an increasing number of groups will have a computer for each member and a hookup among these machines so that everyone in the unit can communicate with everyone else. The members of a group with such equipment need not be in the same room. Thus, they can hold a "meeting" while miles apart. One among many advantages in using such a system is that data relevant to the topic under discussion can be on file in the computers and brought forth where doing so appears to be useful. When this is done, members can interact with evolving ideas as well as with each other. Thus, the advantages and disadvantages of social relations in a group are minimized while participants deal with processing information and generating solutions. Usually, members using these electronic aids develop more ideas than they do in face-to-face groups (Nagasandaram and Dennis, 1993).

Nominal Group Technique. This discussion method takes advantage of research that indicates people are more productive if they perform a task in the presence of an audience, a phenomenon known as *social facilitation* (Zajonc, 1960). The inventors of this procedure (Delbeq, Van de Ven, and Gustafson, 1975) assume that participants will be more comfortable in offering ideas on a topic in need of careful consideration if they have an opportunity to think about and write down what they might say while sitting among persons who will soon hear those ideas. The term "nominal" in the title of this method is to denote that the conferees are often strangers, not a true group. In fact, the method is especially useful when a number of citizens who do not know one another, and may be uncomfortable in that situation, come together to develop ideas on a topic that is important to them.

The procedure moves through four steps after the leader states the central issue, phrased as simply as possible. (1) Those present write private responses; no talk among them is allowed. (2) Each person is then called upon in turn to offer one of his suggestions. This is posted publicly, and no comment is allowed at that moment. Subsequent ideas of each participant are noted until all have been recorded. (3) Those present may ask questions about the meaning of any items on the list that are not clear to them. (4) Participants decide which ideas among the total are most important and rank-order these. The result is a pool of suggestions, ranked according to their significance, ready for comparative evaluation.

The Delphi Technique. This procedure makes it possible for participants to offer ideas anonymously on a question that needs better reasoned answers than members typically can create at a conference table. It allows respondents to comment on ideas proposed by others, at their leisure, without knowing who the authors of those remarks are. The method is especially useful when discussants come from different status levels, have different degrees of expertise or power, or can decide the fate of those involved in the procedure. Usually, respondents never meet face-to-face (Delbeq, Van de Van, and Gustafson, 1975; Moore, 1987).

The process takes time (as long as seven weeks), requires several people to run an operational headquarters, and demands skill in devising questionnaires and coding written answers. Although this method is complicated and slow, it provides thoughtful results no other method can.

The technique employs a series of questionnaires. The first one, containing a few open-ended questions, is sent to the chosen respondents, who return their answers in writing. These initial questions are devoted to problems, goals, predictions, or requests for objective information. After the first questionnaires are returned, the headquarters team summarizes them and returns the results to the respondents with a new set of questions in which they are asked to comment on the main themes among the previous answers. After these questionnaires have been received, a new one is again developed and sent out. This cycle is repeated as many times as necessary to arrive at a reasonable consensus among participants.

The Delphi procedure is especially valuable when it is necessary to learn what a specific set of persons think about a general issue, future goals, or priorities among alternative activities; where disagreement is great or a problem cannot be resolved in objective terms, but judgments on the issue would be useful. The only limits to the number of participants is the time needed for coding questionnaires, and the cost of mailing new versions of these.

Ringi. This procedure is used in Japan in cases where decision makers are stalled or ensnarled in superficial observations, because conferees in that nation do not like to disagree with one another face-to-face (Rohlen, 1975). In order to avoid this discomfort, a written document dealing with the issue at hand, prepared by an anonymous individual, is sent from member to member and edited, by each in turn, without any oral interaction. After each such cycle, the draft is rewritten and sent around again for comments, as many times as necessary, until no more changes are made and all have put their personal seals on the final version. Some groups find it useful to assign separate parts of a problem to each of several subgroups, who prepare a draft of an answer for their section. These smaller reports are then circulated before discussion begins in the larger body.

Group leaders who use structured discussion methods like ones just described assume that conferees will offer relevant information and that members will pool it sensibly. The ideas individuals bring forth may not, however, fit together well. Members can pool their wisdom more effectively if they limit the number of ideas, make each member aware that he or she has unique ideas to contribute, and help everyone know the kinds of information others have that may be useful (Stasser, 1992).

Students of group decision making have done research on the value of preplanned discussion procedures like those just described. The researchers report that groups using such methods probably make better decisions, their members are more satisfied with the group's solutions, and participants abide by their agreements more closely than persons in units that allow discussion to flow in a random manner. Also, preplanned procedures make it more probable that all members will have a say, regardless of their status in the group, and that their ideas will have an equal chance to gain the attention of other members (Pavitt, 1993).

Choosing the Best Answer

When the leaders of a discussion realize that no more alternatives are going to be offered, they turn participants to selecting the best among those on hand. Members begin to test whether a given alternative might provide a sound resolution and to determine the side effects that may occur if it becomes the chosen course. More precisely, they consider such issues as: What gains or losses would the group or interested nonmembers get from each potential solution? What gains or losses will persons served by the group attain? How much will members approve or disapprove of their group after it has selected a specific solution, and why? What will be the reaction of nonmembers?

When working toward a decision, participants often follow the principle of least effort, choosing whatever course is easiest because they used it previously. Thus, one of the first questions raised in a group when its members are evaluating potential solutions is, What has this group done in the past on such a matter? Or members may explore what other committees have done under like circumstances and borrow their solutions. When making their choice, discussants consider the special interests of special persons: constituents whose lives may be touched by the group's choice, experts' ideas, or the preferences of the most respected members.

Ordinarily it is sensible to avoid the requirement that a decision be unanimous, because this hampers the efficiency of members when they choose among available options. A study of hypothetical juries found that the need for a unanimous decision often prevented the group from reaching any decision at all. Seeking a unanimous vote (compared to trying for a majority) caused more conflict between participants, more shifts of opinion, slower movement toward a conclusion, but more confidence in the final answer.

Ordinarily, if all goes well, members have enough commonality among their opinions to agree about which alternatives are better. The way to such an agreement is seldom straight, however, and often is the result of bargaining, arguing, and negotiating among discussants. In addition, members who have more social power tend to have more to say in the ultimate decision.

Sometimes, none of the available ideas for a solution is truly appealing. In such a case they may select the least objectionable proposal. If they do this, they are inclined to justify their choice to themselves and others by inventing arguments in favor of it, a form of rationalizing called *bolstering*. When engaged in this activity, participants try to make their choice appear reasonable by listing favorable consequences that will follow from the decision, minimizing unfavorable consequences, denying any adverse reactions, exaggerating the need for action right away, ignoring the interests of persons outside the group, and playing down the members' responsibility for the consequences of their action (Janis and Mann, 1977).

When a decision-making body makes little progress in settling a difficult question, a skilled officer can move things along by asking deciders to consider what process they might better use on the problem. To sharpen the discussion about procedure, she may ask members to identify the factors contributing to their difficulty in making a selection, such as biases among colleagues, incomplete background information, inability to predict trends in the future, rivalrous subgroups within the entity, unclarity about alternatives, or lack of understanding about the cause of the problem under discussion. On the basis of this diagnosis, the leader and members devise a way of removing the restraints, making them inefficient.

In choosing a procedure to use when making a decision, Fisher, Ury, and Patton (1991) say it ought to have three qualities. First, it should produce a wise agreement—one that satisfies relevant interests of members as much as possible, resolve conflicts among discussants, and give proper weight to the needs of the group and relevant persons outside that unit. Second, it ought to be an efficient method. And third, it should foster, not damage, harmony among members.

When a group has a set of alternative solutions at hand, these authors suggest that it is more sensible for members to avoid arguing over the merits of each solution. They should consider instead what needs or interests will be satisfied if each option were to be chosen. The authors make this suggestion for several reasons. When a participant insists his preference is the best, he locks himself into that view, increasingly defends it against attack or change, and thus becomes more convinced than ever that he is correct. "As more attention is paid to positions, less attention is devoted to meeting the underlying concerns of the parties. Agreement becomes less likely" (p. 5). And whatever agreement members finally reach may simply be a compromise, a splitting of the differences between two unfounded beliefs, instead of a soundly developed solution. Arguing over preferred solutions also makes a group inefficient because members are tempted to engage in gamesmanship, stalling, threatening to withdraw, or offering a tiny concession that only slows things down. Arguing over positions generates a contest within the group.

In order to avoid unfavorable consequences of arguing over preferred solutions, the authors propose a method of negotiation that is intended to produce a sound solution smoothly. They call this *negotiation on the merits*. The procedure has four features.

1.   Discussants must separate people from the problem, because during a lively discussion they tend to become emotionally involved and do not speak or think clearly. They may become angry and say hostile things to those with whom they disagree. They must not be allowed to make ad hominem remarks, so that they will work on the problem, not on each other.

2.   Participants must focus on others' underlying interests in favoring a particular alternative, not the merits of their proposed solution. The deciders are to recognize that a solution must satisfy the reasons people have for favoring a given action by the group. Their interests behind their choice (desires, wants, concerns, fears) are to be the prime topic of discussion.

3.   Participants should develop and weigh many options before making a decision, because members are more likely to strike a useful agreement if they have numerous alternatives to choose among and can look for the one that best resolves differences in the underlying interests of discussants.

4.   Decision makers must, at the outset, define the qualities a sound solution ought to have, because doing so makes it possible for members to select an answer that meets these criteria of merit, selected in advance. Doing so helps them avoid an answer that is pressed upon members with special demands. Another method for choosing an answer from among a number of alternatives—for evaluating potential solutions—is described in Chapter Twelve.

The members of most groups probably believe it is best to keep their emotions hidden during decision-making discussions if they can. Yet expressions of affect are hard to conceal if the group faces questions where there are differences of opinion concerning fairness, justice, morality, influence, or derogation of the group itself. And many groups contain a person who believes it is a great idea for discussants to display their feelings because everyone's thoughts will flow more freely after they have had an emotional catharsis. What helps a group's effectiveness most during a meeting: suggesting that members express their feelings whenever they wish, or suppressing them during a discussion? The results of research on this question suggest that the highest quality decisions are developed in groups where members agree before a meeting to delay any show of affect until after they have reached a decision. The participants in groups with such an agreement also see their associates as more effective and energetic, compared to participants in bodies where members are allowed to express their emotions openly in the meeting. The groups in which members readily express their feelings come up with fewer ideas and do not work as hard (Guzzo and Waters, 1982).

Irving Janis studied the processes groups in natural settings use when making decisions on important matters (1989, p. 30). He says that a vigilant group takes seven separate steps in reaching a solution and that every one of them is a must.

A good decision cannot be attained if any is omitted. In his seven steps, which serve to summarize ideas on preceding pages, a group does the following:

1. Surveys a wide range of objectives to be filled, taking account of the multiplicity of values at stake
2. Canvasses a wide range of courses of action
3. Intensively searches for new information relevant to evaluating the alternatives
4. Correctly assimilates and takes account of new information or expert judgments to which [members are] exposed, even when the information or judgment does not support the course of action initially preferred
5. Reconsiders the positive and negative consequences, as well as positive consequences of alternatives originally regarded as unacceptable, before making a final choice
6. Carefully examines the costs and risks of negative consequences, as well as positive consequences, that could flow from the alternative that is preferred
7. Makes detailed provisions for implementing and monitoring the chosen course of action, with special attention to contingency plans that might be required if various risks were to materialize

The reverse of any of these seven describes a typical mistake a group of deciders might make.

Implementing a Decision

Members of a decision-making unit sometimes forget, after a solution has been made, that implementing actions need to be taken either by a part of their unit or by persons other than themselves. The deciders are responsible for considering what problems implementers might meet when putting the decision into place and what procedures they might use in meeting such dilemmas.

A failure of persons assigned to establish a planned change may be due to their misunderstanding of the group's decision because they received imperfect instructions. The would-be implementers may also demur if the proposed innovation does not fit what they usually have done or if they do not see the importance of the change they are asked to bring about, are anxious about the effects of the proposed transformation, or lack the necessary resources, ability, energy, or time.

Because new plans may arouse anxiety among those who are asked to change their ways, a group may devote extra attention to methods of winning acceptance for their revised standards. Useful procedures include inviting those who are expected to use the change to provide advice on the decision and its enactment or asking discussants to identify the events that might help or hinder their implementation of the change. On the basis of this diagnosis, plans can be made to encourage sound procedures and to avoid useless ones. Such an approach takes advantage of findings from research which show that individuals are more likely to abide by a group decision in which they had a part than a decision they made alone (Lippitt, Watson, and Westley, 1958).

Conditions That Limit Effective Decision Making

Some conditions interfere with the work of a group as it moves toward a decision. Several of these have been studied.

Superficiality of Method. During a meeting, if the agenda is crowded, time is limited, or members are bored with the topic, they may make a decision too quickly. Such a rapid-fire approach tends to be simplistic and based on inflexible rules. As a consequence, conferees may forgo use of good methods (Janis, 1989).

One such quick procedure is to seize the first useful suggestion members develop (ignoring other possibilities) because this notion seems to solve the problem well enough. In a second method, members choose a plan that worked in the past: the current problem resembles a dilemma members recall resolving earlier, fits a maxim that is popular among members, or has become the standard procedure in situations like this one. In such a case, discussants search their memories and choose a solution from among ones they find there. Dependence on the past has an attractive quality: it requires little effort to reach a resolution. In a third superficial procedure, members ask one of their number to examine the problem closely, so they will not have to do so, and to inform them about it: defining it, identifying its source, and offering an array of alternative solutions. The discussants then make a decision on the basis of that person's briefing.

Superficial procedures are used more often when members underestimate the seriousness of an issue, grasp at an "obvious" solution without evaluating it, try to simplify a complex problem so they can solve it more easily, fear that extensive discussion of a question may cause dissension among members, want to satisfy personal motives, or become emotional because of a threat they see in the issue. Superficial methods can be helpful on matters where past experience in the use of them has been good. But they may lead to a poor solution if the problem is complicated and requires clarification as well as background facts before it can be sensibly resolved (Janis, 1989).

Groupthink. This source of ineffectiveness is due to a style of deliberating that members use when their desire to preserve good relations with one another is more important than the quality of their decision. Instead of searching for the best answer, they search for an outcome that best preserves harmony in the group. Five kinds of behavior characterize these attempts to keep everyone comfortable: (1) the discussants consider only a few alternatives and ignore others, (2) they fail to examine adverse consequences that might follow their preferred course of action, (3) they drop alternatives that appear unsatisfactory at first mention without examining them well, (4) they do not seek the advice of experts, and (5) they fail to create fallback procedures in case the chosen solution does not work out (Janis, 1972; 'tHart, 1990).

Five techniques may prevent groupthink or weaken the conditions that arouse it: (1) ask each member to be a critical evaluator of the group's procedure and ideas, (2) request each to discuss the content of their group's deliberations with friends outside the group and to report the results of these conversations, (3) assign the role of devil's advocate to one of the members,

(4) examine the views of persons whose ideas are known to conflict with this group's, and (5) once a decision is taken, have participants consider any remaining doubts at a later meeting.

Status of Group Members. In many groups there is a distinct difference in the status of members. An example is the staff of a law firm in which recent graduates serve along with veterans, or an executive committee of a hospital where nurses sit with physicians. Individuals who differ widely in their social standing are not always comfortable with one another, which may make their interactions stilted, cautious, and less helpful than they might be in a unit composed of peers.

We know from research that higher-status persons talk more often in a meeting and direct their comments mostly to other high-status members, while lower-status participants talk less and also send their remarks to higher-status people. The superior members, moreover, believe that their inferiors talk too much. A group's leader may find it useful to point out this imbalance in participation if it occurs and to ask more powerful persons (outside the conference room) to give more consideration to subordinates' contributions and to direct more remarks to those people. If such suggestions do not make the frequency of comments more nearly equal, a chairperson may ask members of separate status levels to meet in separate rooms on the assumption they will talk more freely in those more homogenous meetings. Later, these groups are brought together to share their ideas. The head of a group need not try to get everyone talking; generally, only 30 percent of those present do most of the commenting in a comfortable and efficient group.

Stress Felt by the Group. Members usually modify how they move toward a decision when they feel threatened because they cannot define a problem precisely, are under attack, need an urgent answer, or have a heavy work load. Under stress they fear they will function poorly and develop an inadequate answer. Their sense of threat is enhanced, moreover, if they are unsure of what causes the problem, wonder whether the difficulty will get worse, or lack control over perceived causes of it.

Ordinarily a group becomes more cohesive when it is

threatened by external agents or states, because participants seek the protection of one another. When cohesiveness is high, members interact in useful ways, as noted earlier, unless participants believe they are being threatened because they are members of that group, and the only way they can achieve relief is to leave the body. During anxiety created by stress, moreover, decision makers tend to be less flexible and imaginative than they might otherwise be (Holsti, 1971; Janis, 1989). Their attention narrows; they pay too much attention to trivial data. Their speed of performance is impaired, but not the quality of the ideas they finally develop, provided they can take their time to reach a good solution (Turner, 1992).

If members of a committee must deal with an emergency such as a storm, strike, earthquake, or fire, they are prone to make errors when choosing a course of action either because the pressure of time makes them consider fewer options or the problem is given to a subset of members that does not include experts on the issue. Moreover, during a critical period, information coming to the group is often of poor quality because messages sent hastily are either badly stated or inadequately thought out. If the issue is significant for the organization, the information available may be biased by the wishes and expectations of those who seek to influence the decision. Members listen to one another more than to the designated leader, and lower-status members are especially inclined to attend to remarks made by higher-status persons (Driskell and Salas, 1991).

When a group is under stress, some members fear that the situation will have unfavorable consequences for them; they ask themselves how they might be hurt and how they can avoid painful personal outcomes. In a case like this, they tend to cope with their needs (for gain or approval) by urging that colleagues use such emotional behavior as relying on unreasoning intuition, not letting attackers get away with their behavior, attacking external opponents, or resigning from the group (Janis, 1989).

Studies of decision making in an emergency, conducted by the Office of Naval Research, indicate that the most difficult part of reaching a rapid answer is diagnosing the nature of the threat and its source. These researchers urge that members of a decision-making unit be trained in identifying and assessing the nature of a problem. A group will do a better job of resolving a problem quickly, these researchers say, if each knows what others' roles are, all have the same information about the problem and share the same understanding about what is being done to solve it, and each can anticipate what others are likely to say or desire to do (Adler, 1993).

Suppression of Minority Dissent. During discussion of solutions for a problem, it often happens that a majority of members argue for one resolution while a minority hold out for a different approach (are dissenters). If the majority will not listen to or consider the views of the minority, the performance by their group is likely to be poorer than if they pay attention to the ideas offered by the smaller set of members (Nemeth, 1992).

Outside Criticism. A familiar cause of inefficiency in making decisions is an attack on a group by critics who have an interest in its conclusions. A city council, for example, considers whether to rezone an area of the city and is exposed to pressures by nonmembers who wish to express their views before that body, with feeling. A faculty committee debates whether research using hazardous materials should be allowed on the campus, and a set of critics who oppose this research complain to the community about that committee's procedures and plans. The critic's comments must be answered if they are incorrect, even though correcting takes time, is embarrassing for the correctors and irritating to the critics, arouses emotional tension, and makes committee members advocates of their own views rather than unbiased problem solvers. Advocacy also slows down the process of reaching a decision. There is much to be learned about what conditions cause critics' comments to hinder rather than help the quality of a group's decision.

People who belong to some groups must settle issues on which nonmembers have both supporting and rejecting views. An example is a board of trustees elected by a popular referendum. Trustees are supposed to ensure that the institution they guide serves the interests of the public at large as well as the needs of persons who have a stake in the institution. To perform their duty properly, therefore, members of the board must know whether the public's interest is pro or con and understand the desires of special groups. If this information is not on hand, members cannot be sure which path to follow. This uncertainty is heightened if board members are in the midst of a campaign for reelection. In such a case, members must make it clear in meetings that they are listening to all sides and being fair in their deliberations. When a decision has been influenced by the arguments of persons who are not in the group, its members must demonstrate that they have been influenced. Such displays take time and contribute little to the quality of the discussion or decision, but they reduce the social pressure felt by trustees.

Legally mandated groups often operate under "sunshine laws" that require all meetings to be open to observers. Members of the audience must be given an opportunity, moreover, to comment on questions under consideration. The effect of this required openness is that those in the group tend to keep quiet on matters they would prefer to discuss in a closed meeting, or they play up to the audience on topics they know their constituents support. The presence of an audience can cause biases and distortions in making a decision; this is especially so when the issue is hard to understand or diagnose.

Tenure of Members. In light of the foregoing, groups whose members have had considerable experience working together would be expected to perform better than ones with a brief history or ad hoc groups created to resolve a specific problem. In a study comparing the behavior of members in twenty long-established committees and twenty groups created de novo, the veteran units were superior in decision making and in dealing with conflicts among their members (Hall and Williams, 1966).

If experience improves the ability of a group, it is likely that a unit's quality of work can be enhanced if members are taught (by a skilled nonmember) how to make decisions most efficiently. To test this notion, a number of groups were told how to deal with differences of opinion among members and how to participate in an open discussion, while other groups were given no instructions. The researchers report that instructed groups, compared to uninstructed ones, made better-quality decisions and better use of resources but took a longer time to complete the task (Nemiroff and King, 1975). Good processes, apparently, cause members to be more thoughtful, and thoughtfulness takes time.

Competence of Members. Although a group is greater than the sum of its parts and often makes decisions superior to those any member would develop alone, it can create even better decisions if members are competent and well-informed about the issue they are to discuss. Sometimes an ad hoc group is created to deal with a controversial issue. In order to assure observers that these decision makers are unbiased, the committee is composed of persons who know nothing about the problem at hand. When the matter is a technical one, the problem solvers are bound to reach a naive solution based on superficial discussion of peripheral topics unless the group is allowed to bring experts before them (Zander, 1979). A leader of a group composed of persons with little skill or wisdom (on either the substantive topic or the group's process) soon sees it is difficult to keep participants on the subject, because much of what they say is not useful in reaching a solution. Members of a group can sense when their solution is not of high quality and are less likely to abide by their unit's decision when they do not think it is a good one.

In a study of the qualities characterizing effective and ineffective groups of many kinds, it was observed that the most successful bodies had a majority of competent members. Such persons had more of the skills, abilities, and knowledge needed for doing that group's work; greater desire to contribute to that effort; and more capability of working with others. Among these three personal qualities, the researchers gave the greatest weight to the latter — the ability to work well with others (Larson and LaFasto, 1989).

Summary

Making a group decision is part of a larger process called group problem solving. Problem solving usually moves through four stages: describing the problem that requires a response, identifying a number of possible solutions, selecting the best solutions from among these alternatives, and taking action to implement that decision. When searching for possible answers, members benefit from using one or more structured procedures: brainstorming, electronic support systems, nominal group technique, Delphi technique, or ringi. In selecting among potential solutions, they will make a sounder decision, more smoothly, if their negotiating is based on the merits of each and on an understanding of the underlying interests of those who advocate different outcomes.

Conditions within a group can limit the effectiveness of decision making. Among such interfering circumstances are use of too superficial a method, failure to evaluate ideas on their merit (that is, groupthink), barriers against participating in the give and take because of differences in status of members, excessive size of group, lack of imagination in developing ideas during a discussion, errors occurring in a group during an emergency or crisis, suppression of dissent by a subset within the group, criticism of the group by outsiders, inexperience of members as a unit, incompetence of members, and absence of an appropriate social policy or set of values.

Implementing the Problem-Solving Process

- Clearly state the problem for the group, explain the significance of the problem, and make it evident what kind of action is needed by the group.
- Keep discussion focused on the issue, stop work on a problem when consideration of it is completed, and call for a vote when the time is right; don't let the discussion drag on when members seem ready to decide.
- Break a complex problem into separate parts and have members make decisions about each part.
- Help members learn how to work with others' ideas so they do more in a meeting than convince themselves that their original ideas were correct all along.
- If no solution is clearly correct or appealing, make the least objectionable choice.

- Where possible, avoid the need for a unanimous decision.
- Use one or more preplanned processes when searching for potential solutions.
- Encourage members to consider any adverse consequences from a potential solution before making a final decision.
- Be sure that those who are to implement a group's decision understand exactly what they are to do.

Overcoming Ineffective Decision Making

- Develop special roles for members, such as devil's advocate, or searcher for needed information, if it appears that group-thinking may make the group inefficient.
- Avoid wide differences in status levels among discussants.
- If status differences cannot be avoided, help members recognize and reduce the inhibitions these differences create in a meeting.
- Use the brainstorming method to help members feel willing to participate, not only to improve the quantity and quality of ideas offered during a discussion.
- Protect the rights of a disagreeing minority among members so that their views will be heard.
- Plan ahead for procedures to use when a decision must be urgently made or a crisis arises.
- Recognize that external critics of a decision-making group can provide useful ideas but that they can also damage the objectivity and effectiveness of those in the criticized body unless members stay calm.
- Plan special discussion methods to use if scientific facts and value judgments must be jointly considered when making a decision.
- Encourage members to evaluate their group's skill and learn ways of improving it.
- If members are incompetent to deal with an issue, get the help of outside experts.

Recommended Readings

Delbeq, A., Van de Ven, A., and Gustafson, D. *Group Techniques for Program Planning*. Glenview, Ill.: Scott, Foresman, 1975.

Presents several straightforward methods for increasing the number and quality of ideas in conferences.

Fisher, R., Ury, W., and Patton, B. *Getting to Yes: Negotiating Agreement Without Giving In.* Boston: Houghton Mifflin, 1991. A highly readable account of methods decision makers may use to reach a resolution that satisfies participants.

Janis, I. *Victims of Groupthink.* Boston: Houghton Mifflin, 1972. This lively monograph describes how important committees in government made poor decisions because of their desire to avoid controversy within their group.

Janis, I. *Crucial Decisions: Leadership in Policymaking and Crisis Management.* New York: Free Press, 1989. Describes procedures required for making sound decisions and ways to avoid poor processes.

Moore, C. *Group Techniques for Idea Building.* Newbury Park, Calif.: Sage, 1987. This book describes several methods for generating, developing, and selecting among ideas in group meetings.

5

COMMUNICATING EFFECTIVELY
AMONG COLLEAGUES

If you watched chemists in a laboratory, reporters in a news-
room, members of a football team at an afternoon practice session, or workers chatting during lunchtime, you would see individuals turning to certain colleagues for conversation but not
saying anything to others. You would also notice that the talk
is sober in some pairs but cheery in others. Suppose, too, that
you could examine notes that employees in an organization send
one another, obtain a record of who calls whom on the telephone,
or find out who types comments to colleagues via a computer
network. Again, it would be evident that some occupants of a
social space more often transmit messages and choose special
targets for their words.

Members of a group initiate communication because it
is useful to themselves or others. Administrators realize that interpersonal talk is necessary in the daily routine and try to help
it occur. This chapter reviews methods officers use when helping associates say what they want to say and get information
they need. We are interested in the direction and flow of messages among persons, not in the acceptance of their content by
one who receives them or in their impact on that individual.
The sites for these communications are, at the outset, anywhere
in a social setting, but not in a group discussion or at a conference

table. Later, we consider the flow of talk when persons assemble to discuss a specific topic.

Freestyle Chatting

We assume it usually is a good thing if members speak freely to one another, because in doing so they accomplish many of their objectives and their group's goals. Examples of personal purposes better met through exchange of words include developing a fuller understanding of recent events, issuing instructions, giving approval to a subordinate, forming a friendship, or helping a colleague solve a problem. Examples of aid to an organization through interpersonal exchange include reducing undesirable diversity in beliefs of group mates, linking a group's separate parts, preventing misunderstandings among persons from different backgrounds, providing an opportunity for members to share special knowledge, helping them collaborate in solving problems, or in making joint products. The group objective a speaker seeks to satisfy may be required by the nature of the job or by the desires of superiors, peers, customers, or clients.

Although an optimal degree of communication is necessary for the good of the talkers and their organization, there is no way to define an optimal degree with precision. Doubtless too little interaction occurs at some times and too much at others. A possible criterion for a satisfactory amount of interchange is that it be sufficient to provide the information, support, and approval (or disapproval) each member needs. Perhaps it is equally important for a member to have an opportunity to share special information he possesses and to offer help to groupmates he wants to assist.

Message Initiation

Being at ease with one another usually increases as members spend more time together, so it is not surprising that messages flow more readily among persons who have belonged to a given group for a long time. Social events like picnics, parties, lunches, or ceremonies help break the ice and encourage members to feel they can talk to each other without hesitation back on the job. Other ways a leader facilitates talk in a workplace are to provide settings for interaction such as committees, task forces, joint assignments, or business trips. In Japan one often sees a small group of businessmen enter a hotel dining room in bathrobes. Their faces are flushed from the communal hot bath they have just finished. Now they eat, drink, and laugh together. These men are from the same office and are socializing with their boss, at the request of their company. A person is more attracted to some colleagues than to others because he believes that outcomes he values are more likely to occur when he is with those people. By getting to know colleagues and learning to be at ease with them, a member identifies which individuals he wants to be around so he can do his job better or enjoy his work more.

When members converse, the intensity and length of their conversation is greater when their ideas are useful to each other. A converser who is aware he is being listened to or who senses that his ideas are well received feels relaxed and thereafter talks often with those persons. It follows that if an administrator needs to increase the frequency of a colleague's oral participation, she helps the individual recognize that his words have been given notice, acceptance, and use by listeners. Or she might put him in a position where such approval is likely to occur. Generally speaking, a person believes that the messages he sends are more important than those he receives.

The amount of conversation among members increases greatly when an important event occurs (a sudden loss of a leader, a spurt in sales, or a threat from a rival organization) and members are uncertain what that event means for them. Their interaction also becomes more frequent when they recognize they have different ideas on a crucial topic. If their ideas are discrepant (but not too much so) they are more likely to talk together. They try to modify one another's views if they feel a uniform notion is necessary, unless of course they dislike one another. As noted earlier, members who have a stronger desire to be together are more eager to be similar in their beliefs. When a difference of opinion exists between individuals and threatens the harmony or performance of their group, the threat stimulates talk among them. Thus, in a friendly group a leader often stirs up livelier communication by showing members where their ideas differ.

A person who has a superior position in a group works harder for that unit, because his post makes him feel responsible for the fate of the organization. Moreover, the remaining members expect him to work in their behalf, and they let him know it. As a result, a member in a central post, compared with one in a peripheral job, talks more often with colleagues both in meetings and on the job. As an instance, a superior typically talks more than a subordinate. In a face-to-face chat with a new employee, a boss talks more than the neophyte. Among office workers, highly respected peers communicate to others more than less respected ones (and they also receive more messages), as do persons who have greater confidence in their beliefs, compared to ones with less faith in themselves. Persons who are provided greater influence by an experimenter, when taking part in a laboratory experiment, talk more than those who are given little influence (Back and others, 1950; Cohen, 1958; Hurwitz, Zander, and Hymovitch, 1968; Kelley, 1951).

It follows that one can reduce a member's inhibitions about conversing by doing things that will improve his or her status within a set of persons. If it is not possible to give him a more important title, he can be asked to become expert in some special set of information. He can also be assured that his contributions are appreciated by associates: they listen to his ideas, are influenced by them, and know he is a reliable and conscientious member. When a member learns he has influenced others, he tends to act like a person with more influence and talks with more confidence to more people. As a member's willingness to express his opinions increases, his faith in his own ideas improves, and he speaks more freely.

Turning to the needs of the organization, if changes in its goals, methods, or structure are proposed, talk increases among those who are affected. Thus, a proposal by an official about new ways of doing work in a group will stimulate reactions. A member who learns that his competence is better than that of groupmates develops a stronger desire for that body to do well, which in turn makes him more talkative about matters useful to the group.

Associates talk with one another more openly when they recognize that their efforts benefit all alike. The frequency of intermember exchange can be increased, therefore, by rewarding participants according to how well the unit does as a whole; the better the group's score and reward, the larger the share for each member. In contrast, when those in a group compete, person against person, they are less inclined to talk, especially if they must continue to work with one another in the future (Zander and Wolfe, 1964). Also, persons are less willing to talk if they must pass along unpleasant news the others have not heard; they fear they may be blamed for being the bringer of bad tidings.

Plainly, persons are more likely to interact if they are physically close to one another or if their paths cross more often. Workers whose desks are nearer a drinking fountain have more conversations with more passersby and as a result may have more friends. People who need to exchange ideas must be spatially situated so that easy communication among them is possible. If they are located close together, they need quiet and privacy for ready conversation. A noisy workplace can be a cause of psychological distance among members and thus a source of low cohesiveness.

Direction of Communication

Whom an individual approaches for a conversation generally depends on what she has to say, what she needs to know, what others want to learn, who is available for talk, what ideas others provide, or what others ought to be told. The person one chooses to address and the topic to be discussed affect each other.

Whether a member wishes to communicate upward or downward within a hierarchy influences what he says or how he says it. And what he wants to say determines whether he more often approaches persons above or below his level. If an ordinary member talks with higher-placed associates, the member usually speaks with caution, says things that might win approval of superiors, and is careful not to antagonize the listeners. If a superior speaks with subordinates, in contrast, he is less concerned with winning goodwill and is prepared to evaluate them or make demands. Requests for help are more often made upward than downward, but not if the superior from whom aid is sought embarrasses the one who seeks it ("Don't you know the answer to that question?").

Emotionally loaded comments like complaints, regrets, fears, or threats are less often spoken or sent upward to a supervisor because a lower-status sender avoids giving a superior a chance to reject his remarks (unless the speaker's feelings are so strong that he ignores the consequences). Instead, a subordinate prefers to bring up neutral or irrelevant matters with a boss that have little significance for joint interests. He tells jokes, stories, and anecdotes about events outside the workplace rather than discussing matters that enable the powerholder to evaluate the speaker's actions on the job (Cohen, 1958; Kelley and Stahelski, 1970). Such tangential statements are made more often by persons who have less confidence in their own ability.

As was noted above, persons with greater influence prefer to communicate with individuals of high status, and members with little influence also prefer to talk upward to those superiors. As a consequence, more communication is initiated upward than downward (Back and others, 1950; Hurwitz, Zander, and Hymovitch, 1968; Kelley and Stahelski, 1970; Kipnis, 1976). Talk flows to the top more readily if subordinates feel sure the boss will be helpful and understanding.

What topics do those in a lower post tend to discuss with persons above them? This depends on how they feel about the discrepancy between their own status and that of superiors. If they think this difference is as it should be, they say things that keep matters as they are. If they value the expertness of the superior, they will ask her questions, seek her advice, or request approval of their plans. If they are uncomfortable with the individual, they will say things that reduce this discomfort (jokes, anecdotes, tall tales). If they would like to increase their own power vis-a-vis the superior or win that person's approval, they demonstrate their attention to important details by describing things that are wrong in the organization. The complaints a superior often hears from subordinates may bother her unless she keeps in mind that complainers usually are trying to show the boss how perceptive they are and how eager they are for their organization to do well.

A subordinate's aspirations for higher status are fostered if they mention the names of high-status friends when they are among lower-status ones or if they demonstrate to associates that they have expert knowledge or a considerable following. Obviously, persons who differ in social power differ in their styles of communication because of how they feel about their own and others' positions.

Helping Members Participate in a Group Discussion

Members of many groups meet merely to discuss things or educate themselves, not to make decisions. Computer technicians convene to examine new ways of analyzing data. Members of a Sunday school class consider ways other classes have helped troubled neighbors. Managers confer about a written report and advise the author how to revise it. Graduate students hold a seminar to think about the meaning of a new discovery. Company presidents jointly study the effects of regulations for disposal of toxic wastes.

A group discussion has three central features. One is that members help each other better understand a problem they all face, but they do not try to reach a conclusion. Another is that each participant is free to take away whatever ideas he or she finds useful and to ignore the rest, if that is desired. The third is that in the long run the group may benefit from the development of its members through discussion, but such aid is not an immediate purpose of the interaction.

A period of discussion serves five purposes for participants:

1. It helps members recognize what they do not know and probably should.
2. It is an occasion for members to get answers to questions.

3. It lets members get advice on matters relevant to activities of the group that bother them.
4. It lets persons share ideas and derive a common wisdom on the topic.
5. It is a way for members to learn about one another as persons.

A discussion is not a debate, an argument, or merely a conversation. It is not the place to reach a decision about actions on behalf of the unit. Moreover, managing a discussion is not the same as running a meeting on the best solution for an organizational problem, because special attention must be given to the discussion's educational and advisory purposes. To meet these aims, a leader must make sure that three procedural problems are handled well: (1) reluctance of members to take part, (2) members' lack of ideas during a discussion, and (3) conditions in the group that restrain ready exchange. We examine each difficulty separately, even though they overlap to some degree, and we consider methods for overcoming each of these problems during a discussion.

Reluctance of Members to Participate

In most discussion groups, one-third do most of the talking while the rest sit silently by. Why do quiet ones stay quiet? Typical reasons: the topic is one they know well, so they leave the floor open for persons who are considering it for the first time; they are shy and do not like to speak in public settings; persons in the room have control over their fate, so they avoid contributing or asking questions for fear they will appear inept in the eyes of the powerful others; newer members feel their comments are naive compared to ones with a longer tenure in the unit; they do not understand the ramifications of the topic, and it has little meaning for them.

The hardest part in starting a discussion is to pose an interesting issue, one that group members want to work on and feel they can handle effectively. Too often a chairman introduces a subject and is met with silence, or a brief response and then silence. Common examples of deadening questions are: "What is hard for you to understand in the report?" "Have any of you ever made such a mistake in calculation?" "How large should this city be?" "Is theory A better than theory B?" The first two questions ask discussants to reveal their own inadequacies, which most people prefer not to do. The third question involves a factual matter and therefore will not invoke much give and take. All the questions are somewhat ambiguous, so a listener is not sure what kind of response is relevant. Better questions are: "In what respects should the report be clarified?" "What errors might a person make in these calculations if he is not careful?" "Why, as you see it, do people propose that this city not be allowed to grow?" "In what ways does theory A differ from theory B?" Stillness that follows a poorly phrased question can itself be a gentle form of pressure on persons to speak, but it will successfully goad them only if the matter before the group is clear to them. Thus, if it is to result in discussion, a topic must be both easy to understand and worth considering, and it should invoke curiosity.

Group members will feel a stronger impulse to speak if the topic has more meaning for them. One way to arouse such insight is to provide an experience relevant to the purpose of the discussion, such as a film, play, excursion, lecture, story, questionnaire, experiment, or role-playing scene. When the demonstration is finished, the leader asks discussants such questions as, What happened? Why did these things occur? What was most important among these events? Such concrete queries can lead into issues of more direct concern to the board. Whether a lively discussion follows depends on how much the shared experience recalls problems for members and how skilled the leader is in recognizing when participants are interested, why they are involved, and what will continue to stir them.

Sometimes it is helpful for a leader to present a question that relates to experiences in another group where those occurrences resemble ones within her group's experience. This approach initiates interaction in a way that is not a threat to discussants while they analyze the behavior of those other persons. Oral contributions can come more easily in such an instance because there are no obviously right or wrong answers, and the discussion can eventually lead to identifying similarities between the others' case and their own. Matters may thus come up for appraisal that probably would have been evaded earlier (as too hot to handle) if they had been posed directly.

A familiar way to identify topics that interest board members is to ask for suggestions. Some of the responses may be poorly worded, so the chairperson writes them on a blackboard or pad of newsprint; participants then modify and choose the most intriguing ideas. Topics may be better stated if members take time to compose them in writing, or if groups of three or so are asked to consider, select, and offer specific issues for discussion. Each subgroup may also appoint a spokesperson who will present the unit's opinions after the discussion period. To create interest in a given topic, get members thinking about the matter ahead of time by posing it, for instance, as a main subject of the next meeting. It may be useful to ask members to keep a diary, observe and rate events relevant to the topic of discussion, comment on the actions of colleagues, complete a planned questionnaire on pertinent subjects, or interview colleagues about topics that can be considered at a coming session.

Members' Lack of Ideas During Discussion

The focus of a lively discussion moves from person to person and topic to topic, returning to earlier comments or initiating new branches of thought that are followed or ignored. A discussion leader is often content to let active give and take continue without much guidance, even though no clear theme is being followed, because the purpose at the moment is to benefit individuals with different interests and questions, not the group. The leader steps in, however, when it appears that the discussion is lagging or members want more discipline so they can concentrate on a single issue until they are finished with it.

Members may have little to offer for any of several reasons: (1) rapid-fire talk leaves little time for members to plan or express their ideas; (2) members are not sure of their views or are afraid of speaking in a group; and (3) members are unfamiliar with the topic being discussed. Let us consider each of these reasons.

1.   A person at a conference table may say little because only one can talk at a time, or ought to, and others block him out by taking the floor before he does. Rapid back and forth among members gives a participant little time to plan what she might say or to choose what words she might use, and by the time an appropriate sentence has been composed, the topic has switched to something else. Each remark by a colleague is, moreover, a distraction to listeners as they rehearse a statement of their own notions while following the talk among others. Thus, a member in a discussion hesitates to speak unless she knows what she wants to say and feels it is important to insert those ideas into the flow of talk.

2.   Other discussants are an audience for each speaker. They stimulate a person to do whatever he is most inclined to do at the moment, to obey his dominant impulse. If he is sure what he wants to say on a given issue, for example, he states these ideas better in the presence of the others; the audience stimulates him to speak up and to talk well. If he is not sure of his views or how to express them (a contrasting dominant impulse), the audience fosters that response. Such a person is less articulate and accurate because the audience arouses apprehension about communicating. One who seldom participates because of fear of speaking before others, or does so in an awkward manner, creates problems for himself because it is hard for remaining members to assess or gratify his needs. Moreover, he is often seen in a poor light by colleagues and himself; he becomes a marginal member (Lederman, 1982).

3.   Sometimes, a group's discussion delves into topics that members have never considered, and these unfamiliar issues make participants cautious about expressing their views or asking questions. Given these three reasons, a wise leader develops a way of instilling self-confidence in members so they feel free to offer comments even when their ideas are not fully formed. He must, in a sense, provide them with something to say.

One way to do this is to divide the group into three or four subgroups, asking each to observe the same presentation while watching for different features during it. The presentation can be a lecture, tape recording, film, panel discussion, or role-playing scene. Separate subgroups could focus on what the presentation omits but should not, what is not clearly stated in it, what derivations follow from the material offered, or what the practical implications are of those notions. Because each division of the larger group takes a separate view of the same material, members in each section see different things. Thus, reporters for each subgroup have something to say that is different from the remarks of people in other small units, even though all have observed the same event. The contrasts among the group reports excite interaction, efforts to understand, and needs to correct one another.

A discussion that starts out well may lose its vigor as discussants run out of things to say and begin to repeat themselves. In such a case, it is up to the chairperson to suggest a new angle, a new question, notable differences among members' remarks, or a new topic. In preparation for such a pump-priming contingency, he arrives at the meeting with notes in hand, or writes notes during the session, about questions that ought not be overlooked in the discussion. A leader can help, at a slow time in the talking, by retracing high points in the topics covered thus far and by asking, "Where do we go from here?" Or he can summarize the previous content of the discussion in such a way that its main issues lead to the next question. As examples: "What other observations need to be made on this topic?" "Why do these things happen?" "How can we improve matters?"

Participants may need help with process, not with the content of ideas, if they are jumping from one topic to another, no topic gets adequate treatment, and no one gets much out of the session. Discussants can develop awareness about what is wrong in their procedure, and how they might better proceed, by appointing a person or two as observers of the meeting. These individuals do not take part in the content of the discussion. They sit at one side focusing on how things are being done, rather than what is being said, and are ready with objective descriptions (not evaluations) of the group's methods of work when asked to describe them. Because observers do not take part in the regular interaction, they can study the group's processes as events that affect later occurrences. As a result, their views are refreshingly different from those of a member or leader. They see things the discussants do not observe. They might note, for example, that a few members are dominating the discussion while others have been ignored, the leader allows the discussion to wander without giving any guidance, the discussion needed a summary but none was made, persons P and Q were misunderstanding each other but nobody noticed or commented on it, things said by a talkative member caused angry responses several times for some reason. Members consider, in light of such information, whether their way of work needs to be changed, and if so, how.

A common way to plant interesting thoughts in a discussion is to ask several attendees to prepare brief talks about opposite sides of an issue, for presentation at the start of the meeting. These short speeches are arousing for listeners because the contrasting ideas reveal that there are no pat approaches and imply that different views are possible. A related method is to ask for brief pro and con opinions about the matter at hand. These statements are listed in parallel columns, one column pro, the other con, and members then choose one pair of pro-and-con items to consider first. Which is more useful? Other pairs are discussed in turn.

A helpful, yet simple, device is for a leader to request a quiet period of a few moments during which those assembled are asked to reflect silently on questions assigned to them, a review of what has been said thus far, or plans for the next step in discussion. During this quiet time, each discussant gathers personal ideas without being interrupted by the utterances of others. After such reflection, members commonly discover they have new things to say, even though they earlier thought they had exhausted their ideas on the subject.

Group Conditions That Restrain Exchange

Lack of talk from or among some discussants may be due to barriers that make it difficult to interact easily, such as authority figures at the conference table, too many in the group, or excessive interaction among a small clique of persons, which leaves no time for the rest to contribute.

A speaker with greater social power (who may very well be the chairman) often says more than all remaining members combined. This potent person makes comments to the group as a whole or in response to participants who address him, while a member more often addresses remarks to the powerful one than to anyone else. Thus, back-and-forth comments occur relatively less often among discussants than between the chair and a member. As a result, a discussion can become a series of two-person conversations between the leader and a conferee, while others at the table listen to that exchange. The central person is the focus of attention, and all who are present seemingly collaborate to make it that way (Bales, 1955; Cartwright and Zander, 1968).

A potential source of inhibition arises when one participant takes more than his share of the available time. If members value the contributions of the talkative one because he is an expert or greatly admired, or if they recognize that the speaker's use of the floor is temporary, there is no problem. But if the talker dampens the interest of others, members may withdraw. Their silence may become emotionally laden, moreover, if the talkative one wanders, utters useless ideas in a dragging fashion, or implies that he knows more than anyone else and demands that others listen to him endlessly.

Although many discussions are burdened by members who derail rational give and take, there are little data on how widespread such problems are. Bales noted, as a result of observing conferring groups in real-life settings (community, military, and industrial), that members of such bodies were more disposed to encourage a state of harmony than disharmony (1955). He coded the interpersonal meaning of each comment in these meetings and reported that members make twice as many positive comments (expressing agreement, release of tension, or friendliness) as negative ones (disagreement, tension, or unfriendliness), and this ratio was more typical of the more effective groups. I observed comparable behavior among members of groups in the experimental laboratory while they worked on tasks requiring close collaboration. There, the number of mutually supportive actions such as praising, approving, agreeing, or helping one another, exceeded nonsupportive actions such as blaming, disagreeing, or coercing.

When they occur, hostile remarks have a greater impact, however, than favorable ones, because the purpose behind an angry comment in a group is perceived more accurately by listeners than the intent inherent in a positive remark, and an aggressive remark stimulates an impatient response more often than a friendly comment generates a favorable one (Bodenhausen, Gaelick, and Wyer, 1978). Thus, even though hostility may occur less often, its effects can be dysfunctional for a group when it does appear, unless participants other than the hot-headed ones keep their cool and cope with others' aggression as rationally as possible. This latter behavior keeps the ire from spreading through the room and demonstrates to the hostile persons that their coercive style is in sharp contrast to that used by others; it is not the tone typically taken in the group. While responding to heat with calmness, members must make sure they are understanding the angry ones correctly by checking their meaning and logic ("Let me see if I understand you correctly; do you mean . . . ?"). Listeners also try to discover what lies behind the others' hostility; do the protesters perceive things the rest have overlooked? What do they hope to gain by attacking colleagues and their views? Sensible members, in short, treat others' objections seriously, answer them calmly, and get to the bases of aggressors' anger where these need to be defined.

We saw previously that the size of a group affects how often a member can talk and how much he expects others will contribute. A large assembly typically requires a speaker to use a loud voice and to stand. These demands intimidate shy members and reduce the proportion who are willing to join in the interaction. Another restraint on speech at a meeting is the scheduling of too little time for what must be done. If the chair urges speakers along because the end of the meeting is nearing, those at the table forgo things they wanted to say or talk so briskly that the impact of their message is weakened. In contrast, meetings that drag on too long eventually cause loss of interest among members.

Interpersonal exchange is more interesting, in the United States at least, if it invokes different opinions among members. Thus, a manager of a discussion encourages expression of thoughts unlike ones already stated, by asking for them, or offering such. A useful argument within a group of learners is valuable, because those who hold one point of view hear the opinions of others and modify their own beliefs or feelings when the weight of the evidence convinces them to do so. It is less likely that speakers in a free discussion, in contrast to those in a decision-making session, will persistently defend their own ideas or become victims of groupthink, because participants are trying to learn what they can, are in a mood to modify their useless notions, and are willing to help one another do the same.

Although those who listen can also be learning, most discussion leaders try to weaken barriers against participation so that quiet people can have a say — assuming they will learn more by taking an active part than by watching others interact. An experienced leader of discussion knows that addressing a question directly to a shy person may pull him into the interaction, but it can be more frightening than reassuring unless that person is on the verge of talking and cannot find an opening. The central person looks for signs of such readiness in the face and posture of a quiet member before calling on him or her. We know that a student will become more ready to respond if a teacher looks him in the eye while making a comment. This readiness grows if the teacher listens closely, maintaining eye contact while the newly stimulated person is talking.

Discussants who speak only to the most powerful ones in the room in an attempt, apparently, to win their goodwill, are not much disposed to help others develop new understandings; indeed, they may see associates as rivals and disparage their ideas. This approval-seeking behavior works against the educational aims of a discussion. A leader can be helpful here if she explains to overeager persons that others deserve a chance to speak, bypasses persons who have had the floor too often, or mentions things members sometimes do that cause groupmates to keep quiet. She may, as an instance, cite the rules for brainstorming (described in Chapter Four), because they illustrate the practices members might follow in helping one another to think and talk creatively. A variation of the protection brainstorming provides for hesitant persons is to ask such participant, in the presence of others, to write a response to a specific issue. These statements are then considered one by one without revealing their authors.

Although a discussion period usually does not try to reach an agreed-on conclusion or a vote, participants nevertheless want to sense they are moving through separate topics toward comprehending a central theme or two, not randomly jumping from item to item without any focus for their talk. The person guiding a discussion can forestall members from making disjointed comments by taking charge at crucial times; precisely defining the matter under discussion and requiring that comments be limited to that topic only until treatment of it is finished or interest in it is exhausted. The chair then identifies the next topic and stimulates interest in it before letting interaction resume.

Two kinds of conditions, we can see, must be equally present in a discussion if it is to help members take part: (1) conditions that foster communication along with creative thinking among discussants, and (2) conditions that prevent procedural confusion during a discussion. Each kind of condition must be well developed if a group is to do its job, yet each, if too strong, can prevent the other from having its most useful impact. To illustrate, circumstances that foster ease of communication reduce restraints on members, generate confidence, and create receptiveness to ideas so that members speak freely. However, such characteristics of style can promote talk at cross purposes or wandering and loss of direction. At the same time, leadership that tries to hold a discussion under close control reduces ease of communication and quality of creative thinking. Thus, these two aspects of leadership can create a circular-causal effect in which each may weaken the value of the other. A leader who wishes to create a helpful group discussion must keep the two emphases in balance, using procedures that foster talk and keeping things orderly without inhibiting freedom of discussion. To support a useful discussion, therefore, an effective chairperson must not be too free, easy, and accepting on the one hand, or too controlling and strict on the other hand.

Summary

Easy communication wherein members say what they want to say and get information they want to have is important for members as individuals and for the group as a unit. An unhindered flow of words helps members accomplish their personal objectives and carry out their jobs. Communication is also necessary for completing the regular activities of the organization. Responsible members and managers use a number of methods to help one another express their ideas and hear the thoughts of colleagues when away from an organized meeting.

Improving Communication Among Peers

- Make sure members know one another's duties, talents, and problems, so that they can efficiently ask for and offer suitable information.
- Help members be comfortable with one another by providing opportunities for them to associate freely at work and on special occasions.
- Make conditions in a workplace conducive to easy interchange by providing quiet surroundings, joint tasks, physical proximity, or committee memberships.
- Demonstrate to a member that his ideas have been influential with colleagues.
- Make differences of opinion visible among members, because if they are friendly, they want to develop a uniform view and talk with one another to do so.
- Promote cooperative relations among members and reduce rivalry among them.
- Press members to modify their ideas and compromise where differences of opinion have caused conflict.

*Improving Communication Among Persons with Different
Positions in a Hierarchy*

- Remind a superior that her greater power can make her a
  threat to subordinates; she needs to make subordinates comfortable when she meets them.
- Demonstrate to a subordinate that his or her superior has
  knowledge, skill, and experience that the lower-status person will find useful.
- Make it evident to a subordinate that doing the job well requires frequent communication with a superior.
- Assure a subordinate that the superior will not use his influence to disadvantage less powerful persons.
- Tell a subordinate that the powerholder is well liked by colleagues and that she can therefore expect to feel comfortable with him.
- Remind a subordinate that it is important for members to
  have similar information and that such similarity can be best
  achieved through face-to-face discourse.
- Explain to a member that the superior often has changed
  her mind, is not a rigid person, and thus can be influenced.
- Demonstrate to a subordinate that the fate of the group depends on members' open communication with the superior.

When members gather for a period of discussion, they
are engaged in a cooperative effort. Members can evaluate their
personal situations, learn from their past, and share their ideas
with others in the group, thus learning from others' ideas and
from studying members' reactions to various contributions.

A leader of a discussion group should be aware of the
problems that can occur in such a group's procedures: members reluctant to participate, members lacking ideas to offer,
and barriers to ready give and take. A skilled chairperson uses
methods for overcoming these sources of inhibition.

Overcoming Lack of Interest

- Pose an interesting issue that members will want to discuss.
- Put the question in such a way that it leads members into

interaction, not into merely giving a simple answer that precludes further talk.

- Create a readiness for discussion by providing examples of prior experiences, relevant to the matter at hand, that stimulate members' interest.
- Make sure the question is pertinent to discussants by having them suggest topics for discussion.
- Have members think about the subject in advance of the group discussion.

Encouraging Verbal Input

- Form subgroups and ask each to observe a presentation, prior to the discussion period, from a different point of view, and have them report on what they have seen.
- Suggest new approaches or topics for discussion when the time is suitable.
- Point out contrasts in stated opinions when they occur and the differences that are being ignored.
- Appoint several persons to be observers of the group's process rather than the discussion's content, and have them report their observations.
- Have members open the discussion with brief speeches for each side of the issue.
- Make use of a brief assigned silence so that discussants can gather their thoughts without distraction.

Dealing with Restraints

- Help shy persons enter the interaction.
- Review the flow of the discussion whenever it appears that the talk would benefit from a summary of where the group has been and is heading.
- Teach members how to use idea-gathering procedures described in Chapter Four.
- Keep things orderly but in a way that does not inhibit participation.

Recommended Readings

Amidon, E., and Hough, J. (eds.). *Interaction Analysis: Theory, Research, and Application*. Reading, Mass.: Addison-Wesley, 1967.
This is a collection of articles on ways of studying the interaction among persons in a classroom and on the results of such studies.

Lederman, L. "Suffering in Silence: The Effects of Fear of Talking on Small Group Participation." *Group and Organizational Studies*, 1982, 7, 279–284.
Why some members fear talking in a group and suggestions for bolstering their courage.

Sheffield, A. D. *Creative Discussion*. New York: Association Press, 1936.
This early classic about the values and methods of group discussion was written when discussion groups were first seen as a special method with special benefits requiring special conditions and leadership.

Stasser, G. "Pooling of Unshared Information During Group Discussions." In S. Worchel, W. Wood, and J. Simpson (eds.), *Group Process and Productivity*. Newbury Park, Calif.: Sage, 1992.
Considers the problem groups have when members fail to share information they bring with them to a meeting.

Whyte, W. *Small Groups and Political Rituals in China*. Berkeley: University of California Press, 1974.
Whyte's book reports on the nature of neighborhood discussion groups, created by the Chinese government in days when Mao was that nation's leader, to influence the beliefs and behavior of citizens.

6

ESTABLISHING STANDARDS THAT SUPPORT GROUP CUSTOMS, GOALS, AND VALUES

As one moves from being a child to becoming an adult, one is increasingly uncertain how to behave, dress, or speak. A teenager desperately desires to "do the right thing" so he or she will not be mocked by peers. Adolescents form cliques where they agree on the currently fashionable "thing" and make it seem important. They faithfully follow their gang's customs even when their behaviors offend parents or even, in some cases, violate the law. Adults say adolescents yield to peer pressure. Youths don't use that language, but they adamantly agree it is necessary to be cool, to be accepted by their peers.

A member of most groups is not always free to act as he pleases. His colleagues expect him to do things for the good of the whole, and he either conducts himself as they desire or earns their disfavor. What is the reason for such social pressures? What makes them strong? How can a member weaken their impact? A participant in a group, especially a newcomer, may sense that certain practices are followed by colleagues and feels obliged to conform to them although he is not directly asked to do so. What makes him aware of these hidden norms? Why does he adhere to them?

Persons in a group commonly agree overtly or intuitively on general qualities they want their organization to have, such as pride in the group's performance, talents for the work to be done, harmony among colleagues, efficient procedures for work, and useful interaction with agents outside the group. Participants also identify unwanted conditions within their unit, including embarrassment over a poor output, unsound procedures for accomplishing tasks, and unfavorable relations with agents who make demands of the group. Some of a unit's characteristics become parts of its way of life without members' open discussion or agreement on these matters; everyone understands these procedures are to be followed by all in that body. Examples of such uncodified practices include holding a farewell party for a retiring member, collecting members' signatures on birthday cards, sending flowers to ill members, avoiding public stands on political issues, or following courteous customs in resolving conflicts.

Once their preferred procedures are in place, members prescribe proper behavior in the group through policies, regulations, operating plans, programs, or guidelines. These joint understandings can concern the group's style in such practical matters as work hours, job procedures, flow of work, forms for paperwork, chains of communication, methods for making decisions, discipline among members, time for coffee breaks, safe methods of working, expected levels of productivity, quality of output, evaluation of personnel, budgets for separate programs, and cost analyses. For simplicity, we denote all these understandings, overt or covert, as *group standards*.

Members intend to have their group benefit from such standards, and it usually does. They hope, as examples, to increase the predictability of one another's behavior, prevent strain in their interpersonal relations, define the group's main values, make the unit more efficient, and ensure that it plans ahead for the good of the body (Carver, 1990; Napier and Gershenfeld, 1993).

Practical Implications of Standards

To keep standards alive, members must abide by them when necessary and pressure colleagues to do the same. The more important a standard is to the group, the stronger the pressure on nonconforming members. A standard is more significant under two circumstances: (1) members value the condition the standard has been established to support, and (2) members believe that adherence to the standard will help maintain this valued condition. To illustrate, suppose an organization establishes policies for recruiting new members. They decide they will search for persons with general ability rather than specific training, and that these recruits will be in their early twenties, graduates of one of three specific colleges, and able to speak Spanish. Once the organization implements such standards, they are important for members provided the latter believe the organization needs recruits and that the kind of persons described in the policies will help the group.

Groups teach new members the value of established standards. In organizations that place special emphasis on values or ideas, such as political clubs, communes, cults, or self-help units, neophytes are urged to commit themselves to its beliefs. To do this, persuaders ask new members to devote time and energy to the study and support of these ideas, to invest money or other resources in the group's programs, or to renounce competing activities. In many cases, pressures are applied to members during initiation rites, sales conferences, annual meetings, dedication ceremonies, or confrontations (group versus member) intended to demonstrate to listeners the importance of creating certain characteristics within the group (Galanter, 1989; Kanter, 1972).

During the ordinary give and take within a group, a standard is invoked with such phrases as: "In accord with our earlier agreement . . . " or "As is our usual practice in this club . . . " This reminder of the standard's content justifies behavior being proposed, and if listeners accept the standard, they will be likely to endorse action taken in its behalf.

A member who does not behave according to a group's standard may be ignored at first, because saying nothing to him about his deviant conduct is easier, more kindly, and less embarrassing than pressing him to change. Steering clear of such a member does not, of course, correct his behavior or reinforce the relevant standard. Groupmates are more likely to ignore a deviant act when the violated standard is not critical for the fate of the group. If they feel they should not condone a person's deviant behavior, they may try to change him by some means that cause little strain for themselves. They talk, for example, about his undesirable activities outside his range of hearing, assuming that rumors about this conversation will reach his ears. If this does not work, they talk about him where he can overhear what is being said. If this ploy has no impact, a few members speak to him directly about his behavior. If none of these approaches is effective, they ask an official to meet with the misbehaving member or turn to a disciplinary measure established for such a situation.

If none of these approaches can make a misbehaving member conform, self-appointed enforcers may try their hand. In the United States Senate, for instance, an informal set composed of well-accepted veteran members ensures that each senator adheres to established practices concerning privileges or social power, and it punishes those who are not properly senatorial. In churches, schools, clubs, or workplaces, volunteers curb the actions or thoughts they disapprove of in colleagues. In Japan, workers in a section of a factory set their own standards for quality or production in that unit and control conformity to these standards without involving managers in these efforts. The quality of work in the firm is the business of these quality-control circles, as they are called, not of higher officers (Zander, 1983).

A more complex procedure to enforce standards is necessary when members' behavior is not visible, such as when participants perform their duties hidden from one another or the standards are contained in members' private thoughts. In such cases an organization must develop methods to make these unseen acts observable. Where members deviate from standards but cannot be spotted doing so, they may be secretly observed via informers, hidden microphones, or one-way mirrors. And if the deviance consists of improper ideas, monitors may try to get confessions or watch for subtle signs of unorthodox beliefs. However, such surveillance generates discomfort and distrust that may be more harmful to a group than the deviant behavior being detected. Secret measures for monitoring are usually used, therefore, only where mutual trust is not especially important.

We observed earlier that members will support a group's standard more vigorously and conform to it more closely if they are convinced that doing so will encourage valued conditions within their organization. Thus, members need to understand the reasons behind a standard and why a group will benefit from it. One method for helping participants appreciate these matters is to give them a say in deciding what the standard is to be. Those who take a more active part in such a discussion adhere more strongly to the joint decision they helped establish.

As an indirect step in getting support for their group's standards, members try to strengthen the cohesiveness of their unit, because persons who are attracted to membership will try to do things that help the organization and win approval from colleagues. Responsible members strengthen cohesiveness by choosing persons who fit together well, explaining to the chosen ones what they might get out of belonging to the group, demonstrating to the recruits that the group is meeting their needs, and showing them that they will derive more satisfaction from this group than from others.

When a group's standards require behavior that participants do not like, or when members are not greatly interested in the fate of their unit, they can be encouraged to conform nevertheless by offering them a reward for obedience or a punishment for nonconformity. A reward can be a word of praise, public recognition, time off, promotion, or something more tangible. A punishment can be a rebuke, repetition of a training program, assignment to a different job, demotion, or exclusion from the group in ways we examine in a moment. Neither rewards nor punishments can be effective in inducing conformity if those exposed to such pressures do not wish to remain as members and feel free to leave the group whenever they wish.

The standards of a group are not always formally stated. They can develop under cover as a result of custom, tradition, experience, or habit, and they can be passed along orally from member to member. Informal traditions in a family or seasonal customs in a company may be as strong as established rules. Violations of informal standards are disapproved of as much as violations of more formal ones.

Regardless of whether groupmates place pressures on a person to conform, a member may feel compelled to act as others do if he observes that he sees things differently from colleagues in a situation where all are dealing with the same phenomena. As a result, he is faced with a cognitive conflict. Should he believe his own perceptions, or should he trust the views put forth by others? Because all aspects of this situation are identical except for his own idiosyncratic outlook, the individual feels he must try to see the situation as others do, in order to support mutual understanding and joint action within the group. He must make such a change, moreover, even though this shift contradicts the evidence as he sees it. This kind of conflict is more likely to arise on matters that involve the senses or rational thought than on matters of preference or aesthetics, unless of course autonomy among members on such issues is central to the group's existence because it is, for instance, an art appreciation club or one for sampling gourmet foods.

A deviant is more likely to shift his views so they agree with the opinions of others if a number of persons disagree with him, the information available to members is ambiguous, the changer is not certain his ideas are correct, he knows that others are aware his opinion differs from theirs, and he recognizes that he and the others are members of the same group (Cartwright and Zander, 1968; Napier and Gershenfeld, 1993).

Consequences of Group Standards

Consider a member who is being pressed by associates to meet their expectations. In response, she can ignore these pressures, conform to them, try to modify them so she likes them better, or oppose them and seek to have them abolished. Most often a member abides by them and does not anticipate approval from others for doing so. She accepts the group's rules more readily if she wants it to be successful, believes that adherence to stated standards is good for the group, is committed to helping that unit, or has little power to resist because of her low position or status in the group. As already implied, the power of a group over the behavior of a member is proportional to the attractiveness of the unit for the member. A member's conformity to a group's standards, I suspect, determines her actions and expressed opinions, in the presence of groupmates, more than do her past training, experiences, or motives away from the group.

A person is more likely to conform to a group's standards if he is immersed in that one group and no others. The group may be composed of residents in a monastery, soldiers in a platoon on patrol, sailors on a ship at sea, believers living in a commune, boys in a home gang, workers in a department, brothers in a secret lodge, or those in a society that forbids social interaction with the outside world. Because he associates only with these members, few competing demands reach him. As a result of this membership, moreover, he loses interest in his own needs, sees himself primarily as a part of the group, and automatically does what it requires. Cults, criminal gangs, or extremist political groups commonly try to eliminate the individualism of members by demanding that members not associate with anyone outside their organization or by making them pledge total loyalty to this group and no other (Festinger, Pepitone, and Newcomb, 1952; Galanter, 1989; Kanter, 1972). If an individual is a member of several groups and the requirements of these sets contradict one another, she adheres most closely to the demands of the group that attracts her most.

An entire group may support a specific standard of performance or behavior for a particular member who has a specific position. These are called *role expectations* (Kahn and others, 1964). A leader, for example, is expected to start a meeting on time; a bookkeeper, to keep accounts straight; a shortstop, to make no errors; or a program chairman, to plan suitable activities. If the member accepts a given requirement for his role, he usually works hard to fulfill it and continues to do so even if he fails. Failing a group's standard has a greater impact on a member's self-regard when he is more attracted to the unit. He feels worse if he fails the demands of a group that he deeply respects than he does if he fails a group he does not admire (Zander and Quinn, 1962).

A deviant act by a member is more objectionable to associates if it fosters unwanted group qualities and if they think the act will be repeated. As an instance, if a member has engaged in inappropriate behaviors for some time and is not willing or able to drop them from his repertoire, his groupmates assume he will probably break the rules again. The unattractiveness of a given member's behavior to colleagues is determined by the unfavorableness of those actions multiplied by the perceived probability he will repeat them in the future. A confirmed deviant is more disapproved than a new offender.

A member whose behavior is unsuitable for an organization becomes a target of increasingly stronger pressures to change. He is urged to give up his deviant ways and to adopt ones compatible with the group's standards. Some bodies, like fraternities, religious bodies, cults, or firms that sell services, have formal procedures for pressuring a nonconformist to get in line. Members exert these pressures as long as the deviant is acceptable as a member and as long as there is a reasonable chance of changing him. If a target of such pressures does not listen, however, efforts to correct him become weaker. Members eventually stop talking to a deviant who shows no signs of yielding to persuasion. A case in point occurs in a meeting when discussants ignore the comments of a person who is too different to be acceptable (Festinger, 1950; Shacter, 1951).

If a participant becomes especially unattractive to associates because of his unwillingness to abide by the group's standards, his colleagues may consider designating him as no longer a member of that body. Avoiding the person, refusing to talk with him, or shunning him are preliminary to such a process, but its ultimate form is more extreme. A group may reject a deviant member by arranging things so that he can no longer depend on that group and the group can no longer depend on him — the conditions for belonging are abolished. He is expelled. He is fired, drummed out of the corps, excommunicated, exiled, or disenrolled.

In some situations a deviant is allowed to remain in a group for a while simply because persons who are supposed to remove her cannot bring themselves to do this directly. Instead, they may use indirect ways to get rid of her, giving her few duties, trivial assignments, a job that isolates her from colleagues, or advice about a new occupation available elsewhere so that the deviant eventually drifts away from the group of her own volition (Zander, 1977b). In quite opposite groups, participants are actually encouraged to come up with ideas that violate set standards. Such liberty is fostered in units that are growing rapidly, creating new jobs, engaging in research, developing new information, planning creative programs, or responding to changes in their environment—in groups, in sum, where standards must not be so rigid that they interfere with effectiveness. In such instances members appreciate useful deviant behavior, even though it is unorthodox. They nurture rebels and view them as saviors to be followed. Rebels can inspire desirable change.

An individual's deviancy may be tolerated if it is taken to be a minor matter because it does not interfere with ongoing activities or weaken ties among members. Even when failure to conform harms the unit somewhat, it is overlooked if the body is successful overall. A maverick who resigns voluntarily is forgiven and forgotten, not punished. Unacceptable acts are not taken seriously if they are unintentional and if their perpetrator says he is sorry. Some members earn *idiosyncrasy credit,* the right to be deviants because they occupy high-status positions in their organizations or have served these units well in the past (Hollander, 1958; Kahn, 1964). But such members must not be too deviant too often. Members also ignore associates' nonconforming acts if the members themselves are not attracted to the group and thus do not care to protect its standards.

A deviant is under emotional strain if he is questioned for breaking the group's rules or for trying to change important group standards. He may be plagued by feelings of guilt if he has harmed or embarrassed his mates and by low self-esteem if he does not perform as well as expected or is asked to leave because of incompetence. Because guilt and low self-regard are difficult feelings to control, officials in some organizations interview and counsel departing members to lower the impact of their rejection (Goffman, 1952). The irony for a member who is expelled is that he can feel rejected only if he wants to remain (otherwise he would have left the group earlier when he sensed that he did not agree with others). Also, rejection means to him that a number of persons have turned away from him. A shunned person has no recourse but to look for a new group, even though he is still attracted to the one that dismissed him (Zander, 1977a).

Opposition to Group Standards

Although group standards foster valuable characteristics in a group, some persons do not conform to them because doing so is a form of surrender. A vivid display of this view was presented by Whyte in his book *The Organization Man* (1957) in the days when Senator Joseph McCarthy declared that the federal government was infested with persons who had been lured into joining the Communist party. The senator's claims aroused widespread worries that individuals in groups too often lack the courage to think for themselves or to stand up against their group's demands. Whyte said: "He [the individual] must fight the organization. Not stupidly, or selfishly, for the defects of individual self-regard are no more to be venerated than the defects of cooperation. But fight he must, for the demands for his surrender are constant and powerful, and the more he has come to like the life of the organization, the more difficult does he find it to resist these demands, or even to recognize them. It is wretched, dispiriting advice to hold before him the dream that ideally there need be no conflict between him and society. There always is: there always must be. Ideology cannot wish it away; the peace of mind offered by organization remains a surrender, and no less for being offered in benevolence. That is the problem" (p. 448).

A participant is more likely to share Whyte's view if her personal goals and those of the organization are incompatible and if she derives no sense of pride from being in the group. Or a member may be more involved in attaining her own ends instead of those of the group because she is not a full-fledged member, has a minor role, is not needed by the body, or finds few satisfactions in membership. A deviant will believe that the price of conformity is too high if expectations for her are too difficult, against the law, harm her health, lower her self-regard, hurt her career, or damage associates.

An individual may refuse to conform when colleagues' efforts to influence her are not compelling, even though these persons win her affection, offer her a reward, or threaten her with punishment. Members are not inclined to abide by a group standard, even one they helped define, if they believe the standard is based on an unsound decision. And they will feel free to ignore their group's plans and even seek support for deviant actions if they assume their nonconformity cannot be detected. Members are more likely to ignore a group's standards if their unit is very large because deviant behavior is less visible in such a body.

If a member is an effective agent of influence, he can convince groupmates to abolish certain standards and replace them with ones he advocates. We do not know how often a member convinces colleagues to drop an established rule and go along with a different idea; it probably happens frequently in creative or broad-minded groups, but because the odds against it and the risks of advocating change are great, members may establish procedures that let a participant complain against a standard without danger of retaliation. These procedures are followed by appeal boards, grievance committees, review councils, panels for resolving conflicts, or suggestion schemes. Some deviant members express their displeasure about a group's standards not by breaking rules but by withdrawing to the margins of the group. They may carry less than their share of the group's load, avoid its social activities, remain silent during its discussions, stay away from work when not sick, or dress in an unacceptable manner. By such actions they indicate their dissatisfaction and their interest in a new way, but are not openly subordinate.

The strength of a member's opposition to a group's standard is determined by the size of the gap between his personally preferred behavior and the actions expected of him multiplied by the value he places on his own preferences. Thus, a member of a neighborhood group for social action who discovers that his views are different from those of the majority will be more likely to express his feelings against others' plans if he places greater value on his own ideas. To oppose a group's pressures with confidence, then, a member must define the difference between his personal wishes and those of the group and decide how much weight he puts on his own desires. The more his preferences differ from the group's standards and the more he values his own notions, the stronger his opposition to the group's demands is likely to be. Deviants are, or soon become, marginal members; every lively group has some.

A striking characteristic of group standards is their enduring quality and their resistance to change, partly because members know they will meet pressure and disapproval if they move to modify the group's established policies. The usual stability of a standard has led to a number of experimental demonstrations in which it has been shown that if an entire group discusses and makes a decision about a change in behavior that members might undertake, the agreed-upon change will be more readily adopted than if each person were asked to change on his own without any group discussion. A group agreement describes new expectations members have for one another, thus creating forces on each member to comply with these group supported sentiments — a new group standard. It has been observed that the acts of making the decision and reaching an agreement that has a high degree of consensus among members are more important in getting participants to comply with a new standard than merely participating in the discussion or making a public commitment to abide by a new norm.

How can responsible members help colleagues be aware of the need for reappraising an established standard without their being seen as rule breakers? One familiar method is to sponsor a review and evaluation of the unit's methods so that problems in the group's way of life become visible and discussion of them becomes legitimate. Such an evaluation will be more useful if it is done via an anonymous written questionnaire. Another approach is to ask superiors outside the body, if there are such, to ask for an appraisal of the group's policies that seem due for rethinking. It is sometimes helpful to bring in a consultant who can find what the facts are and comment on these without fear of retribution. Finally, officers of a group may introduce a discussion of questionable standards by describing the successes that groups similar to their own are having with quite different methods or policies and by asking if such procedures "would be suitable for us" (Drucker, 1993).

It is helpful when planning to implement a new standard among members, or persons outside the group, to recognize that a standard persists unchanged over time because forces directed toward changing it are countered by forces directed toward preventing that change. The standard thus endures because it is in a state of equilibrium between contrasting sets of forces. A policy that limits the size of a university's board of regents to twelve, as an example, does not change even though some members believe it should. Those who argue for a larger board assert that it can recruit more experts in relevant fields if it raises the membership limit, can obtain more financial contributions for the university from regents and friends, can increase the number of contacts with powerful decision makers, can have more and larger subcommittees of the board, and can have greater racial and ethnic diversity than now exists. Those who oppose such arguments say that a larger board will reduce the involvement of members, crowd the room in which the board meets, increase costs of paying travel expenses for board members, and make discussions more difficult during meetings. The two sets of contrasting notions are equal in strength and thus cause the board to stay with the current number. The standard is frozen in place.

Clearly, if they wish to change the size of the board's membership, decision makers must reduce the strength of forces acting against a change and increase the strength of forces in favor of a change. They must unfreeze the current state of equilibrium, by changing the field of forces working for and against change. They then can introduce the change and refreeze the forces for and against the new practice by making these equal once more so that the standard is set at a new and stable level (Hawkinshire and Ligget, 1990).

Summary

A group needs to establish standards for its way of life if it is to be a viable entity. Most members support and follow their group's standards. Persons whose behavior deviates from them are pressed by colleagues to keep in line and, in the extreme case, are removed from the group if they will not conform. Standards stating how members should behave are created to ensure that valued qualities will be present in those units. Responsible members exert social pressures to support the group's standards and do a number of things to increase the weight of their pressures. Yet not all members conform; some can, if they are able, resist their group's pressures or even change the standards in ways the members come to see as desirable. Certain members in a group may be allowed to ignore its standards because they are especially valuable persons for that body.

Enforcing Group Standards

- Arouse a desire in members to remain in the group, because the power of a group over its members is greater when the group is more cohesive.
- Show participants how the group's standards contribute to the achievement of important qualities in the group and how adherence to the group's standards facilitates movement toward its goal, maintains the body's unity, lets members develop clear opinions on issues, and helps the group maintain good relations with other units.
- Increase each member's involvement in the group's work by asking target persons to give up individual gains in favor of the group's success.
- Show a member, where possible, that the difference between what the group asks and what the member prefers is not large and that there is thus little need to resist group pressures.
- Help all members see how their contributions help the group accomplish its purposes.
- Give participants a say in establishing standards, because they are more closely obeyed by those who help make them.
- If conformity of members cannot be detected directly, develop a means for determining whether members have done what the group's standards require.
- Develop a method for rewarding and approving persons who

conform to the group's standards, such as a bonus payment, a place on the honor roll, a gold medal, a membership in an honorary society, or a public recognition day.

- Establish for a member goals he can attain so that he derives pride in his work for the group.
- Encourage members to come up with new ideas (even if these do not suit established standards) when creativeness is needed to develop new aspects of the group's life.
- Make it known that any colleague who does not conform to the group's standards will be disapproved.
- Do not reject a deviant from the group if he or she has a history of helping the body, holds a high-status position, deviates on matters that are not critical for the fate of the group, or if the group has a tradition of helping rather than shunning deviants.
- Help one who deviates from the standards to deal with the strain, guilt, and loss of self-esteem that accompany removal from the unit.

Opposing Group Standards

- Decide which of your beliefs are important, what goals you propose to achieve as an individual, and what goals you want the group to achieve. Do your views cause you to be less willing to conform to the group's standards?
- Identify the rewards and coercions offered by colleagues and decide whether you will ignore or accept their appeal.
- Recognize the weight associates place on their urgings as they claim their expectations need immediate attention.
- Do not give up on legitimate personal preferences merely to prevent disharmony in the group.
- Recognize when you have lost interest in a group, because this reduces the threat of being rejected by that body should you not conform to the group's standards. If you do not wish to remain, you need not abide by standards you dislike.
- Recognize like-minded members and join forces with them, to feel support from hearing their views and to develop with them plans for joint opposition to the standards.
- Determine what forces are directed toward changing a stan-

dard and what forces oppose such a change. How strong are these contrasting forces? Decide how you can strengthen supporting forces and weaken opposing ones so that a static standard can be changed.

Recommended Readings

Cartwright, D., and Zander, A. "Pressures to Uniformity in Groups." In D. Cartwright and A. Zander (eds.), *Group Dynamics Research and Theory.* New York: HarperCollins, 1968.
This essay summarizes early research on the origins and effects of group standards.

Galanter, M. *Cults: Faith, Healing, and Coercion.* New York: Oxford University Press, 1989.
Describes why cults and charismatic groups develop power over their members and why members abide by the extreme demands of such groups.

Hollander, E., and Offerman, L. "Power and Leadership in Organizations." *American Psychologist,* 1990, *45,* 179–189.
A review of writings on persons who have enough power to support or ignore group standards.

Kahn, R., and others. *Organizational Stress: Studies in Role Conflict and Ambiguity.* New York: Wiley, 1964.
Some group standards define roles separate members of an organization must play. The research described in this book reveals the sources and effects of these pressures on members.

Kanter, R. *Commitment and Community: Communes and Utopias in Perspective.* Cambridge, Mass.: Harvard University Press, 1972.
Shows the ingenious ways standards are enforced in closed communities where members must obey the commune's rules.

7

FOSTERING HARMONY
AMONG MEMBERS

During a board meeting the other day I realized I was having a good time, the meeting was a pleasant occasion, and others around the table apparently felt the same. The talk was quick and pointed; differing views arose because problems were being solved, not because intellectual turf was being defended. There was good humor, but work was being done.

A board member is supposed to be bored. Why was this session a rewarding one? The unit's purpose had much to do with it. The group is the governing body for a club interested in current affairs, and it met to collect ideas for the coming year's programs. Tentative suggestions included examining a local scandal concerning disrepair in the town's sewers, financial problems of the schools, crises in the Balkans and Middle East, issues in a coming election of city officers, and fears that the town was growing too fast. There were more than enough in these and other ideas for a good menu of sessions. Choosing among the topics would be a simple and straightforward task. However, several members of the board had in mind a different approach to program planning that they wanted colleagues to approve. Their notion was to transform the group into an informal grand jury that would spend months investigating the facts in the sewer scandal, determining who was at fault and exposing these guilty souls. This unusual way of examining a local issue appealed to many at the meeting but finally was dropped after a brief tussle for fear it would get them into blaming city employees and questioning their integrity on the basis of information that might be incomplete or biased. We could end up doing more harm than good to neighbors and discussants because of half-baked detective work.

There were several reasons, beyond interest in the board's task, that caused members to work together well on the program selection task. Some of the participants were friends. The members had to move quickly because plans were to be finalized soon. And members were alike in trying to preserve effective and harmonious relations in their meetings: this shared sensitivity inspired loyalty to the group and a desire that it prepare a good report.

The meeting of the current affairs board was not an unusual one; most people who work with others enjoy making things go well in their collective efforts and get satisfaction from developing a sound product. To illustrate, when a meeting room door opens after a committee session, the comments often are lively, and members show they are pleased with how things went and with their product. Yet the sources of such cheer are seldom studied. *Joi de group* is commonly thought to be a side effect that does not warrant examination, even though in many groups it is the most striking feature of their unit. In this chapter we examine the origins of group harmony, defined as a condition conducive to comfort among members and in their interactions. Then we consider how harmony can be restored when disagreement among members is causing enough tension to threaten the group's existence, efficiency, or effectiveness.

Sources of Harmony

In a college rooming house, the residents took delight in insulting one another and in quarreling about political matters on which they were ill informed. I never decided if these men were so joyously abrasive because they had little skill in human relations, were tired from their tough schedule of studies, or were sorry they fell in with this bunch. In a company devoted to developing new products for use with computers, the employees in one department were in a constant state of anger because of the way a supervisor disparaged subordinates' ideas. The climate in the place changed to one of joint collaboration and support when the hostile supervisor departed.

Although there are unhappy entities like the ones just described, members of most groups, as I said, are more disposed to encourage a state of harmony than of disharmony. When hostility arises among them, they are more interested in removing it than in continuing it, and members' efforts to reduce disharmony in a group become stronger (within limits) as the friction among them is greater. We noted earlier that there is empirical support for these assertions, based on observations made years ago of conference groups in military, industrial, and community settings. In a more recent study of groups whose members held contrasting views and who tried to persuade one another, the chances were good that their disagreements might become heated. Yet even in such a hot situation, members were more likely to use reason, requests, or attempts to make the opposition feel good than lies, threats, or appeals based on their position and authority. They sought, in short, to avoid a quarrel in favor of a well-tempered discussion, presumably because a softer approach is more useful to the group (Savard and Roger, 1992). In some cases, of course, members are not able to create conditions they prefer because sources of discomfort in their unit are too entrenched to remove.

Harmony among members is facilitated if they agree about goals, either for themselves or the group, and if their acceptance of and adherence to the group's standards is strong. If members are alike in hopes, ambitions, or goals and in acceptance of their group's standards, each knows what to expect from the other and why a participant acts as he does. Most members' moves aid actions of colleagues; they are aimed in similar directions, which generates cooperation among them.

In accord with this line of thinking, responsible members often do things that foster harmony. One useful approach is to make sure members understand what is behind each others' intentions and actions. Such understanding can be generated by selecting recruits who are similar to the group's current members, because commonality of belief preserves loyalty and pleasant interpersonal relations. This kind of selection procedure is especially common in fraternal associations (Scott, 1965), clubs, or research units. The rosters of newly created committees may likewise be assembled on the basis of who will work well with whom. And ability to get along with others, it has been reported, is more important than talent or productivity in determining which scholars are hired for teaching positions in colleges.

Harmony is facilitated by encouraging participants to develop personal motives that are relevant to the group's purposes and to drop those that are not. Most commonly, defining of most appropriate objectives is accomplished when a member is recruited and learns, during a period of orientation, that some things he hopes to obtain in that group are not obtainable because members are not interested in them, or will not tolerate them. In other cases, members are taught to want things that are acceptable to colleagues (Moreland and Levine, 1980).

Harmony is fostered if members conform to social pressures placed on them by peers to follow the unit's standards, instead of violating these agreements and inviting disapproval. Those who make decisions for a group want to ensure that it has enough power to determine the intentions and actions of its members. One way to strengthen the power of a group over members' behavior is to increase the participants' commitment to that body. Some organizations work to foster this commitment (Galanter, 1989; Kanter, 1972; Moreland and Levine, 1980). They tie participants to the body by asking members to make sacrifices for it, invest time or money in its actions, or undergo a confrontation session in which they are told how they can become more valuable to the group. They may also solidify group ties by demonstrating to members that they derive benefits from this body which cannot be found elsewhere, or by generating a perception of unity among members. Groups with greater unity have a stronger influence on the beliefs of members and are more attractive to them.

Harmony is encouraged among members by developing

in them a stronger desire for achievement of group success — a disposition to develop pride in their group's accomplishments. When this desire is stronger, a group is more productive, and members work together better as each participant seeks an end that is also sought by groupmates. The desire for group success increases in strength, moreover, as a group is more successful. Measures that generate more of this desire help create harmony.

Smaller groups tend to have more harmony than larger ones. Members in large groups, compared to those in smaller ones, are less likely to participate, pair with others, or work hard on the group's task, and are more likely to reveal aggressive behavior. Those in smaller groups tend to be more active, cohesive, and productive than in larger ones (Wheelan and McKeage, 1993). As groups increase in size, a smaller and smaller proportion of members run the organization, make decisions for it, and talk to the total. As a consequence of such tendencies, more members become marginal and engage in activities that are less useful for a group's outcome. Larger bodies more often depend upon impersonal means for communicating rules and policies such as published statements, memoranda, or notices on bulletin boards than do smaller organizations. This impersonal announcing of group rules is made necessary by the greater centralization of authority and the complexities of reaching the many members. As a consequence, pressures toward uniformity have less weight for members as an entity increases in size. The evidence is strong that larger groups have more absenteeism as well as turnover of membership. It seems evident, all in all, that members find participation more satisfying in smaller groups than in larger ones and that conditions conducive to harmony arise more often in units that are not too large (Zander, 1977a).

Leaders of a group foster harmony by recruiting desirable members. The attractiveness of an individual in the eyes of group members is determined by the positive value of his particular acts or attributes in light of the group's selection criteria and the probability that he or she will reveal these characteristics in the future. Personal qualities a group appraises in a member include skills, abilities, talents, income, experiences, training, physical attractiveness, willingness to work, or lack of undesirable attributes. In some associations a potential member does not need many qualities to be attractive; it is enough if he or she has the initiation fee, a registration to vote, strength to march in a demonstration, an alcohol-soaked liver, or a soul to be saved. In other kinds of groups, the attractiveness of a potential member depends on the fact that he or she needs the group or that the group will do the person good — members welcome the chance to help.

An invitation to a recruit, unlike the removal of a member, requires assent by the invited one. Thus, recruiters must convince a potential recruit that he will benefit from joining. Such an appeal is made in various ways. The newcomer is shown that the group's programs are important to the community of which it is a part and that the neophyte will help outsiders by joining. He is shown that the group provides opportunities he values, such as a chance to use his skills, to practice his profession, to accomplish personal goals, to have fun, to be wanted, to earn money, to have security, to be personally changed in some way, or to escape humdrum parts of his existence. He is shown that the group contains members who will be compatible with him and who presumably will work well with him. He is told that the organization will defend or protect him against fearful adversaries: liberals, sinners, reactionaries, or racists. The new one is gently drawn into the group by being asked to do a small job for it, in the hope that a minor involvement will convince him that there are appealing qualities in the unit, that he will benefit from full-fledged membership, and that he would like to join it. It can happen, in contrast to the above, that members make their selections of newcomers on grounds that may not foster desired conditions within the group: they like the looks of the recruit; or the person is related to important individuals, is wealthy, is supported by powerful backers, strongly desires to join, promises to help the group in influential places, or is supported by an officer of the group.

As we noted, members sometimes protect the harmony of their unit by removing deviants, even though this is a distasteful task because advocates of rejectees may defend the latters' actions.

The issue of fairness can arise if the standards by which a member should abide are stated in such ambiguous terms that it is hard for associates to determine whether a given person's actions are living up to the letter of the rule. Thus, when members prepare a statement of appropriate conditions for membership in their group, they may express them as negative injunctions; that is, in terms of what shall not be allowed or tolerated instead of what shall be approved or welcomed. A person has fewer excuses for failing a negative injunction than for an affirmative one, because what should not be done can be precisely put and observed, and the liability of an actor depends on whether his behavior has had undesirable consequences, not on whether he failed to do good. As an example, eight of the Bible's ten commandments are stated as negatives; that is, as "thou shalt not."

Some bodies — college faculties, psychotherapy groups, creative teams in research or writing — tend to be tolerant of those who transgress their injunctions, because they recognize that members of their units need an open mind and a willingness to examine unorthodox ways of thinking or acting. In such bodies, participants who too slavishly stick to the unit's usual practices are less useful to the group.

Studies of the kinds of members more often removed from groups and of reasons for their removal reveal that conditions other than productivity or conformity to a group's rules often help decide who is to be set aside. These include discrimination on the basis of age, gender, race, or ethnic origin; status in the group; failure by that body; or need for the unit to win approval by outsiders. Also, groups with higher cohesiveness may be more ready to dispense with members who threaten that desirable state.

Members who violate prohibitions agreed on by a group may be retained if the rule breakers keep their misconduct undetected, members dislike to speak ill of another, removal of a person exposes the group to retaliation by that individual's supporters, or the individual is valuable to the group despite eccentricities that offend some. Most groups have one or two of these kinds of members.

Dealing with Disagreements Among Members

Members of the board for a community of condominium owners
met to decide whether they should sign a revised contract with
a company that specializes in maintaining the buildings and
grounds of such developments. The newly worded agreement
was the product of a joint committee composed of a few condominium owners and officers of the firm. The president of the
community board asked for comments on the contract. The
offered statements revealed that some on the board were uneasy about whether several sections of it were strong enough
to protect the village against poor workmanship, liability law-
suits, and problems that arise because board members are not
able to discern if the agent is doing a good job. They said, "Let's
not sign it." Another set of members declared that they cannot
know if the contract is suitable until they have experience working with the agent under this new agreement. They urged that
the contract be approved. The board was in a bind because of
contrasting opinions among the members. Neither side was willing to change their views.

Such a disagreement is not uncommon within groups
created to make decisions. It can be called a conflict if two or
more parties disagree over what the other ought or ought not
do—when each side *knows* what should be said or done and *knows*
that opponents' views on these matters are wrong. I have seen
a conflict arise within a group because of the unwillingness of
some to accept persons nominated for membership, different
views about allotment of funds in the budget, disagreement
among officers over who should speak for the unit, contrasting
ideas about the way to settle a lawsuit, doubts about a plan to
create a new official position within the entity, or feelings among
a clique of members that the group is ignoring the needs of certain departments. It is noteworthy that members may differ with
one another but never express these views because rules or traditions in that body forbid overt dissension. These unexpressed
disagreements can nevertheless affect members' interaction and
the quality of the group's performance. A dispute, whether overt

or covert, may make the group unpleasant for both participants and observers (O'Connor, Gruenfeld, and McGrath, 1993).

Several conditions within a group make it more likely that a disagreement will arise among members. One such condition is a lack of regularized procedures for conducting its activities, which may result in members doing unexpected things that appear to be at cross purposes (O'Connor, Gruenfeld, and McGrath, 1993). Another situation is competition among participants because they have different goals or plans for themselves or the group that are not blended into an aim accepted by all. Sometimes one set of members wants one goal and a contrasting clique wants another. For instance, members want their association to take action against undesirable qualities in the unit's surroundings, while a competing coalition wants the group to study the causes of these characteristics and to report its findings.

A strong source of conflict exists when members of a cooperative unit are faced by scarce resources: for example, all members of a cattle-raising community have to share the same pasture, as no other good grazing land is available; or the income of a city arts society decreases, and backers of separate kinds of performers must decide how the smaller budget is to be allocated. In such a case, if members act to serve their own needs and ignore the desires of others, they reduce the supply of resources for all, including themselves. If a few ranchers allow more cattle in the pasture for more hours than the rest of the animal raisers, they reduce the supply of grass for others and for themselves (Lohmann, 1992). When resources have to be shared, then, there is an inherent conflict between individual and group interests. An individual can control his own behavior but not the behavior of others, unless all agree that the group's interest will be protected first (Kramer, 1990). There also is, in this situation, a temporal conflict between short-term and long-term considerations. Some members will want to satisfy their own needs first (seize short-term gains), because doing so will increase their influence, wealth, and status. In view of such a need for haste, a member may find it hard to justify self-restraint. Also, if members give more support to the needs of the group (favor long-term gains), there is a risk that some will take advantage of "share and share alike" rules by working for their own good while colleagues are taking no more than their allotted amount of resources. They take a free ride.

What makes members greedy and willing to face disapproval by associates if caught? When the total amount of resources is small, some are eager to fill their own desires as soon as they can. The same consequence occurs if the pool of resources is not being replenished fast enough. If a group is growing, members recognize that their share is bound to become smaller and that they had better get theirs soon. If some members are inclined to think of their own needs first, regardless of the wants of their group, they may assume it is proper to ignore objections from groupmates. If a member is extraordinarily valued by the group or has a high position among the unit's officers, he may believe it is appropriate to take a larger share than others. A member who suspects that others are greedy may try to get his before the others do. Finally, if a member can quietly take more than his fair share and no other member will know he has done so, he may be more inclined to grab what he can (Kramer, 1990).

Another circumstance that fosters conflict among members is the presence of a person or two who are disposed to be hostile toward colleagues, to confront any opposer and make him recant his notion while rejecting the willingness of the other to compromise. Interpersonal hostility is also more probable within a group if one party uses procedures that are intended to coerce resisters into submission (see Chapter Eleven). Interpersonal hostility arises if some members believe they have the right to take part in a decision but are not allowed to do so, or if they expect that others will be helpful but those persons provide no assistance. Members who are concerned with achieving good results for themselves and who ignore others' desires or feelings tend to generate conflict between themselves and colleagues.

Situations within a group that generate tension among members make conflict among them likely. These situations include not being given an opportunity to speak in a meeting, being pressed by associates to produce, being uneasy about the reactions others will have to one's comments, having one's ideas or behaviors criticized in public by groupmates, being unable to understand what others are saying, or being the scapegoat of fellow members (Napier and Gershenfeld, 1993).

Sequence of Events in a Conflict

If an interpersonal conflict is allowed to flower untouched, it proceeds through several stages like the following (Forsyth, 1983). First, members recognize they disagree. Then one or more confront their opponents and try to persuade the others to change their views. Those on each side become more attached to their initial positions and more eager to defend these notions as a result of arguing in favor of them. Their rationality in thinking and in style of speech lessens, and they allow hostility to enter into their manner. Whatever one side does when trying to coerce the other is imitated by the ones to whom it is directed. As those in each party speak, they use increasingly strong language, and the anger in both cliques escalates. Each side wants to win, not work toward an answer that will be acceptable to both. Neither party now trusts the intentions of the other. Tension aroused among those involved in the contest eventually begins to flag, because the arguers cannot maintain their emotions at a high level for a long time. In addition, bystanders make it clear that the disagreement is unpleasant to them, is not getting anywhere, and is unacceptable as a way of behaving in that body. They urge the rivals to "cool it."

Steps in Resolving a Conflict

Participants may stop talking to one another, allow long pauses to settle on the group, or in other ways withdraw from a stressful situation if they see and accept that a conflict is not useful to themselves or the group. In the heat of a disagreement, dissenters usually are not willing to hear the comments of peacemakers who press them toward rational discussion. As their anger wears thin, however, they begin to consider the advice of the observers.

Conflict resolvers in a group can be helpful toward restoring calm by asking those involved in the fight to describe what needs they hope to satisfy by clinging to their own view and not listening to the opinions of rivals. If such motives can be identified, peacemakers may foster movement of the disagreers toward a resolution by helping them discern how they might meet these prime desires in ways other than insisting on the correctness of their favorite answer. The interveners, in effect, help disagreers adopt procedures used in problem solving (Fisher, Ury, and Patton, 1991). We can see that a conflict and efforts to resolve it tend to reduce the quality of a group's performance (O'Connor, Gruenfeld, and McGrath, 1993).

Qualities of a Useful Conflict

Although a conflict among members is uncomfortable for both those involved and those who observe it, groups often benefit from a heated airing of contrasting views, because such interaction arouses interest in finding the best resolution to the disagreement. It is notable that conflicts can be keener among members of cohesive groups who tend to have strong group standards and who therefore press one another to abide by the rules. Persons who wish to change standards of a cohesive body meet opposition. Clearly, a group's cohesiveness and stability may be threatened if members do not work through differences of opinion among them and decide whether the standards ought to be changed or kept as they are.

A useful conflict, in contrast to a useless one, has a number of qualities that need to be encouraged by responsible members (Witteman, 1991). They include the following:

- Members critically evaluate one another's ideas.
- Members generate more ideas than in less useful discussions.
- Participation among members is widely shared.
- Members are flexible in their ideas and actions; they do not insist on one view or behavior.
- Responsible members try, as necessary, to summarize where the discussion is heading.

- Members deliberately work to find a conclusion they and others can accept.
- Members successfully influence colleagues and are influenced in turn by them.
- Members seek and underscore their agreements with one another.

Summary

Sometimes harmony among members is the outstanding feature of a group. Members in most units are more disposed to encourage harmony among them than disharmony. They foster it by

- Ensuring that members agree about goals for the group
- Selecting recruits who are similar to members in their beliefs and values
- Selecting recruits whose skills and aims are relevant to the group's purposes
- Ensuring that members accept and conform to the group's standards
- Arousing members' desire for group success
- Facilitating success by the group

A conflict can arise within a group if two or more members disagree over what the other ought or ought not do — when each side knows the other is wrong. Such friction is more likely to occur when members are rivals rather than cooperators, the unit has no regularized procedures for its activities or for dealing with conflict, members must share resources which are in short supply, or they are disposed to distrust the intentions of colleagues and anger easily.

A conflict within a group tends to move through a series of phases in which hostility escalates on each side until it eventually fades so that participants become willing to listen to members who are not involved in the tiff, and the arguers become able to reason. Most conflicts among members are wasteful, but some can arouse curiosity and willingness to learn or consider changes. These become valuable events in an organization.

Recommended Readings

Blake, R. R., and Mouton, J. S. *Solving Costly Organizational Conflicts: Achieving Intergroup Trust, Cooperation, and Teamwork.* San Francisco: Jossey-Bass, 1984.
The authors describe a procedure for replacing chronic conflict with rational understanding and cooperation.

Felson, R., and Tedeschi, J. (eds.). *Aggression and Violence: Social Interactionist Perspectives.* Washington, D.C.: American Psychological Association, 1993.
This book contains a number of articles discussing the kinds of social interaction that precede aggressive behavior in a group.

Horwitz, M., and Berkowitz, N. "Interpersonal and Intergroup Methods of Managing Social Conflict." In S. Whelan, E. Pepitone, and V. Abt (eds.), *Advances in Field Theory.* Newbury Park, Calif.: Sage, 1990.
A review of research on methods for resolving conflicts.

Pruitt, D., and Rubin, J. *Social Conflict: Escalation, Stalemate, and Settlement.* New York: Random House, 1986.
The authors describe the origins of conflicts, the behavior that typically develops during a conflict, and procedures that help in resolving them.

Ury, W. L., Brett, J. M., and Goldberg, S. B. *Getting Disputes Resolved: Designing Systems to Cut the Costs of Conflict.* San Francisco: Jossey-Bass, 1989.
A book-length treatment of many methods for dealing with conflicts within groups in varied settings, from playgrounds to coal mines.

Part Two

EFFECTIVE
GROUP
MEMBERS

8

DEVELOPING AND EXERCISING
PERSONAL POWER

Group life gives an individual many opportunities to influence others. A member wins an argument with a colleague. A school principal teaches staff members how to motivate pupils. A star of a team is imitated by younger players. A platoon leader issues orders. A supervisor rewards the "worker of the month." A bully threatens schoolmates to make them do what he wants.

One who is capable of influencing another to change in a particular way has *power* over the other in that specific instance, even when one's words or deeds are copied by observers without one's intending them to be. A tactful person seldom mentions his personal power, because doing so implies to a listener that the speaker is primarily interested in his own gains, treating associates in ways that are satisfying to himself and ignoring of others' needs. Instead of saying that he influences associates, a powerful person usually says that he guides, counsels, advises, or assists others, because such terms for encouraging change are more acceptable designations than the words "power" or "influence." Despite the dislike of these words, ordinary citizens admire powerful persons and encourage young people to strive for an influential station in life. It is fashionable, moreover, in discussions of modern management methods, to speak of "empowering" one's subordinates. Thus, popular attitudes toward social power are mixed: a person may want more power, but he should not make this wish too obvious or selfish.

This chapter and Chapters Nine and Ten discuss several aspects of social power. Here we concentrate on power among individuals in a group and consider the methods members use to exercise their influence, why they choose a given procedure, and what power does to a person who has it. Chapter Nine discusses how influential agents make their actions count, and Chapter Ten examines good and bad consequences for a person being influenced.

When a group tries, as a unit, to act as an agent of influence, its decisions in doing so are made by individuals. These persons acting in concert use the same approaches, for the same reasons, as any of them would when working as a solo agent of change. How a group attempts to change other groups is not discussed in this book. The topic is treated in two volumes: *Effective Social Action by Community Groups* (Zander, 1990) and *Making Boards Effective* (Zander, 1993).

Several features in the nature and use of social power are worthy of our notice (French and Raven, 1959; Kipnis, 1976; Raven, 1992; Savard and Roger, 1992). Persons who wish to change others and have power in their relations with those individuals are ordinarily able to influence them only in specific matters, not in all. For example, they may be able to influence colleagues on an executive committee to act in matters concerning the organization's programs or finances but cannot have this effect in respect to leisure activities of members or their choice of a wife. It follows that an agent of change is not influential in every case and place. Moreover, persons with power to affect the views of an executive committee may have no influence at all with persons in the personnel department.

Initiators of efforts to change others who know they can influence a specific person in specific matters may choose not to use their power at the moment; instead, they may keep it in abeyance until they need it. Thus, merely possessing a given sort of power does not mean that it will be used often or even at all. In addition, some persons with power to influence may not realize they have it. We see examples of this when members quietly adopt the views or style of a given person — the imitated one is a model for the imitators without realizing this is the case. Some kinds of power come to a person simply because he is expert in a particular type of information, even though he is not trying to influence others. An expert's power derives from the tendency of uninformed persons to ask the wise individual for information or advice. He or she has no influence (sadly enough) if no one knows that he or she is well informed or if no one listens to what he or she says because the expert is a marginal member.

Power is a two-way proposition. Persons seeking to spread a given idea may cause others to change in certain respects, and the informers themselves may be influenced by the target persons. As illustrations, in negotiations, bargaining, or problem solving, participants on each side recognize that listeners intend both to influence and to be influenced, to inform and be informed. Thus, participants change their minds during a discussion and simultaneously change the beliefs of others. Target persons often develop more or less opposition and resistance, to protect themselves from being influenced or from being made uneasy by the style the influencers employ. The exercise of power in a give-and-take discussion can be seen as an ebb and flow, as a sparring match. For the moment, we concentrate on influencers. Later we shall attend to the responses of target persons.

Methods of Being Influential

A person who wishes to influence another may go about it in a variety of ways. Which method he chooses depends on his judgment about what will work. How might an individual try to change another?

Giving a Reward

A would-be influencer may ask a person to do a particular thing and make this request acceptable by providing an object or circumstance the recipient would welcome — a reward for the person's help or obedience. The agent of change may promise to approve of the actor, to praise him publicly, or to express appreciation and gratitude. He may proffer valuable prizes, such as money, a gift, or a new job, unless he fears that these will be perceived as bribes and thus rejected by the receiver. He may give rewards to an influenced one without advance notice after the individual has completed what was asked. This after-the-fact reward, called a *reinforcement,* is a potent method of influencing that can be used effectively only if the recipient happens (or is urged) to do the things the agent of influence wants, and the agent knows that the person has done so. To be an effective reinforcement, a reward must be linked by the receiver to his performance of the act.

Persons who move into action solely because of an offered reward are ordinarily motivated to earn that benefit, not to carry out an action that is valuable or satisfying in its own right. The reward, not the change, is the incentive. When this is the case, people do only what is necessary to get the gain. They behave in ways requested by the reward giver. They make these actions visible so that the agent of change knows that their behavior deserves to be rewarded. The influencer keeps an eye on target persons to be sure they do the things that warrant a prize. Because the latter's overt acts can be observed, rewards are useful ways to make sure that innovations occur. If a reformer seeks transformation of the beliefs or attitudes of receivers, however, it is difficult for him to determine whether those addressed have in fact made such changes. People can say they have revised their thinking in order to win a reward when they actually have not adopted new beliefs.

Being Coercive

An influencer becomes coercive when he intends to constrain the freedom of choice among persons he wishes to induce. In using coercion the initiator threatens to punish target persons if they do not do what they are asked or do not stop behaving in undesirable ways. The coercer inflicts a penalty or punishment on the ones being coerced until the latter change their behavior. He may do this by saying he will disapprove of the one being pressured, make the latter's unwanted actions widely known, or reveal his disappointment in the one being targeted. He may threaten loss of pay, denial of privileges, physical restraint, even pain. These forms of coercion are seldom well received by the person on whom they are imposed and often accompany a demand for actions that the influenced person is not pleased to perform.

Considering within-group coercive actions in general terms, we can see that devotees of such tactics may use one of three types. (1) They interfere with the actions of target persons so that the latter cannot perform well for themselves or the group. They engage in a sit-in, sabotage machinery, take over a meeting, boycott services offered by the one under pressure, or mount a hostile demonstration. (2) They physically limit the freedom of target persons or hostages by seizing one or more of them and keeping them under isolation or under guard, until the kidnapped ones or authorities meet the demands of the hostage takers. (3) They threaten harm or inflict it on target persons, other individuals, or things of value to the one under the threat. The latter will be publicly ridiculed, demoted, sent messages promising them harm, physically assaulted, or their dear ones hurt unless they change their ways as being pressed to do.

When using either rewards or punishments in order to generate change in others, the initiative is in the hands of the agent of influence. He desires that the influenced persons act without question. He develops the idea of making the change, presses the others to act, and tells them what the consequences will be if they refuse. He monitors the others' behavior to see whether to administer a reward or punishment. Because the ones being pressed to change know that their actions are being observed, they endeavor to make it appear that they are doing as asked — either by making obedient behavior visible or by hiding deviant actions. Thus it can be seen that rewards and punishments have less effect in changing easily concealed forms of behavior, such as personal beliefs, feelings, or attitudes, than on overt actions, because the former cannot be monitored as well as the latter (French and Raven, 1959; Raven, 1992).

Being an Expert Informant

An individual can be influential on certain matters because listeners perceive him to be well informed in that field. He may provide his wisdom in a lecture hall, at a conference table, or in writing, and he may do so on his own initiative or at the invitation of those seeking his help. An expert is more likely to change the views of audience members if several circumstances exist: (1) he presents his ideas, (2) listeners want his views, (3) they believe the idea provider is an expert in the matter at hand, and (4) they consider his thoughts to be good ones. If any of these conditions is missing, the influencer will not be successful in his attempt to change others' views.

In some groups, target persons do exactly the opposite of what an expert suggests—the influencing agent causes a "boomerang effect" among listeners. This negative result occurs if those exposed to the expert's ideas believe he is using his expertise in his own interests, not in behalf of listeners (Raven, 1992).

Making Oneself Attractive

In some settings a person may be influential as a result of being attractive to the one to be changed so that the latter wants to associate with the attractive person or do and think things the attractive person does. A friend can be more influential than an acquaintance. The power of such a valued model over an admirer persists even when the admirer does not know the agent of influence. In such an instance, one who copies the other asks oneself what the attractive person might do in the given situation and then acts in ways that fit that hunch. Because the attracted one uses the other as a source of reference, this kind of influence has been called *referent power*.

Note that a person may be influential without intending or planning to be. Her ideas, attitudes, dress, or gestures are adopted by others, who may observe without ever talking to her. She is a source of change by others because she is imitated by them, even though she may not know this is happening.

Others copy qualities of a model because those traits are perceived as valuable and because the agent of influence is respected as an expert, is liked, or is the kind of person imitators hope to be some day.

I have a friend who decided in his adolescent years that he would guide his behavior by doing the opposite of whatever his older brother did. He made this decision because the older one was constantly getting into trouble in school and community. My friend perceived the brother as an unattractive model. The older brother had negative referent power over the younger one (Raven, 1992).

Appealing to Important Values

One of the ways an individual bolsters an influence attempt is to convince a listener that the requested change in behavior will help him live in accord with values he wants to obey. The agent may, for example, assure the person to be changed that he will be braver, more rational, more kindly, more outspoken, or more honest if he acts in ways advocated by the inducer.

Not uncommonly, a holder of power justifies his influence attempts by appealing to norms or customs of society. One such norm is *fair reciprocity* — an influencer declares that she has done certain favors for the listener and it is now fair to ask for a return of that favor. A person who is attempting to be influential may also say that he needs help, is not able to do what he wants to do, and badly needs the target person's assistance. This is called *dependent power,* an influence attempt by a powerless person. A would-be influencer may ask for *equity in costs,* declaring that he has spent time, energy, or money in behalf of the listener and therefore has the right to ask the receiver for a payback (Raven, 1992).

Within a hierarchical organization, a superior may ask, instruct, or order a subordinate to do specific things in certain ways. Both the initiator and the receiver understand that the higher-status person has the right to make such demands and that the lower-status one has the duty to obey. The superordinate individual, in this instance, has *legitimate authority* to act as he does in the organization; this is granted to him by the charter and bylaws or the support and approval of superiors.

Offering General Information

Some agents of influence do no more than supply information to anyone who will look or listen. They offer a more or less factual statement by way of memorandum, announcement on a bulletin board, newspaper story, speech, or other means of communication. They do not try to persuade listeners or inflame them with propaganda; they merely impart knowledge. They assume that these ideas will show target persons that times are ripe for a change, or that the information furnishes a sensible answer to a question that is before the persons reached by these ideas. Those who distribute this information take it for granted that some members of the audience are interested (or could be) in the issue at hand and are looking for thoughts that will help them understand it better.

Changing the Environment

An agent of influence can generate changed behavior by modifying others' surroundings in ways that require them to act differently. Often such changes are ones that target persons oppose. As illustrations: an assembly line is set at a faster pace so that workers will produce more per day, a ward room door in a mental hospital is locked so that patients cannot wander, a busy legal office is flooded with gentle music so that lawyers will treat clients courteously, or service representatives in the telephone company are told that some of their conversations with customers are tapped so they will follow the firm's policies when dealing with callers' complaints.

　　　The influence strategies described thus far are ones researchers developed on theoretical grounds and studied in an experimental laboratory or a natural setting (Cartwright, 1959; Kipnis, 1976; Raven, 1992; Savard and Roger, 1992). When people are asked what methods they most often use to influence others, they describe additional procedures. The self-reports of executives, as instances, include the use of reason, bargaining, forming a coalition of like-minded persons, friendliness, and making the listener feel good about himself or herself (Kipnis, Schmidt, and Wilkinson, 1980; Littlepage, Nixon, and Gibson, 1992). The processes administrators use least often are sanctions, blocking of freedom, bargaining, or reminders of one's authority. When college students are asked to describe "How I get my way," they add the following to the methods already mentioned: making the other feel bad about himself, deceit, manipulating the listener's thoughts, evasion, pulling a fait accompli, hinting, or persisting with a request until the other gives in (Falbo, 1977).

It is worth noting that each among many methods of influence has a place at some point along a scale depicting, at one extreme, a change agent's degree of encouragement to take action on one's own and, at the other extreme, the strength of pressures a change agent places on a target person to act as told — from methods likely to stimulate autonomy in the person being addressed to ones least likely to allow any free choice at all. Such a scale suggests that inducement strategies may vary from being quite permissive with receivers (general information, modeling, or expertness) to being a source of direct pressure (coercion, rewarding, or appealing to important values).

Inducers who use direct-pressuring methods usually want a specific result and try to make sure they get just that, even if they must monitor the behavior of the target person to be certain that the one they put under pressure behaves as he or she is urged to do. They will observe the target person's apparent motives, goals, and procedures, as well as his or her way of interacting, and try to influence those factors. Initiators of change who use less constraining methods, on the contrary, want a situation to be improved in whatever way makes sense for and best satisfies the target persons. Their influence attempts provide ideas, information, and good models so that the listeners can choose the course they think is best. Such permissive influencers are interested in the responses of those they address and are willing to accept a result quite different from one they may initially have favored.

We see that in each method of influence a change agent is offering an inducement to a recipient with a view toward arousing his interest in doing what is asked. The agent stimulates the other's readiness to change by offering him approval, pride, gifts, ideas, an answer, friendship, fellowship, or assurance of moral fitness or by threatening to withhold incentives like these. An inducement is necessary because, strictly speaking, a change in a person's behavior or beliefs can be made only by the person himself, and therefore if one wishes to influence another, one must give that individual cogent reasons for changing. In a hierarchical organization, those in superior positions have more resources to offer and more freedom to provide them than subordinates do; thus, higher-status persons are more often influential than lower-level staff are.

Choosing a Form of Influence

In many organizations there are rules to restrict how one may exercise influence, and these limit one's freedom of choice in such matters. Most teachers are not allowed to spank students. Some supervisors may not fire workers. A manager must consider the feelings of employees when directing their work. In addition, a change agent's views of human nature may cause him to prefer one method of influencing more than another. For instance, an individual who trusts colleagues to behave in desirable ways tends to treat them with dignity and give them autonomy or a say in decisions (Hollander and Offerman, 1990; Likert, 1959; McGregor, 1959), whereas a person who does not trust associates is inclined to hold them under control. If he believes that people are inherently bad and cannot be expected to do the right thing, he compels them to act as he wishes. If he thinks that people are naturally good, he gives them an opportunity to do well on their own. If he assumes they are neither good or bad but can learn to behave in a suitable fashion, an agent of influence will teach listeners how to behave.

Before deciding on a method, she makes a diagnosis of her and the receiver's situation on the basis of three considerations: (1) whether a given procedure is likely to influence the target person successfully, (2) what benefits the influencing agent might derive from a given method, and (3) what costs she (the influencer) will experience with a particular procedure (Kipnis, 1976; Savard and Roger, 1992). Each of these three factors deserves a bit of discussion.

Probability of Successfully Influencing the Other

By the time an agent of change is deciding what method to use, he knows what kind of change he wants the target person to make and assumes his success during an influence attempt is to be measured by the influencee's movement toward that end. Such knowledge is not very helpful in choosing which tactic to employ, however, because any method of influencing can, in principle, be used to reach any kind of objective. Thus, an influencer typically will judge the probability of being able to induce a desirable change in a target person by considering the following issues:

- What method can he perform well in this situation? He may recognize that he cannot pose as an expert and that he is not a model the listener will wish to imitate. He may feel comfortable in praising the target person or in offering him a reward in order to generate a readiness to change in ways the influence agent suggests. In considering his ability to use a specific procedure efficiently, he also considers whether he has in hand the necessary resources—such as space, supplies, data, time, skill, or self-confidence—to press for action. When a would-be inducer becomes aware that no other method will work, he is likely to use a coercive procedure as his last resort.

- What kind of behavior will the other welcome most? Perhaps the listener is used to being told what to do and prefers a direct order from the agent of influence. Or perhaps the target person prefers freedom and having some say when deciding if and how he should implement a proposed change.

- What ideas will the listener be least likely to *oppose*? The content of ideas the influencer wants the receiver to adopt can help determine what influence method to use. A notion that surely will be popular with the receiver can be offered in a way that allows the target more or less autonomy. An unpopular notion may need a bit more pressure, even coercion plus monitoring, to be sure the receiver does what he is told.

• What will the person on whom power is being placed be least likely to resist? *Resistance* is a target person's emotional reaction to the style used by an agent of influence. A receiver may resist if the influencer is deceitful, aggressive, unclear, derogatory, or selfish. If resistance occurs, an influencer must modify his way of delivering his message so that his manner is less likely to arouse such a response. The one being induced may also resist because he feels that making the requested change requires too much work or other costs. An influence agent therefore may have to use persuasion or a threat to get his way. A receiver may resist because he fears he does not have the ability to implement the change he is to make. When this is so, a pressure exerter may act as an expert, a teacher, or a coach so he can help the receiver overcome his hesitation to try the new way (Kipnis, 1976).

Perceived Benefits of Using a Given Method

An agent of influence will prefer a method of influence that he estimates will provide benefits for himself. He will consider which procedure is most likely to fulfill the motives he wanted to satisfy when he decided to press target persons toward making a given change. Does he want to dominate the others? Give them assistance? Limit their freedom? Or does he want to act in ways that best fulfill the definition of his duties? An influencer judges which way of influencing will grant the most desirable side effects for himself, such as experience, learning, improved relations with target persons, fun, long-lasting modifications, or a better reputation in that group.

The choice of a method for creating change in others is guided by the influence agent's intentions concerning who is to benefit from the change. If the actor thinks of himself as a reformer who is working to improve things, it makes a difference whether benefits he seeks will reward himself, others, both himself and others, or the group as a whole. His intention can lead an inducer to be either permissive or pressuring in the procedure he adopts. If the change agent wants to gain an objective that will benefit himself and no one else, he probably will assign most weight to those desires and use procedures that allow him to put pressure on target persons in the direction he and no other desires, unless of course the target persons assent to the self-serving request. If, by contrast, the reformer intends to benefit other persons, he will devote most attention to the needs of those individuals and will attempt to influence and assist them by offering advice, information, or the results of investigations he has made into the issue at hand. The intended beneficiary of an influencer's actions may be as important as the effects of estimated success, gains, or costs in determining how he chooses to go about exercising his power (Zander, 1990).

Costs of Using a Given Method

An influencer will derive less satisfaction from an attempt to induce another if the method he employs is costly for him or her. These costs may be expenditures of time, energy, or money; loss of friends or reputation; or violation of values that the actor tries to abide by in his behavior.

In addition to those described above, other factors affect a person's choice of a power procedure. Persons low in self-confidence, compared to those high in this characteristic, are more likely to employ bargaining and to make requests of individuals they wish to influence, whereas those high in self-confidence more often depend on their expertise in attempting to influence others (Savard and Roger, 1992).

Administrators in a formal organization commonly take their cues on how to influence from their superiors. The people at the top of a hierarchy set an example that extends down through the organization. A chief executive who shouts at colleagues spawns hoarse subordinates, and a boss who listens to the ideas of co-workers stimulates rational behavior. Therefore, to change managerial methods within an organization, we do better by starting with those in the biggest offices; we cannot have much impact on middle managers if the chief supervisors will not change their ways or will not let associates do so. Indirect or interest-arousing forms of influencing, such as requesting, informing, or reminding members of established standards, are more commonly used in business offices, college faculties, and hospitals, whereas more direct methods, such as rewarding or coercing, are more commonly used in military units and industrial workplaces. The nature of the setting, in short, often determines the style of power an administrator will employ.

If you have worked in a hierarchical organization, you probably noticed that members use a different kind of behavior when addressing a superior than when addressing a subordinate. In one investigation, the frequency of attempts to use three gentle approaches (reason, request, or making the other feel good) when a subordinate tries to influence a superior were compared to the frequency of the subordinate's pressuring actions (assertion, threat, and claiming the legitimate right to make an influence attempt). As you would expect, there was a contrast: subordinates used the former three much more often than the latter three when trying to influence bosses. In the same study, influencers invoked the legitimacy of their authority (in order to be influential) less often with superiors than with subordinates, promised rewards more often to workers than to the boss, and acted in an assertive fashion more often toward employees than superiors (Savard and Roger, 1992). In sum, a member is more likely to use pressuring methods to gain the compliance of subordinates as his position is higher within a hierarchy of an organization, even though he has a greater variety of influencing methods available to him because of his position (Kipnis and Lane, 1962; Pruitt and others, 1993).

In a relevant laboratory experiment, a participant was asked to take the role of a boss who was to increase the productivity of those he supervised. He was allowed either to give information to his crew or to threaten them with punishments. He was not allowed to use any other style of managerial intervention. Some of the supervisors had groups that performed poorly because they were inept individuals; others had groups that did not do well because they were lazy. The supervisor more often gave information to groups whose members had little skill and more often threatened when a group's members were lazy and did not work hard (Kipnis and Lane, 1962). In investigations of leadership styles used in natural settings, it was repeatedly observed that persons who direct workers in tasks that require physical labor were much more likely to be direct and pressuring in style than officials who deal with ideas and decisions in a conference setting.

In a variation of the above laboratory experiment, poorly performing groups differed in size and in the amount of time they had to complete their job—ample versus rushed. Some of the supervisors were known (on the basis of a previous measurement) to have high confidence in themselves; others were low in self-confidence (Goodstadt and Kipnis, 1970; Kipnis and Consentino, 1962; Kipnis and Lane, 1962). The supervisors were allowed to use either persuasion or coercion, and no other method. In these investigations the boss was more likely to use persuasion than coercion when the group of workers was small (a smaller number allowed better discussion of the supervisor's inducements), the time for the task was sufficient (a hurried task made the supervisors more petulant), the workers were interested in what they were doing, and the superior had much confidence in himself.

It seems reasonable that an influencer would be more willing to give information if she is better informed about the topic at hand, others recognize her as an expert, and they want her ideas. Giving advice is a comfortable way to influence others. The agent of change is not under pressure, the procedure is orderly and predictable, her pronouncements require minimal staging, and, best of all, she need take no responsibility for decisions of the listeners; the latter are free to accept or reject her ideas as they wish.

Members probably prefer to be supervised in one way rather than another. Can their preference affect the way their leaders exercise influence? Apparently it can. If members want a say in their group's decision and make this known, officers are more likely to use democratic methods, even if these leaders are not ordinarily inclined to do so. And if members want their supervisor to be in charge and an issuer of orders, the executive is inclined to make decisions for the group and keep things under tight control regardless of his usual disposition. If members believe their colleagues cannot be trusted to do their part well, they favor the boss's use of rewards or punishments. If they believe their associates will naturally do the right thing, members will want the boss to support their efforts rather than limit them. Briefly put, members often press their superiors to behave in ways that suit the members' preferences (Crowe, Bochner, and Clark, 1972).

When a holder of power believes that others' compliance is temporary or that permissive methods of influencing will not work, he tends to turn to stronger means. In such a situation, if the supervisor is not sure that employees can be trusted to perform at their best, an increment of pay is promised workers who will achieve a given standard of work. Such extra pay is less likely to be offered if the superior is sure subordinates will produce at a given level (Kipnis, 1976). Because democratically run groups engender more trust among participants, rewards are probably employed less often in such groups.

In groups where agents of influence are free to use any among many ways of exercising power, they commonly prefer to appeal to reason. Or they try to ingratiate themselves to listeners, display their expertise, or request the others' cooperation. These latter three account for 40 percent of the methods employed in experimental studies of managerial methods (Kipnis, 1976; Kipnis, Schmidt, and Wilkinson, 1980; Savard and Roger, 1992).

Fashions in how influencing should be done change over the years. The Old Testament contains more than a dozen assertions that God loves a servant who is obedient to his superior even when treated unfairly by that boss. Perhaps more persons lived up to those admonitions in earlier days than they do now. Fifty years ago, a manager was usually ruder and harsher than today because it was then thought that only that kind of leader could be effective. In some cultures, managerial behavior patterns are quite different from what they are in other cultures; administrators in Sweden or Israel are not like those in Italy. Japanese managers are surprised by (and critical of) the methods of supervision used in rival Western countries (Lebra, 1979; Vogel, 1975; Vogel, 1979).

Why a Person Tries to Influence

How often do powerful persons use their capacity to influence others? In face-to-face groups (such as committees, conferences, or classrooms), individuals with greater power talk more often than anyone else and usually think they have the right to do so, which may in fact be true (Cartwright and Zander, 1968; Goodstadt and Kipnis, 1970). Those with greater power also make more attempts to influence co-workers in day-to-day communications at their place of work. The tendency of powerful persons to talk more often has been observed in relations among workers in mental health clinics (Zander, Cohen, and Stotland, 1959), industrial supervisors in factories (Goodstadt and Kipnis, 1970), boys in a summer camp (Lippitt and others, 1968), and subjects in laboratory experiments (Cartwright and Zander, 1968; Savard and Roger, 1992). Apparently a majority of members approve of frequent talking by persons with greater power because they elect more talkative individuals to be the leaders of their groups (Morris and Hackman, 1960). Also, members who increase their talkativeness over time are increasingly likely to be chosen for higher offices by their peers. And the frequency of talking is more important in these elections than the quality of things they say.

A member may be stimulated by particular conditions. Superiors may ask her to do something (for example, "Why don't you try to make your influence felt?"), or her duties may require that she supervise others. She may exert power because she depends on colleagues in her work and believes they will not perform adequately unless she urges them to do so. If disorganization threatens a group, she may assume command to prevent confusion. An agenda's topics affect those who have expertise on the matters under discussion, and these persons feel free to speak because they have useful things to relate and know their words will be welcomed. Within a larger entity, a unit's problems enable particular people to have a stronger hand in deciding its course. For instance, a company's legal staff becomes more influential if the company is sued; financial officers have a louder voice if the company needs capital funds; professionals in a firm's health clinic are asked what improvements ought to be made if work conditions make employees ill. The actions of a potential power wielder are affected by her views about current circumstances. If she believes that changing others will be useful, she does whatever she can to create these changes.

Regardless of whether an agent of change works toward accomplishing his own goals, meeting others' needs, or serving his group's objectives, he tends to make the simple calculation I described earlier before he takes action. First, he estimates whether his attempts to influence (regardless of method) are likely to be successful — whether the target person will accept his request. Such readiness may develop in a recipient because he is in a subordinate position, is in a role that requires him to depend on the work of the agent of influence, or is by nature an acquiescent individual. A person who weighs the chances of influencing a colleague feels more sure he can do so if he is more confident his aims are proper in the eyes of the person he intends to induce. He will be more certain he can get another to change if he knows that the target person's colleagues also want him to change.

Second, he assesses whether his gains from making an influence attempt will exceed his costs. Thus, he encourages a person to change if doing so will make his own work easier, more satisfying, or more efficient. But these gains must not be accompanied by excessive costs to himself, such as a loss in the quality of work he performs or a long-term reduction in productivity, which wipe out the benefits he seeks.

Why does a would-be influencer want to make another do something he might not wish to do? He does so when he realizes he can achieve a specific satisfaction only if the other does certain things. The power wielder is dependent on the target person to behave in ways that fulfill a motivation of the inducer (Kipnis, 1976). What kinds of motives might an agent of change satisfy if a target person modifies his behavior in ways requested by the influencer? A supervisor may desire to have his staff improve its productivity so that he will appear to be an effective boss. Or he (the supervisor) may be pressed by his superior to have the workers pay closer attention to rules within the organization. An influencer may be motivated to overcome fears that he is a weak boss by pressing others to modify their actions, or he may enjoy determining what others do and how they do it — he likes to push others around.

An inducer may develop greater self-esteem, security, or self-confidence as a result of determining what others think or do. And often, a holder of power wishes to show a receiver who is boss by making the latter comply against his wishes (Kipnis, 1976; Raven, 1992). In brief, a person's motivation to change the behavior of another is more likely to arise when he develops a need that can be best satisfied by influencing a particular other to take an appropriate action. An individual will attempt to press another unless he is inhibited because personal values prohibit him from using the kind of power that seems to be needed, he is not physically able to take the required steps, the costs will be too great for him or colleagues, he is not sure he can make his influence felt, he does not have confidence in his ability as an agent of change, or standards within the organization forbid display of overt pressures (Savard and Roger, 1992).

Selection of an Inappropriate Influence Method

A resident in a condominium was offended by the noises a neighbor made, most of which were the day-by-day sounds of an ordinary household. Instead of speaking man-to-man with the allegedly noisy one, the complainer appealed to the president of that neighborhood's organization. His wife had earlier agreed to be chairman of a committee to plan the condominium's Christmas party, so the complainer began his request of the president by suggesting, "You don't want to lose the chairman of your Christmas committee, do you?" He repeated this threat a number of times while urging the president to discipline the noise-making resident. The president was not convinced he should intervene on the basis of the complainer's whining because he did not believe the noises were bad enough to warrant such a move; furthermore, the complainer had grumbled over other matters, refused to try for a friendly settlement with the neighbor, and weakened his pleas with his repeated threats about his wife's readiness to resign her Christmas-party post if the president did not act as requested. The accuser's style in trying to be influential offended the president and caused him to reject the complainer's bleating. The complainer used an inappropriate method of influencing.

An inappropriate attempt to influence, in general terms, is one that does not help an inducer to convince a listener because the speaker cannot perform as required. He cannot write, speak, argue, vilify, charm, or persuade, or he does not have the resources he needs.

Why does an influencer select an ineffective method? One reason is that the agent of change cannot judge whether one procedure is better than another because his own objectives are not well enough defined to guide such an appraisal. If he is not sure what he wants to accomplish, he cannot plan how to reach that objective or help an inducee move in that direction. In addition, the success of a change agent in influencing a decision maker depends in good part on how correctly he estimates which ideas or style of delivery will be most acceptable to the target person. For example, if the change seeker thinks a listener will appreciate lots of background information, whereas that person actually wants straightforward ideas about what specific steps he ought to take, the listener will believe the inducer is too vague about what should be done. As another example, a speaker may propose a solution when the listener only wants facts about the issue, so that she can choose her own answer in light of that information. An agent of change may use a wrong procedure because he has not properly diagnosed what would best appeal to the listener.

An advocate may choose an inappropriate power strategy if he fails to recognize that the costs of a given procedure will cancel many of the gains he had anticipated. He may find, as an instance, that threatening to expel a member who does not do what he is asked causes the coerced one to resent, resist, and return such behavior. Or a change agent may overlook losses he will incur from excessive use of time, energy, funds, or emotional strain. An influencer may make faulty calculations as he estimates whether a given method can succeed or whether the gains following that procedure will exceed its costs.

A further reason for choosing an inappropriate method is that the agent of change becomes defensive, angry, or suspicious toward the target person because the latter responds in similar ways to the initiator's style. The pressure exerter thereupon tries to defend his honor, assuage his anger, or confirm his suspicions. Even though such emotions are legitimate reasons for trying to influence those who cause them, they usually lead to behavior by a change agent that makes the target persons want to defend themselves.

Effects of Having Power

An individual who perceives he has power over particular persons because he has been able to influence them successfully, without generating much opposition or resistance, usually benefits from this state of affairs. He can achieve personal objectives because he can make things happen as he wishes. Moreover, while serving his own needs, he can command the help of less powerful others toward these ends. He is often treated deferentially by subordinates and is approved, complimented, and offered privileges by them. It is not surprising then that a member likes his status better as his power increases. Consequently, he comes to see possession of power as a valued end in itself and a natural part of his office. He develops an attachment to power, does not want to lose it, and works to preserve it (Cartwright and Zander, 1968; Kipnis and Lane, 1962; Raven, 1992; Zander, Cohen, and Stotland, 1959). Because of his control over his own fate when interacting with less influential others, he is comfortable with them and enjoys contacts they initiate, even though he does not often seek out subordinates. He is not at ease, however, with subordinates who ignore his greater influence. To illustrate, a manager who is new in his job will not feel at home with a worker who knows more about the manager's duties than the boss does himself, or with a member who is more popular than the supervisor among groupmates or more expert in the work of that group.

A good proportion of powerful persons become self-centered because they can use their power to deprive others if they wish.

They can allot more rewards to themselves than to groupmates and can justify this behavior as proper and deserved by a person of their status; they are entitled to special treatment (Messé, Kerr, and Satler, 1992). In addition, one who sees himself as an equal among equals soon learns that his power provides the means for excessive personal comforts. A Japanese government official wrote about the "indescribable pleasure" of becoming a person of power. "In the course of such experiences — like starting to smoke or taking up the habit of an evening drink — one at first feels a little ticklish, but before long it begins to feel good, and one feels that something is missing if he isn't treated in this way. Next, one feels an inward dissatisfaction, and in the final stage, one advances to the symptom of imagination. It is exactly the same as addiction to a drug. . . . The more one is a petty, self-righteous type, the more likely he is to fall prey to this disease of 'bureaucratic mentality' and the worse will be its ravages . . . and almost no one is entirely immune" (Craig, 1975, p. 9). Even in a bureaucracy created by pigs, as Orwell relates in *Animal Farm* (1946), the more powerful swine give themselves many special benefits on the grounds that they deserve such privileges while lesser hogs do not.

An administrator often must make decisions that put the needs of the organization first. Not uncommonly, she assumes that meeting her own wishes is exactly the same as meeting those of the unit. Thus, a subordinate who dislikes actions by his boss might be told that his beliefs are contrary to the best interests of the group (not of the superior). Frequently, individuals with little power act toward a superior in ways that help the latter become more self-oriented. They let a high-status person behave in ways they would not tolerate in a lesser member and grant this freedom to the influential one as a payment for her help to the organization (Wiggins, Dill, and Schwartz, 1965). As a method of self-protection, subordinates often tell a manager they agree with her when in fact they do not, so she believes her ideas are popular and has no means to learn otherwise. An individual in a powerful post usually does not pay much attention to the views of others, because there are too many subordinates and differing opinions among them. As a result, he develops stereotyped, unfavorable views of the others that confirm his belief that he has a right to ignore their views and to exercise control over such incompetent persons (Fiske, 1993). As a response to infrequent connections with subordinates, a powerful person may develop an informal clique of colleagues. He encourages these followers to be loyal to him by using his power in their behalf. In exchange, the followers give him information, support, and access to channels beyond his immediate social environment.

Everyday events in a group help managers believe their ideas, acts, and skills are of superior quality and that they are wise and effective administrators. If these self-views are based on responses of subordinates and are not in accord with the way subordinates really feel, the superiors get from these associates little feedback of the kind that helps them correct erroneous self-appraisal. The possession of power can therefore help people develop exalted views of their own value (Cartwright and Zander, 1968; Kipnis, 1976; Zander, Cohen, and Stotland, 1959) and make them feel sure of themselves in relations with subordinates. Along with favorable self-regard, persons with power realize they are able to determine what happens to their colleagues and whatever the colleagues accomplish is, in good part, because of the powerholder's influence and help.

Not all people with power are made self-centered by owning it. Because powerful persons are able to make things happen as they wish, they can and do use their weight to help others. This assistance can be as full and compassionate as they want because they have the freedom to implement kindly desires. Persons with greater power have more self-confidence, are not defensive in the ordinary course of events, and can easily be understanding and supportive of subordinates, if they wish to be so.

Summary

We examined how persons attempt to influence colleagues, why they choose one method rather than another, and the effects power has on those who own it. Let us summarize the points made under these topics by stating them as matters to keep in mind when one seeks to be influential.

Whether to Make an Influence Attempt. A member of a group cannot always be sure when it is appropriate for him to try to change others and when not. He can be more confident that it is proper for him to exercise his influence if conditions like the following exist:

- Members deviate from the behavior expected of them in their group, and it is his job to modify their behavior.
- Members need help in carrying out activities for the good of the group, and he is to provide assistance.
- Disorganization or failure is threatened within the unit, and he must help prevent this.
- Superiors request the person to act in an influential way or they support his efforts to be an agent of change.
- Rewards or punishments must be invoked to influence colleagues, and he is the only one near at hand who can offer these.
- The would-be influencer estimates that his attempt to influence will probably be successful and that his gains from doing so will exceed the costs.
- The influencer is dealing with persons who are subordinates, and he has a legitimate right to make demands of them.
- He has done favors for the listener and now asks for a return of that kindness.

What Form of Influence to Use. He will use one form of influence rather than another under certain conditions.

- He will try to persuade the others if he believes that recipients are misinformed and not trying to correct their misinformation and if he is confident of the correctness of his ideas on the matter under consideration.
- He will offer his ideas to listeners for what they are worth if he realizes they respect his expertise and are seeking correct answers to their questions.
- He will merely associate with others if he realizes that they wish to be like him and want to model their behavior after his.
- He will try to get others to like him if he wants target persons to give serious weight to his influence attempts.
- He will appeal to values listeners respect when suggesting

ideas or behaviors if he knows that values are most important to them and judges that they want to live in accordance with those values.

- He will more often threaten to punish members if they are lazy or uninterested in completing tasks assigned to them when no other form of influence works, the need for change is urgent, potential receivers of a given punishment are known to fear and dislike it, and he is higher in the hierarchy than those he is addressing.
- He will be more ready to coerce colleagues when he has little confidence in his ability as a supervisor, fears that he might be losing control, can monitor the target person's behavior, and has adequate means for coercing them; and when individuals in the environment approve of coercion as a method of influence.
- He will promise a reward when he believes it will work best, has an adequate supply of rewards, can monitor the recipients' behavior, is not embarrassed to offer a reward, and is willing to meet the demand for an increase in rewards over time.
- He will merely impart information to listeners if he believes they want such.
- He will modify the environment of target persons in ways that unfailingly restrict their behavior if he suspects they will not obey verbal demands.
- He will be selective in using methods of influencing if he realizes that he employs some more skillfully than others and is prepared to choose those that suit him best.
- He will use the style of influence that fits the expectations of those he attempts to influence.

Preventing Adverse Effects from Having Power. An influential individual tends to develop a favorable opinion of his own value. Because he may not receive accurate feedback from subordinates, he cannot always know whether his view of his worth is shared by them. If he uses power in ways that disadvantage target persons, he may not be told he is doing so or recognize this. Both a false self-evaluation and damage to colleagues are adverse consequences of having power. A powerful person can reduce the weight of these consequences by taking certain actions.

- Use forms of power other than reward or coercion as often as possible; that is, try to arouse internal incentives among listeners.
- Identify the needs of those to be influenced and help them meet those needs.
- Recognize that subordinates want to win and retain his goodwill. Accordingly, they will give him more attention, warmth, approval, and acceptance than his behavior may deserve. A sensible person of power understands the purposes that may lie behind those friendly actions.
- Take steps to ensure that his evaluation of his performance is not inflated because of the goodwill-winning actions of those with less power.

Recommended Readings

Cartwright, D. (ed.). *Studies in Social Power.* Ann Arbor: Institute for Social Research, University of Michigan, 1959.
The studies in this early book stimulated wide interest in social power as a field of research.

Kipnis, D., *The Powerholders.* Chicago: University of Chicago Press, 1976.
Summarizes a program of research into the behavior of persons in powerful positions. Describes how persons with much power act toward others and what power does to one who has it.

Raven, B. "A Power/Interaction Model of Interpersonal Influence: French and Raven Thirty Years Later." *Journal of Social Behavior and Personality,* 1992, *7,* 217–244.
Summarizes many of the most important findings from research on social power in the last thirty years.

Savard, C., and Rogers, R. "A Self-Efficacy and Subjective Utility Theory Analysis of the Selection and Use of Influence Strategies." *Journal of Social Behavior and Personality,* 1992, *7,* 273–292.
Describes why persons use certain tactics rather than others when attempting to be influential.

9

BECOMING AN
AGENT OF INFLUENCE

When Socrates lived in ancient Athens, many residents spent their days hanging out in groups at the marketplace discussing issues of concern to mankind, such as questions about the nature of piety, justice, sanity, courage, art, government, and science. Socrates often inspired talk in such groups by prowling through members' beliefs, prodding their thinking, demanding definitions of terms, and describing the illogical derivations following from answers he could not accept. He responded to a question with one of his own, saying he knew only questions, not answers. He was accused of tearing down, of never building up, and was both hated and loved by members of these intellectual struggle groups. His prime concerns, he said, were ethics, politics, the use of pure reason in such activities, and serving as a midwife for others' ideas. He eventually was executed by city officials because they believed he had an undesirable influence on the minds of young men. Yet today, his comments, preserved for us by Plato, are still influential, and the Socratic method of teaching is used in schools where students are taught to think, not merely memorize.

As we have seen, a person of power may prefer one method of influence in one situation and a different method in another. But he is not always sure which approach is best; neither is anyone else. In a utopian society, an agent of influence might confidently estimate the comparative effects of different methods of influence and in light of these hunches select a procedure that suits a given setting. There is not much evidence from research for this thesis, however, because most studies of the procedures used by holders of power have been conducted by scholars who advocate that one method be used in all times and places. For example, one should always be strict with subordinates, reward or praise them, or give them a say. Few students of power or leadership have compared the effects of ways of influencing, like those described in Chapter Eight, to see which are best under what conditions.

What must an individual do to be an effective agent of influence? Generally, he must make appropriate resources available (ideas, models, approvals, dollars) or imply that these will be provided if the listener acts as the powerful person prefers. At the same time, before the person addressed will take the desired action, he must covet the resources the influencer offers, and believe he cannot obtain such benefits elsewhere. Plainly, an agent of change can have a greater effect if he has more resources, provided these are the kind valued by the one to be changed. However, there is more than this to a successful influence attempt. One who plans to foster a modification in others must be prepared to accomplish five additional tasks, each of which will facilitate the alteration.

Presenting Clear Information

The success of an influence attempt, assuming it is more than a simple request or a model to be imitated, depends on the assumption that receivers will act on information they obtain. One who wishes to transform particular individuals must therefore give them ideas they need in order to act appropriately. Thus, she may tell them how the quality of their work suffers when they move too rapidly, describe why their organization needs new members, or explain the advantage of following a particular plan in a specific way. Yet even when declarative statements are clearly presented and understood by listeners, or even when observers like the actions of a model, members do not always act on these notions. Why?

Part of the explanation lies in the ideas a recipient already has about this matter and the pattern among these ideas — called a *cognitive structure*. An individual with a well-organized cognitive structure is already equipped with wisdom about the notions under consideration, understands them, and realizes that they fit together sensibly — for him. A person with a poorly organized cognitive structure knows little about the topic at hand and has no strong beliefs about the connections among these notions. A financial officer, as an example, can have clear and well-organized thoughts about how his company should invest its profits but be vague about how to train new employees. A bridge player can easily comprehend comments that fit the system she uses in playing the game but not understand a friend who speaks about a different method. Members of fundamentalist religious bodies cannot fathom the practices of those in more liberal congregations. And an individual with well-organized ideas on a given topic can describe the more central categories under which his notions are organized. One who has a loose cognitive structure, however, is not sure which of his ideas on the subject are major and which are minor, because they are assembled but not arranged.

When an observer is given or comes across new information, she pays little attention if it does not fit one of the categories she heretofore used to store her ideas. Or, equally common, she may distort the new information to make it fit her prior structure of beliefs and thus in effect change the content of the original message. As an illustration, think of instances in which an associate appeared to understand you, but in later conversations it was evident that he had heard something different from what you had said because he "does not think about such matters in the terms you use."

A person with loosely organized concepts will readily accept new information if it appears to be useful to her. One with a well-organized cognitive structure will consider and accept new information, too, but only if the message fits into his system of ideas on that topic. Thus, a wise influencer plans her presentation to suit the cognitive structure of listeners. To do this, she must determine what the receivers already know, how they have arranged these beliefs, and thus what terms the message provider should recognize or use.

If the recipient's knowledge of the topic is thin, loose, and flexible, an information provider will be most effective if she furnishes a well-organized set of facts, presenting a fairly complete way of viewing the matters under discussion and indicating the most important ideas among these (for example, the major and minor topics in an outline), the sources of parts of the presentation, and the consequences from each part. In brief, she provides ideas arranged in a clear pattern, organized around several main features, as a proposed cognitive structure. In contrast, if the recipient's knowledge of a topic is already rich in content and tightly arranged under several headings, a sender will be more effective if she directs her information and arguments toward changing only the main categories. If the central categories can be modified, the ideas within each can be changed. As an example, members will better improve their group's rate of productivity if they are told the group's purpose, activities, and goals than if they are shown how to improve their personal skills, because group-oriented ideas are more important to a group's performance than are personal styles. On the whole, a recipient's beliefs are more amenable to change if he knows he must make use of new notions in the future than if he is simply asked to hear these ideas or to think about them (Zajonc, 1960). A major problem for an agent of influence then is to choose a strategy that will prevent a listener from ignoring or distorting the content of his influence attempts.

Arousing the Interest of the Person to Be Changed

When attempting to change a listener it is necessary that the proposed action be seen by the observer as a means to achieve an end he values for himself or colleagues. Or he must develop a belief that the advocated change is necessary, for his own good and the good of others. A wise influencer therefore learns what is important to the member to be induced: what does that person want to know, need to learn, or have to get into his head? Having done so, the agent seeks to demonstrate to the other that what the influencer suggests or exemplifies is relevant to the other's attainment of his purposes. As an illustration, the target is told that he will become wiser, richer, more skillful, better liked, or prouder of himself if he acts in ways he is being shown are worth following. Then the change agent encourages the listener by emphasizing the likelihood that the latter will be able to make the change proposed. The inducers build the observer's confidence in succeeding by helping him obtain needed skills, outlining procedures, and bolstering the target person's courage to try a new and uncertain action. The more a listener wants to fulfill such motives, the greater the number of aims a given action will benefit, or the easier the proposed action is compared with other possible actions, the more the receiver is likely to make the recommended changes.

Converting Interest into Action

Persons who become interested in changing themselves or events around them may accept what is suggested and be willing to make the modifications proposed yet take no action. If asked why not, they say other matters seem more important. To make sure that persons act in accordance with their intentions, it is necessary to help them see what steps they must take and how they must take them. It is also important to emphasize the need for prompt action. If the path they are to move along is precisely demonstrated, requires few choices, and is simple to follow, target persons are more likely to make the necessary moves.

Suppose, as instances, a subordinate is asked by a superior to provide specific information. He is more certain to obey this request if he is given a form for his answers, an addressed envelope in which to return the form, and a date as a deadline. Or if a person is asked to speed up his rate of productivity, he will move more rapidly if he is given reports on his output over a series of trials. A person more readily takes a health examination or signs a pledge to give to a charity if the means for doing so are close at hand and the individual is asked by an agent of influence to take action here, and immediately, rather than doing it later, elsewhere, or at her convenience. Influenced persons adhere more fully to a change if a single decision controls a sequence of later steps, as in agreeing at one time to payroll deductions over many months in contributing to a welfare fund; they will soon stop making such contributions if they must decide whether to contribute anew each month (Cartwright, 1949).

After an individual has been influenced by a specific other on several occasions, he is more readily influenced thereafter by that person; the readiness of his response to the influencer improves with practice, unless of course his response barely overcomes a desire to resist.

Recruiting Social Support

A wise agent of influence within a group makes sure that members welcome the change she proposes for a given participant and that the person who is to be changed knows of this approval by his mates. One way to generate a similar view among members about changes that a colleague should make is to privately consult each member ahead of time to get their advice about how the colleague needs to improve his knowledge or actions. The group as a whole may discuss the matter and advise the agent of change. Or the group may meet with the person and give him suggestions. But such discussions can be successful only if the target person wants their help and the discussants are able to give it in a way that does not make the subject defensive. If an influencer has no specific behavior to recommend to a listener but feels strongly that some change is necessary, she may let the group independently develop its own plans for one another. Such a method generates greater adherence to and greater social support for a decision than if the person decides privately how to change his or her personal behavior.

Members more readily support one another, either to accept a change proposed by an influence agent or to oppose it, if they are aware each participant depends on the other, that the efforts of each are necessary for the gain of all, and that members will be rewarded to a similar degree as a result of the group's achievement (Deutsch, 1949, 1973, 1990; Zander and Wolfe, 1964). Interdependence can also be stimulated when a large task is divided into smaller parts and each part is assigned to a member. A participant then recognizes that he cannot do his share without the help of other members. Interdependence among participants creates readiness to trust one another's intentions. As a result, each person supports the actions of group companions.

Sets of social supporters are created when citizens jointly work for local changes they believe will improve things. The members recognize that they cannot make the transformation they seek on their own because they are not equipped to do so, a set of decision makers is in charge of the situation to be modified, or the activists need the support of neighbors. Thus, a group of change agents tries to persuade everyone who will listen that the proposed reform is wise. Usually, they do not have enough power to convince either neighbors or officials, so they have to figure out how they can become influential, to develop a voice that cannot be denied by decision makers in their town (Zander, 1990, 1993).

Establishing the Change

After a person has been influenced, he may be uncertain and uneasy about the effects of his being changed. Such unsureness tends to occur if the person who has adopted a proposed transformation recalls positive aspects of behavior he had to drop from his repertoire as a result of his change and begins to note negative features of the shift he has accepted. This dissonance is uncomfortable, and the partially undecided person will want to eliminate it. He can do so in two ways: (1) by thinking of the negative qualities in the behavior he dropped and (2) by discovering favorable features in the change he has adopted. An agent of influence can help a target person carry through this process by following suggestions made by Festinger (1957) for reducing one's uncertainties after making a decision:

1. Point out the attractiveness of the changes made and the lack of value in the rejected alternatives.

2. Convince the undecided person that the alternative plans
    and those chosen are similar in important respects.
3. Provide information that helps the influenced one alter his
    views of the dropped behavior until his beliefs are in ac-
    cordance with his decision.
4. Assure the person that he is a desirable associate, so he will
    remain available for further influencing.
5. Provide no social support for forms of behavior already
    rejected.
6. Decrease the importance of issues involved in the dishar-
    mony between earlier behavior and newly adopted forms.

Strength of an Influencer's Power

A person who is being subjected to an influence attempt may
be unsure about adopting the action proposed. Often, such hesitation causes an unwillingness to do as the influencer proposes.
The strength of an agent's effort to be influential is equal therefore to the pressure she can exert on the hesitant person minus
the latter's opposition or resistance to changing as requested.
If a target person's heel digging is stronger than the agent's inducement, the recipient will not change or may even oppose
the author of the influence attempt.

   Talking in more general terms, the reactions of an individual to a change agent's attempt to influence him depends on
how he sees the consequences of accepting or rejecting it. He
will be more likely to adopt the proposed change if it is in his
best interest to do so. He will not be attracted to the change
if it is liable to do him more harm than good, unless he intends
to right a wrong that others have had to endure and, in so doing, reduce personal costs of his action.

   Most persons who want to stimulate another to change
recognize that the listener needs to know what is in it for him
if he makes the transformation being proposed, so an inducer
frames his influence attempt in a way that he thinks will help
the receiver in this respect. He tries to arouse a motive or desire
in the listener and tries to convince him that the suggested change
will satisfy that desire. For instance, he proposes to the colleague
that he pay more attention to what others say in a meeting or

try to develop a problem-solving discussion rather than get into an argument with others. The agent of change presents his case in a way that causes the listener to care about the views others have of his behavior, to be concerned about the feelings of colleagues he has pressed into quarrels, and to be aware of the satisfaction associates will have after modifying his membership manner: "The other members think you are arrogant and that you look down on them. You could change the opinions they have of you." "You will feel better in this group if you take the lead in encouraging rational discussion, and so will the rest of us." (See Chapter Thirteen).

The general rule agents of change seem to follow is this: The stronger the motive or desire that change agents arouse among target persons, and the stronger the probability that this motive or desire will be satisfied through doing what the initiators propose, the more the agents of change will influence the target persons. In accord with this rule, the wise influencer strengthens a relevant motive or desire in the others by making it seem important to them or by helping them recall the value they have placed on it in other situations. An agent of change also helps target persons see that attainment of the proposed objective will give them satisfaction. I suspect that not all change agents operate as directly as these statements imply. Indeed, some adopt no strategy at all, let alone the ones to be discussed here.

Persons of power need to decide, therefore, how they will go about trying to influence target persons. What method they choose, among possibilities noted earlier, depends on what they are capable of doing well and the kinds of responses they believe listeners will have to different kinds of advocacy. They ask themselves several questions: Shall we try to influence target persons by encouraging their freedom of choice, putting no direct pressure on them, and arousing their internal motivations as they respond to our proposal? Or shall we use methods that limit target persons' freedom of choice by offering them incentives they will win if they go along with what they are asked to do? In what follows I recall some of the ways an agent of change can go about influencing others (mentioned in Chapter Eight) in order to illustrate how each of these is used effectively.

Methods That Encourage
Freedom of Choice in Target Persons

In a common approach, an influencer has no face-to-face discussion with one he hopes to influence. Instead, he talks privately to that person's peers about the latter's unwanted behavior in the hope that one of these individuals will speak to the target person or that the latter will overhear that his style is disapproved by colleagues or has caused them pain for which they ought to be compensated (Raven, 1992). An influencer may use this indirect method if he fears retribution for confronting the one he intends to influence or if he does not want to be a source of criticism that may cause colleagues to disapprove of him. An indirect approach is effective if it makes the focal person realize he is to blame and should feel guilty for his actions. The desired change is justified on the grounds that members dislike the target person's inappropriate behavior.

In another indirect method for fostering change, the agent serves as a model of good decorum and action in the group. He volunteers for demanding assignments, participates actively in discussions, stimulates enthusiasm for tasks the group undertakes, or approves of actions by separate members. Sometimes a potential model acts in such ways without intending to demonstrate an ideal style. His actions are so attractive to members, however, that they wish to be like him and thus they copy his style. An influencer who uses such a method does so because it is a comfortable way of exercising influence and does not embarrass others. It is a wise approach when observers of the model are newcomers or are known to be uncertain about how group members should act. How can a model be most effective? Ordinarily, the exemplars must be visible to those who are to be influenced and must be attractive to them. Thus, well-known or popular people often are models.

In another approach that encourages receivers to develop their own motivation toward a change, an influencer provides information to a target person and to anyone else who will look, listen, and benefit. He does not try to persuade or inflame a listener; he merely imparts new knowledge. He may use any of a variety of means to put forth important facts: a memorandum, report, speech, display, exhibit, hearing, street performance, workshop, or conference. He uses such means because he believes the others want special knowledge and will trust him as an unbiased source. He may heighten his credibility by describing his training, relevant experience, and the high quality of the sources and data he cites. It is a safe form of behavior because it requires no face-to-face confrontation with target persons. The message is most convincing if it is addressed to persons who have curiosity and desire to know the facts, it is presented clearly, the presenter is known to be a legitimate source, the facts are correct, and it proposes an objective along with several courses of action.

Methods That Provide External Incentives

Some procedures, in contrast to ones just noted, are used by influencers when they believe target persons will not be satisfied simply by making the change asked of them. So the inducers offer an incentive that will increase the target person's motivation because he or she wants that gain. The methods used here put direct pressures on those who are targets to do what they are asked or to stop doing something undesirable.

A not uncommon approach is persuasion, a deliberate effort by an agent of change to control the beliefs or behavior of a target person by making comments that are deliberately one-sided and self-serving. A persuader intends to convince listeners that no views or actions other than ones being advocated are acceptable; thus, he does not closely consider contrary statements or arguments by the other side. Because persuasion is an effort to convince, a persuader depends on facts that are inherently compelling. If he shades the truth, exaggerates the unfavorableness of current conditions, or arouses fear or greed in listeners, he is using propaganda. In either persuading or propagandizing, a speaker benefits most from the change being pressed (Zander, 1990).

How is a persuader most effective? He uses special rhetorical devices such as having his ideas dominate the give-and-take, giving little attention to rebuttals, demonstrating how listeners will benefit if they do what is proposed, citing as many gains as possible, identifying many persons who will be pleased by the change, or speaking in emotional terms that overwhelm the use of reason because reason may lead to questions and hesitation rather than acceptance.

Another way a person tries to influence colleagues is to offer them a reward if they do as they are asked. They are told that their actions will be appreciated by others or that they will be given a better duty, higher pay, relevant training, or other kinds of benefits. A reward may be used in order to arouse the attention of uninterested persons, underscore that past behavior should be repeated, or demonstrate to observers the kind of actions that will be most welcomed in that body. This method is most effective if the reward is valued by a receiver, it is not provided too often, the agent of change can observe the target person's subsequent behavior, the persons being rewarded know why they have won approval, the reward is made public, and it rewards overt behavior rather than hidden feelings or beliefs. A rewarder's offerings will gain value if the agent of change recalls for them the type of benefits he has provided in the past.

One more way to pressure others directly is to threaten, or actually inflict, a penalty on the ones being coerced until the latter change their behavior. They demote the others, reduce their pay, confront them publicly, reduce the size of their workspace, give them boring duties, demand apologies, or exclude them from membership. They do these things in order to get the undivided attention of the persons being influenced and to create a negative incentive that receivers wish to avoid. Such methods are most effective if the penalty is repelling to those affected by it, the coercer can keep the transgressor under observation, the target person knows why his actions are disapproved, the penalty is public, the punishment is for overt behavior rather than beliefs or attitudes, and the objects of the coercion are not controlled by a third party such as a workers' union, church, or secret society. One who uses coercion is more likely to be effective if he has a past history of doing what he says he will, he has a high position in the organization, his approach does not generate too much opposition or create too many undesirable costs for him or the group, and relations between the coercer and the punished one will continue into the future (Pruitt and others, 1993). An influencer may strengthen his hand by making clear to the one addressed that he has the means for penalizing him and would not hesitate to use these methods regardless of their cost (Raven, 1992).

Sometimes it becomes necessary for an agent of change to increase his power, compared to that of target persons, not by enhancing his own credibility but by reducing the power of listeners. As examples, the influencers may decrease social support of the target persons, dismiss or demote them, or enter into a conflict with them.

Are persons who are asked to behave in a given way more likely to do so if the change agent uses one style of induction rather than another? The handful of investigations in which the effectiveness of different influence procedures has been compared have been conducted in natural settings, mainly because it is difficult to create realistic differences in social power among participants in the laboratory. The problem with studies in real-life settings is that it is difficult to be sure what actions lead to what results because too many things go on at the same time.

Granted that these studies are preliminary in nature, it is nevertheless noteworthy that one result is often repeated in them: when an agent of change acts as an informed expert or as an attractive model observers would like to imitate or be with, target persons are more likely to be influenced and respond more favorably to the influence attempts than if the influencer relies on rewards, punishments, or appeals to recognize the rank of the influence agent.

As an illustration, faculty members in twelve small colleges were more satisfied with their respective deans' management methods if they believed the dean depended more on his expert knowledge or on acting as a good example in exerting social power, and they were less satisfied if the dean depended on rewards, coercion, or recognition of legitimacy (because of his rank) when making attempts to influence the faculty. Likewise, in a high school classroom, students chose personal goals

similar to ones they believed were set for them by the teacher
if they judged the teacher to be a skilled appraiser of student
ability and a model scholar, but they paid less attention if the
teacher used threats of punishment more than other bases of
influence (Rosenfeld and Zander, 1961). In an insurance firm,
salesmen sold more policies if the manager of their office frequently acted as an expert informant or a model worthy of emu-
lation than if the manager more often rewarded, punished, or
pointed to the propriety of his actions when bolstering influence
attempts.

Although these results are statistically reliable, there is
reason to wonder how widely they apply. In a body of well-
trained and conscientious members, regardless of the setting,
it is probably wise for a supervisor to depend more on expert
and referent power, simply because such methods are liked better
by influenced persons, are less disruptive of operations, and are
less likely to arouse resistance among the influenced. A manager need not reward or threaten subordinates if they are already doing a good job (Likert, 1959; McGregor, 1959). A
review of several studies summarized the characteristic behaviors
of group supervisors (Kahn and Katz, 1960). The authors report
that leaders of more effective groups were better able to use different styles of supervision in different situations, delegated more
authority to others, were more supportive in their manner, and
helped their groups develop more cohesiveness. A program of
studies on leadership repeatedly found that heads of more effective groups are more concerned with successful completion of
the task and the use of strong leadership methods when the situation is either very easy or very difficult for them to manage.
But when the task is of intermediate difficulty, the most effective influencer devotes his attention primarily to friendly interpersonal and supportive relations among group members (Fiedler, 1967).

Conditions That Work Against
the Effectiveness of a Change Agent

A person who tries to influence others may not be as successful
as he wishes if (1) his proposal is opposed by those addressed

or (2) his style when presenting his ideas causes listeners to develop an emotional state of resistance.

Opposition

Suppose an influencer presents a proposal for change. The
listeners ask questions, weigh the pros and cons, and say they
oppose the idea. Their opposition is based on the substantive
content of the proposal, not on how the change agent acts as
he offers his views. The proposer must overcome the others' opposition if he is to have any chance of inspiring the change he
advocates. To transform the beliefs or behavior of target persons, the agent of change must counteract the target person's
reasons for refusing to change their views. Otherwise, those reasons will continue to be used in opposing the plan. Whenever
target persons yield to an influence attempt, they must give up
ideas and objectives they previously prized. The strength of their
opposition depends on three factors: the amount of difference
between the change proposed by the innovator and the views
of target persons; the degree of satisfaction that target persons
derive from the current state of affairs; and the features in the
change agent's plan that are not attractive to persons being influenced. In ordinary language, target persons will oppose a plan
if it asks them to make too great a change. They like things as
they are, or they see too many unfavorable features in the proposed innovations. The influencers have to counter these three
sources of opposition.

Influencers overcome the first complaint, that the innovation is too different from past practices, by making this claim
appear not to be true. They aver that the new plan at first appears quite different but actually has many similarities with past
practices, and they identify these similarities. The proposed
change, they say, is a small one. Any differences that do exist,
moreover, are at the heart of the new plan; they are invaluable,
even if unusual. The inducers meet the objection that past procedures are satisfactory by pointing out ways in which this has
not been the case and by explaining why satisfaction with prior
practices could not have been great; the new change, when put
in place, will provide more favorable outcomes.

An innovator tries to prevent listeners from fearing unpleasant side effects that might follow a change. To do this, he counters claims that target persons may make about the new idea: that it is too complex, too hard to implement, unlikely to work, arouses anxiety, or violates a tradition. Or he asks target persons to give up control over their own actions. Fear that the proposed change is too difficult can be met by deliberately suggesting an obviously too difficult but ideal solution that listeners will oppose and then indicating that the influencer will lower his demands and be satisfied by a change that is easier to bring about, which in fact is the one he really wanted in the first place. This switching method is known as the foot-in-the-door technique (Goldman and Greason, 1981).

Change seekers meet the opposition of target persons in other ways. They cite contrasting facts and give counterarguments. They describe the problem that indicates a great need for change and press for a joint problem-solving session. They suggest that a written version of the joint solution be prepared that will have the force of a contract, or they treat the target persons in ways that develop mutual trust and confidence, using an impersonal style that prevents negative emotional reactions.

Resistance

A change agent evokes resistance in one he hopes to influence if he presents his case in a way that arouses anger, fear, or defensiveness in the listener. Resistance in itself is not bad or lacking in excitement or interest. It tends, however, to reduce the chances that a target person will respond rationally. Worse, a resister's behavior can be contagious among fellow members, who begin to behave as the resister does and to reinforce one another's emotional reactions.

The style of an influencer's behavior, rather than the substantive content of his ideas, causes target persons to resist. Examples of resistance-triggering actions by an initiator include making arbitrary demands so that acceptance of them is tantamount to admitting defeat, ridiculing the ones addressed, making ad hominem or disparaging remarks about listeners, showing anger toward target persons, talking loudly, pitching one's voice high, displaying facial and postural signs of aggression, threatening the focal persons, pressing them to engage in illegitimate acts, or using dishonest or distorted information. In all these, the influencer is trying to restrict the freedom of the target persons or is using emotional and false means in his attempts to be convincing.

An agent of influence ordinarily tries to prevent resistance among persons she wishes to change, unless she is confident she has enough power to overcome it or unless it pleases her to make the other persons angry or fearful. She avoids behaving in ways that generate resistance. She takes steps to prevent the anger or fear that may cause the resistance and attempts to get the receivers engaged in a rational discussion by describing the change being advocated as a problem for discussion rather than by pressing the other to adopt a stated solution. She may, for example, list a number of alternative changes and, while stating no preference among them unless asked, propose a procedure that could be followed to make a choice. A major consequence of such moves is that target persons are assured their freedom of choice is being respected — they are not being pushed around.

A different way for an influencer to prevent resistance is to diagnose ahead of time the possible origins of resistance in those addressed. To do this, the change agent gathers information that helps him understand why listeners may become hostile, defensive, fearful, or evasive. Once she understands the sources of these reactions, she tries to eliminate causes of them in her style of presentation and attempts to convince potential supporters or the target person that she is asking for rational treatment of an issue that is worthy of discussion. She may ask that her idea be given a tentative trial, that only some of what she suggests be adopted at first, or that the advocated change be introduced one step at a time (Rothman, Erlich, and Teresa, 1976).

Such ways of preventing resistance may be too bland if refusals by target persons cause an agent of change to keep up his pressure for a transformation, come what may. In such a case, a two-sided resistance may develop in which the behaviors of the one being addressed mimics the resistance-arousing behaviors of the influencer. The latter, in turn, imitates the target person's unpleasant style. Mutually hostile feelings (or other emotional responses) escalate as resistance on one side causes similar behavior on the other. A circular-causal interaction develops. The behavior of persons on both sides causes misperceptions, misunderstandings, or deliberate efforts to coerce (Pruitt and others, 1993).

In a situation like the one being considered, discussants tend to see malicious intent in the actions of the other side. They distort the comments by their opposite numbers, do not listen to the others, do not try to understand what they are saying, see one another as selfish and untrustworthy, and make no conciliatory moves for fear that willingness to compromise will be taken as a sign of weakness. They threaten, emphasize how far apart their ideas are, make excessive demands, and try to deceive rivals into giving up. Each side is out to win. Nevertheless, there are actions those on the two sides can take to inhibit or dampen such double-edged resistance (Deutsch, 1973; Fisher, Ury, and Patton, 1991; Pruitt and Rubin, 1986; Ury, Brett, and Goldberg, 1989). These include the following:

1. Both the agents of change and the persons exposed to pressure state at the outset that they intend to be rational and control their tendencies to be fearful and hostile — each side tries to assure the other that they will try to remain reasonable.
2. Participants prepare to prevent resistance by organizing their own views clearly.
3. Before a meeting, the agent of change and the target persons agree on how they will conduct themselves. They agree to not ridicule opposing comments, to pay close attention when rivals speak, and to recognize that others are justified in presenting their views as they see things.
4. Discussants work to develop bases for being trusted and for trusting members of the opposite party. For example, they provide evidence for factual information, bring in wit-

nesses to support ideas that may be questioned, and refer to similarities in the views, experiences, friendship, and motives among target persons and change agents.

5. Participants agree on which values are most important, such as fairness, justice, and equality.
6. Everyone promises to abide by these values.
7. Members on both sides identify similarities between the objectives of reformers and those of target persons and declare that all participants are therefore in a cooperative relationship. Each can help the other reach a common goal. Rivalry and competition are inappropriate and irrelevant.

Following steps like these can prevent each side from becoming too coercive on the one hand or too passive on the other. If all goes well, a constructive problem-solving relationship is created, in which the parties coolly consider a proposal for change. The result is a solution-finding process rather than a contest in which the strongest or most abrasive side wins.

Summary

An influencer takes a number of steps to generate change: he makes his ideas acceptable to others, arouses the others' interest in these ideas, converts that interest into action, obtains social support for change in the target persons, and establishes the change so that it will endure. More specific actions include the following:

- Make the new ideas fit the influenced person's way of thinking.
- Tell the influenced person of the need for action and show the path to be followed to attain this action.
- Generate social support by fostering cooperative relationships among members and ask them jointly to plan how they can change themselves.
- Help the influenced ones overcome any misgivings after changing.
- Promise the target person individual rewards for changing in the ways advocated.

- Be attractive to the target person.
- Tell the one addressed exactly what will and will not cause punishment.
- Coerce a person only when his behavior warrants such action.
- Keep in mind the contrasting consequences of methods that encourage freedom of choice in a target person and those that provide an external incentive.
- Counteract the listener's reasons for refusing to change his views, thereby preventing his opposition to a proposed plan.
- Adopt a style of behavior that is known to avoid resistance in the listener.
- Follow this rule: The stronger the motive or desire that change agents arouse among target persons, and the stronger the probability that this motive or desire will be satisfied through doing what the initiators propose, the more the agents of change will influence the target persons.

Recommended Readings

Cialdini, R. *Influence: Science and Practice.* Glenview, Ill.: Scott, Foresman, 1985.
A highly readable account of how agents of influence operate.

Kipnis, D. *The Powerholders.* Chicago: University of Chicago Press, 1976.
Examines the ways that persons with power choose to influence and make their efforts count.

Raven, B. "A Power/Interaction Model of Interpersonal Influence: French and Raven Thirty Years Later." *Journal of Social Behavior and Personality,* 1992, 7, 217–244.
Describes the motives causing agents of change to influence others. Contains an extensive list of references to studies of social power during the past thirty years.

Zander, A. *Effective Social Action by Community Groups.* San Francisco: Jossey-Bass, 1990.
Discusses how groups of citizens with little power strengthen their ability to influence powerful decision makers.

10

RESPONDING TO
THE INFLUENCE OF OTHERS

I met years ago with officers of a utility company to consider how their firm might make better use of groups in its operations. Eight of us sat in a conference room making small talk while waiting for the organization's president to arrive. After a bit, the door suddenly opened and their youngish leader strode into the room. All the managers rose and greeted him as "Mr. President." After the sound of welcome died, I found myself still sitting, surrounded by standing men. I had, moreover, greeted him as "Bill" instead of "Mr. President."

Why did I act in such a carefree way? Was I simply being cheery toward the CEO, whom I knew was not a stuffy person? Was I trying to show others in the room that I did not have to kowtow to a boss? Didn't I know any better? I do not believe an affirmative answer to any of these questions characterizes my actions. I acted differently from the rest because I was not a member of their hierarchy. Bill was not my superior. I did not behave as a subordinate often does toward a power-holder because he did not control my fate, and I had no need to make sure that he had good feelings about me. It was proper for me to address him as a sociable person would.

A member of a group directed by a powerful person seldom feels neutral toward that individual. Her reactions are likely to be at either of two extremes: she feels friendly and comfortable with him, or unfriendly and uncomfortable. In either case, relaxed or cautious, she reacts to the powerholder in ways beyond the day-by-day demands of her regular role. A subordinate is at ease with an instigator of change if she derives from that person benefits she could not obtain for herself. For instance, her superior informs, teaches, or advises her and speaks up in her behalf; praises or helps her get things she needs; acts as an advocate for her with persons at a higher level; gives her autonomy, a say in decisions, or an opportunity to develop pride in herself; and assures the subordinate that this behavior is his regular style.

In contrast, a member is uneasy if a superior causes disadvantages the member would avoid if he could. The influencer points out the member's faults or inadequacies without demonstrating how to improve, provides no help toward ends the target wants to achieve, keeps a close eye on him so that the product of his effort meets the superior's demands, threatens to punish him if he does not do well, offers rewards for behavior the official approves, and leaves the lower-status person uncertain as to whether the influencer will act consistently or unpredictably on any given day. Although it is said there is nothing as funny as unfairness, this maxim holds true only when others are victims, not oneself.

An influenced member doubtless has an easier time with an agent of change who makes him comfortable than with one who does not. However, a problem for a relaxed member is that he may be so well protected by the powerful person that he loses his capacity to take care of his own needs: the eternal aide, assistant, or second in command may not wish to leave the comfort provided by the sponsor. But more often, one who is well supported by a superior develops self-confidence to take care of himself without requiring help from the influencer. He is therefore of less interest to us. An individual who is insecure, tense, and dissatisfied because of the way his boss uses her power has a more complicated problem. He cannot, by definition, easily persuade the influencer to change her ways. He must try to reduce his discomfort. Here we concentrate on uneasy members and how they cope with their anxiety.

An Uncomfortable Relationship

When members are insecure in their relations with persons of greater power, their first reaction may not be due to what the influencers have done but because they do not know the power-holders well and seldom associate with them freely. Bosses and workers more often meet when superiors are ready to do so, not when employees wish. As a consequence, members cannot confidently anticipate what style higher-status persons will use when exercising their power. The subordinates' uneasy reactions to this uncertainty are compounded because they realize that powerful persons can use their influence in ways that satisfy themselves alone, ignoring the desires or displeasures of subordinates if they wish.

Avoiding the Powerholder

A simple way for an influenced member to reduce discomfort, if he can get away with it, is to make it difficult for the superior to have access to the member. A subordinate can do this by avoiding situations in which the superior has control over defined relations in the duties of the two. A member can escape such role relations by avoiding face-to-face contacts with the other person or by limiting the contacts to occasions that are absolutely necessary. Where these contacts cannot be canceled, the member tries to have them in a conference setting where colleagues are present, rather than one on one, because an audience may inhibit a superior's derogatory use of power.

Another way to avoid the impact of a powerholder is to become passive and uninvolved in matters under the superior's control. The member withdraws so that the superior's orders are not perceived as limiting or as derogating the member's actions. Because the subordinate has no investment in the situation, he does not feel forced to do things he does not want to do. Subordinates who are required to converse with a boss during an unplanned encounter, in the lunchroom or hallway, often tell jokes and engage in cheery banter in order to avoid more weighty topics and to show the listener that they are friends and allies of the higher-status one. An additional method of avoiding discomfort caused by an agent of influence is to change one's appraisal of how that person acts. A subordinate looks for evidence that the superior uses her weight in a benevolent manner. (Tyrants are seen to be most kindly by persons who fear them most.)

Winning the Powerholder's Approval

A second way to reduce uneasiness in relations with a superior is to win her approval so that she will exercise her influence in a supportive rather than a restrictive manner. To earn the superior's goodwill, a target person may praise the superior, say he admires the boss's ideas or skills, listen to her intently, laugh at her jokes, rise when she enters the room, introduce her to relatives, send her postcards from the seashore, agree with her in meetings, offer to do favors for her, suppress a desire to disagree, ask her advice, tell others how much he likes the superior, tell others how much the superior likes him ("I am a friend of Hillary"), and generally demonstrate that this subordinate is worthy of support by the superior (Jones, 1964; Zander, Cohen, and Stotland, 1959).

Although flattering the boss is a common form of coping, one researcher who studied its value concluded that its use increases one's chances of advancement by only 5 percent. The most effective stroke one can give one's boss is praising him to his superior. Next best is complimenting the supervisor on how he handled a tough problem. The most important rule in the use of flattery is don't fake it (Schnurman, 1993).

Changing the Powerholder's Style

A third approach for relieving discomfort is to persuade the influencer that he is too strict, abrasive, or self-centered. A member can strengthen this persuasion by giving the boss a statement describing what members feel is wrong in their relationship with him, a petition with the signatures of associates who are aggravated, or a committee report containing a catalog of complaints; by holding a conference with the superior and a set of individuals who try to convince him how he should change; or by conducting a mass meeting in which the manager is invited to respond publicly to suggestions. An air of confrontation is minimized in favor of logic and credible evidence.

Gaining Group Support

In a fourth method of coping, a subordinate gathers the support of her peers to reduce adverse responses to the powerholder's behavior. She might assemble a group of colleagues to discuss and interpret actions of the boss, console workers who are mistreated, or reduce the tensions of lower-status members. She could also establish a unit for planning ways of changing the organization's practices or of getting leaders to accept training in methods of management (Zander, 1990).

Regaining Autonomy

An influenced person is more likely to be unhappy with restrictions on her movements or beliefs if she does not expect, when joining the group, to have her freedom closely limited by a superior. A common reaction to such strictures for one who dislikes them (not everyone does) is that she try to restore her autonomy (Brehm and Brehm, 1981). The strength of her effort to recover greater freedom of movement increases as it becomes more important for her to do the things she is pressed to abandon, as the number of behaviors she must change increases, and as she perceives that the supervisor is more likely to carry out his threats. To regain autonomy, she may refuse to change her behavior as asked by the boss, or she may abandon changes she has already made. As an example, imagine that a union member is told by local officers that she must adopt a particular stance on a political issue in an upcoming election and vote for a particular candidate. Suppose, too, that the member believes her political preferences are private decisions and that a union should not try to affect what she does in such matters. In this instance, she is likely to resist pressures from officers so that she can maintain her area of free movement. She may even do the opposite of what she is being pressed to do (Brehm and Brehm, 1981).

Appealing to Authority

The help of others in actions against a strong agent of influence can be sought by asking an organized authoritative body, perhaps a city council, state legislature, labor union, or board of directors, to undertake formal efforts on behalf of disadvantaged persons. Examples of such tailor-made bodies are ones created by a legislative unit to resolve a conflict, plan a new contract, or hear citizens' grievances. Members may also appeal to a mediator, arbitrator, or court (see Chapter Twelve).

Threatening

A further procedure for instituting change in a powerholder is more aggressive. Here subordinates try to generate in the powerful person a fear of unpleasant consequences unless he becomes more supportive of subordinates. Extreme techniques in such instances include arson, sabotage, injury to bystanders, the taking of hostages, kidnapping, robbery, or other forms of intimidation (Zander, 1990).

Preparing to Protect Oneself

In some cases, a subordinate with little influence is able to negotiate a change with a powerful person. Examples are a worker negotiating a grievance with a supervisor, a student brought before a dean to discuss the scholar's undesirable behavior, or a research assistant who questions a theory being advocated by his mentor. All things being equal, we expect in such cases that the influential one will be more likely to have his way. The weaker party may strengthen his hand, however, by negotiating on the merits of the case or on the principles involved.

To foster negotiation on the merits of the case, the target person defines ahead of time the worst possible outcome he would accept — his bottom line. Such a decision helps the less influential person resist lures he might regret accepting. A variation on this approach is to identify the best outcome one might expect during a negotiation, or what one will do if an agreement is not possible (Fisher, Ury, and Patton, 1991).

If a potent person refuses to consider any position other than the one he has stated, the weaker one would be wise not to criticize the rival's grasp of that position, refuse to accept it, or defiantly defend his own stand. Instead, the less powerful participant might do better by trying to discover why the superior wants his approach and no other. What is he trying to accomplish by his plan? What other way might work as well, or better, to satisfy the superior's interests?

Opposition by the Target Person

As we saw in the previous chapter, an individual often copes with unwarranted ideas by opposing them. Clearly, a person with little power would risk expressing contrary ideas to a superior only if he feels sure the other will not be insulted by the opposer's forwardness and if the refuser believes he is able to oppose in a manner that does not arouse a negative response among superiors.

A target person may oppose a superior's request for any of a number of reasons. He may think it is a bad idea, is contrary to his own experience, or will not work. He may believe that the new plan defies logic or good sense. He may feel there is no reason for changing things, since all is going well and complaints about the current state of affairs are not valid. He may be offended by the innovation because it is unethical, immoral, illegal, plainly dumb, or breaks with long-standing tradition. He may reason that the intended effects of the proposed innovation are uncertain, will create a bad precedent, or can do good for a few people but harm to a greater number. He may decide that the change will be too difficult or costly to implement or that he may lose self-regard if he tries to do what is asked and fails in doing so. He may view the influencer as a complainer who has no support from other members, or he might sense that others would be offended if he complied (Raven, 1992; Zander, 1990).

When a person is pressed to adopt a change she cannot accept, she must make the reason for opposing it clear and convincing. She has to refuse in a way that persuades the influencer to take no for an answer. This is not easy to do if she has to state her arguments against the initiator's plan in a public meeting, without prior preparation, or while colleagues are watching. Accordingly, she may stall, request time to consider the matter, ask for definitions of terms, state reasons for opposing the plan, encourage the influencer to respond to her comments questioning the change, or describe limits on her freedom to transform things. Or she may postpone making any change on the grounds of pressure from regular duties or a need to think more about the issue at hand.

A prime concern of a target person when pressed by an activist who makes his requirements widely known is dread of the public consequences that might follow if he makes a blunder. He may feel some success if he implements the ideas offered by the agent of change. More commonly, however, he derives little pride from such an action if he is proud of his current practices and did not develop the idea for a change. He may be criticized by constituents who believe that his decision to change is unwise. Moreover, rejection of a proposal may cause public disapproval of the opposer if it is a popular idea among associates, and a refusal will arouse anger among those who support the change. All in all, an activist has little to lose and much to gain from putting forth a change proposal; a target person has little to gain and much to lose by accepting such a proposal.

Resistance by the Target Person

When a target person resists, he defends himself from the feelings aroused by the innovator and at the same time uses methods that will limit the influence of the change agents. Toward this end, he may appeal for help from colleagues, third parties, or those who can help weaken the power of the change agent.

A target person resists another's proposal for one or more reasons. He decides that the person pushing a particular plan wants primarily to benefit himself or to deprive the one he asks to make a change. He does not trust the validity of the information used by the initiator in support of his case and believes these data are deliberately based on misinformation. He perceives that the proposal offers a solution but does not indicate what problem it is supposed to solve. He sees the advocate for change as abrasive, discourteous, uncivil, hostile, or loud.

A person may also resist because colleagues welcome such a reaction to the change agent's style, dislike the person making the suggestions for change, or feel that the target is being put under unfair pressure and ought to reassert his right to determine his own behavior (Brehm and Brehm, 1981; Pruitt and others, 1993; Raven, 1992; Zander, 1990).

If a target person develops both opposition and resistance, which has the greater impact on his behavior? A target person who opposes a proposal from an agent of change usually does so on rational grounds. When arguing against the other's ideas, he employs facts and logic in explaining his stance. His opposition becomes less objective, however, if he also resists and reacts emotionally to the sender's style. His resistance reduces his rationality. Resistance is often a more powerful determinant of behavior than opposition, as it interferes with sensible give and take.

Two-Sided Resistance

When a target person is faced with an influencer who uses unpleasant behavior, his impulse, as we have seen, is to counter these actions with similar ones; like is met with like. Emotions increase on both sides if the obnoxious coercer, upon receiving a dose of his own medicine, feels impelled to return more of the same. Such interactions can lock competers into a cycle of coercive actions that escalate as persons on each side try to defeat their rivals. These behaviors interfere with mutual influence because each party rejects the other's ideas.

More often than not, the ones involved, or bystanders, eventually recognize that calmer forms of interaction are needed and that otherwise hostility will continue to grow and waste one another's time, that it is unwise for a discussion to remain caught in a cycle of coercion, and that it would be better to develop rational efforts among participants. Before he can develop a more thoughtful demeanor, however, a target person must curb his own feelings. He can do so by facing the mindless nature of his behavior and diagnosing why it occurs. He tries to figure out why a need to win is dominating his moves and urges the agent of change to make a similar review of his own feelings, asking himself what the target does that arouses resistance. Each tries to describe these actions and reactions to the other.

Ideally, after such two-sided evidence is assembled, a target person can do several things to foster constructive problem solving and to minimize defensiveness between the sides. First, he suggests that the tone of discussion (about whether the target person should comply with the sender's request) be kept away from rivalry, pressuring, or efforts to outdo others and move instead toward a cooperative approach that will improve the chances of a mutually beneficial outcome. He explains that he supports such intentions, not because he feels too weak to resist but because he believes it is the wisest procedure to follow and will facilitate constructive conferring. He makes it clear that he is willing to change his goals if he is convinced it is wise to do so and if such a change does not violate his basic values or principles. In addition, he states that cooperative efforts to choose a wise course toward change, if any, will likely lead to solutions both sides will appreciate. He describes what virtues he sees in the ideas being proposed by the agent of change and emphasizes that he himself has wondered if a change was necessary in the matter under discussion. Statements like these indicate that the target person is willing to talk openly and make changes if and when he is convinced they are useful.

If neither side will engage in such a discussion, the person under emotion-arousing pressure may take unilateral steps to prevent escalation of resistance. At the outset, she may avoid contact with the agent of change, listen to the reformer's ideas as little as possible, make no coherent response to the other's notions, postpone consideration of the proposal, and avoid behavior that mimics that of the influencer. She may point to the abrasive ways of the change agent by publicly declaring that his procedures are unfair. The weight of such an accusation can be enhanced by suggesting that the powerholder use more acceptable manners and by asking colleagues to help both the influencer and target person define what kind of behavior is off-limits. If associates act on such a suggestion, they inadvertently become a source of social pressure against using behavior that arouses and fosters two-sided resistance.

Sharing Influence with Target Persons

In recent years many managers of large organizations have become interested in the wise use of groups and teams. This interest has been inspired by the group-oriented supervisory styles observed in Japan, Sweden, and companies within the United States. These management methods, variously labeled as participative leadership, participation in decision making, empowerment, or quality circles, are intended to give subordinates a say in controlling their own fate and a share in influencing the way of life within their group and the larger organization. In the terms we have been using, such encouragement of two-way influence is an effort by an agent of change to help lower-status persons increase their influence and cope with an agent's directing behaviors. The powerholder develops a role for followers in the leadership of their unit (Hollander and Offerman, 1990; Zander, 1983).

Why do influential persons grant groups of subordinates the means to affect the nature of their work and environment? Several reasons seem likely. One is that such supportive activity makes it possible for less powerful persons to express their personal needs and goals and make their self-oriented aims fit the requirements of their group. Members, in brief, devise means for increasing their own satisfaction. Another reason is that a supervisor may not have as much detailed information about a given issue as persons who regularly deal with it; thus, the latter can help him delineate a wiser plan where a change seems necessary. In Japan, for instance, groups of workers meet regularly to identify and find solutions for problems they discover in maintaining the quality of products they make. Members of these quality circles inspect their own output and feel free to make changes in their group's procedures without telling managers of new methods they are using (Zander, 1983). A further reason is that participants who have a share in setting objectives for their organization are more attracted to those aims and work harder to achieve them. Finally, a sensitive person of power may recognize that he and his actions represent a threat to members and that this uneasiness can be lessened in decision-making sessions where participants have an effect on the outcome. All in all, having a say on goals and activities within their group makes members more motivated to perform well, unless of course their decisions are weak or never put into practice (Hollander and Offerman, 1990; Vroom and Yetton, 1973).

Despite the evidence that sharing power with subordinates may be useful, more than a few managers are unwilling to try such a procedure. They fear that the supply of social power within their organization is limited and that if subordinates are granted control over certain matters, they, the superiors, will lose power over the workers, who will then ignore the boss. It is more likely, however, that both the superior and subordinate gain in influence when the latter are given a share in making decisions, that power is not a finite entity in which one loses if others gain (Likert, 1959; Tannenbaum, 1968). I mentioned earlier that it is useful to think of leadership as any act by any member (including the designated leader) which moves an organization toward attainment of its goals. Thus, sharing power is a way of making sure that persons who can contribute to the group's progress have a means for doing so. Probably, persons who have a lust for strong power are most likely to be threatened by sharing power; they believe they must maintain tight control over events around them or chaos will develop. Some persons in positions of power have no idea how to run meetings where they ought to listen to what others say, or they feel they will be blamed if the persons they empowered make poor choices or use their freedom as an opportunity to do shoddy work. Doubtless, decision making by subordinates goes better if they have a desire for pride in their group's actions. In such a case, they are eager to work on behalf of their group and welcome the freedom to do so.

Coping with the Effects of Influencing Others

An influencer may have problems because he often cannot avoid thwarting and discomforting subordinates. How shall he respond to the realization that he has frustrated group members? Such a realization may cause him to feel guilty because he has hurt colleagues. Or he may fear retaliation from those he has harmed. He may attempt to reduce his distress in several ways. In one method, the superior lowers his guilt by justifying his actions. He tells himself and listeners that the victim deserved the treatment because he is an unworthy individual who ought to be derogated. He denies he was responsible for hurting the person influenced, saying the harm was caused by others or by circumstances beyond his control. Or he declares that the injury of target persons was small and therefore not a serious concern. In quite a different approach for reducing his distress, he compensates the harmed individual in some way, reasoning that both the sender and receiver will then be disadvantaged alike. He may punish himself so that he no longer feels shame for the harm he has done, because he the guilty one is now equally harmed. Which of these several methods an agent of influence uses depends on which one he thinks will best reduce his uneasiness over having hurt a subordinate (Walster, Berscheid, and Walster, 1971).

Summary

A group member who is influenced by a more powerful colleague may be pleased with that relationship because he receives useful advice, information, help, or rewards. He may, moreover, be dependent on the agent of influence for these favorable events or for protection that person provides. In contrast, a member may be unhappy in his association with powerful others because he is threatened with or receives restrictions, disapprovals, or punishments. He must somehow cope with a situation that is not easy to change. There are a number of ways he can try to deal with this state of affairs. The one who makes him uncom-

fortable may also respond to the fact that he has created stress
for another person.

Coping with the Effects of Being Too Heavily Influenced

- Avoid face-to-face interaction with the person of greater power.
- Conceal behavior that might cause the powerholder to punish
  or retaliate.
- Reduce own uneasiness in relations with a superior by seeking evidence that the latter really uses his weight in a benevolent manner and in behalf of less powerful persons.
- Withdraw interest and concern in tasks you are pressed to
  perform so that the other's pressures do not appear to limit
  your autonomy.
- Oppose the content or logic of the influencer's ideas in ways
  that make it possible for that person to take no for an answer.
- Demonstrate resistance (displeasure or anger) to unpleasant
  manners used by the change agent. Make it clear that you
  do not intend to imitate his behavior.
- Act toward the superior in ways that cause the superior to
  respond with goodwill.
- Persuade the powerholder that his behavior is too strict or
  derogatory.
- Recruit the help of peers who feel that individuals with little influence have more impact on a superior when a number of them make a joint request of a higher-status person.
- Ask established bodies to urge the influencer to lighten his
  demands or to create special groups for that purpose.
- Get the influencer to change her style by intimidating her
  through threats or attacks.

Helping Subordinates Deal with Their Status

- Develop a procedure that empowers subordinates by giving them a say over their own fate or an understanding of
  why they can have no say.
- Recognize that one's possession of greater power may represent a threat to subordinates.
- Recognize, accept, and take appropriate supportive actions
  when individuals with little power try to cope with their
  insecurity.

- Give subordinates praise, approval, or respect when they deserve it.
- Make it clear to influenced persons that the agent is willing to change and benefit from their advice.
- Employ indirect forms of power (expert, referent, legitimate) more often than rewards or coercion.
- Use rewards and penalties when they are earned—not for unspecified reasons.
- Reward people after they have done good work, not before.
- Avoid rationalizing acts that were harmful to receivers; do not assert that victims deserve to be hurt, were not badly harmed, or that the harm was not caused by acts of the change agent.

Recommended Readings

Brehm, S., and Brehm, J. *Psychological Reactance: A Theory of Freedom and Control.* San Diego, Calif.: Academic Press, 1981.
An explanation of how persons of little power behave in order to free themselves from others' control.

Hollander, E. "Conformity, Status, and Idiosyncrasy Credit." *Psychological Review,* 1958, *65,* 117–127.
The author explains how and why some persons are allowed to ignore a group's rules or the power of its officers because of their special value to the group.

Jones, E. *Ingratiation: A Social Psychological Analysis.* New York: Appleton-Century-Crofts, 1964.
Describes how subordinates try to win the approval of superiors.

Nemeth, C. "Minority Dissent as a Stimulant to Group Performance." In S. Worchel, W. Wood, and J. Simpson (eds.), *Group Process and Productivity.* Newbury Park, Calif.: Sage, 1992.
This author demonstrates that members within a group who disagree with the majority can be useful for that unit.

Zander, A. *Effective Social Action by Community Groups.* San Francisco: Jossey-Bass, 1990.
This is a book-length discussion of how sets of citizens can earn power for themselves to influence local holders of power.

Part Three

WORKING EFFECTIVELY WITH OTHER GROUPS

11

UNDERSTANDING THE ORIGINS
OF INTERGROUP CONFLICTS

In Pleasant Valley, a residential community of condominium homes, employees care for everyone's buildings and grounds. A board of directors, elected by the residents, monitors the work of a general manager who supervises these workers. The village contains a dozen neighborhoods, each with its own governing board. One day, representatives from several of these local boards met to consider complaints that the maintenance of their property was too expensive, slow, and poorly done. The complainers formed an ad hoc association to finance a study of how managerial methods might be improved, upkeep done more efficiently, and neighborhood directors given more say about such services.

After months of discussion, the members of the ad hoc unit put their plans before the valley-wide board of directors and, to their surprise, were rebuffed. The directors said that the quality of work done by the hired staff needed no improvement, that the directors' devotion to duty was being derogated, and that the complaints were the work of a rebellious minority of residents who were violating the charter and bylaws of the corporation. Angry words brought things to an impasse.

At first, those on neither side would meet with the others. Later, when tempers cooled, bystanders urged the rivals to work together in planning how to improve maintenance matters. After agreeing on a problem-solving process, and after considering proposals and compromises, the two parties shaped a plan that promised to provide more satisfactory work by the staff.

Members of a group within a larger organization or a community containing many groups often must collaborate with nearby entities. Salespeople consult with designers in the advertising department, executive officers meet with the directors of their organization, and union leaders confer with members of management. Interactions like these, across the boundaries of groups, can develop in unexpected ways if participants are not clear what rules should be followed, who should have a say, who is in charge, or how to proceed. Such ambiguities may lead to strong responses among those involved, and the groups may be unexpectedly burdened with conflict and hard feelings or lifted by mutual help and graciousness. We need to understand both discordant relations and pleasant alliances between groups, but scholars devote much more attention to bad intergroup actions than to good ones, so we have more to consider about conflict than about peace. Our examination of intergroup dissension will help us speculate about the nature of good intergroup relations if we assume that harmony may be based on conditions opposite those that cause and encourage disputes.

Nature of Intergroup Conflict

A conflict develops when two parties disagree about what the other ought or ought not do (Horwitz and Berkowitz, 1990). A committee to plan an addition to a building offers their ideas, but the administrative committee says these are too costly; the board of a hospital decides to close the unit for emergency care, but a nurse's association opposes this action; a curriculum committee recommends changes in their school's course on social relations, but a group of parents does not like these suggestions.

Conflict can occur between groups when purposes and activities in one group are at odds with those in another. An event generates dissension when it prevents, obstructs, interferes, injures, or in some way makes actions less effective in another body (Deutsch, 1973; Likert and Likert, 1976). The source of such ill-fitting activities may be competition for scarce resources (such as office space, funds, tools, or influence), barriers to self-determination by members, differences in basic beliefs, or fears that actions by those in one group will create discomfort for those in the other.

Conflict occurs in some cases because rivalrous units have very similar needs or interests; both want a given gain but there is not enough for all. Thus, if members in one body are satisfied, those in the other cannot be. Where two groups seek similar benefits from a short supply of resources, members of either body have to change their aims or find a larger supply of resources. In other instances, the desires or plans of members in both sets are opposite: pressure applied in a given direction by group A is met by a pull in the opposing direction by group B. Where groups seek similar results, members of either unit have to change their aims or find a greater supply of resources. Some conflicts are primarily psychological: members have negative, often unfounded, feelings or beliefs about adversaries and act according to what they fear rivals will do. Other conflicts are overtly hostile face-to-face actions. Some are brief, others enduring. Some are destructive, others are useful sources of desirable change.

A conflict is *wasteful* if the tension it generates prevents discussants from thinking clearly or making sound decisions. It is *useful* if it awakens interest and curiosity that lead to the airing of problems that are being ignored and to efforts toward improving things. In the next chapter we consider ways of resolving conflicts. Here we examine the origins of disputes, what causes them to become wasteful, and their effects.

Conditions That Make Intergroup Conflict More Likely

Conflicts occur more often when certain conditions exist. A few of these states absolutely must be present if disagreements are to develop; others increase the probability of difficulty between units; and still others increase the strength of a dispute once it is under way.

Minimally Unsettling Conditions

The minimal circumstances for a rupture to occur are those that create an anticipation of rivalry between separate units. First, participants in a given group acknowledge the other group's existence. Next, those in each unit recognize or suspect that events in the other body will affect themselves and that things done in one unit will be incompatible with preferred moves in the other. To cite a simple example, it is enough that participants in a group know that those in the other *may* (not *have*) become rivals for observers to feel that the potential adversaries are unlikable. In a study that examined this point, members of a group were asked twice how well they liked persons in a separate unit (both bodies were temporary, recently formed, and visible to the other). The first measurement was made before respondents knew that representatives of each group would toss a coin to see who would win a prize; the second measurement was made after members had learned the coins were to be flipped (but no contest had yet taken place). As soon as members learned about their upcoming rivalry, their liking for the future competitors decreased sharply from what it had been a moment earlier. Persons in a group usually believe that members of a rival body will take steps that can interfere with the observers, and vice versa, before a conflict arises.

Even when circumstances most conducive to intergroup disagreement exist, bad relations between two bodies will not blossom unless a trigger situation develops. As more of these stimulating situations occur, difficulties are more likely to follow. In addition, a disruption more certainly will take place if units are fairly equal in power, because if one group is stronger than the other, those in the more powerful unit can limit dissension started by rivals. Or those in the stronger body can have their own way if their actions are resisted by a weaker unit.

Fuzzy Definition of Roles

Groups are more likely to develop bad relations if members are not sure which team has the major responsibility for specific tasks in which both have a part. Ambiguity about domain of authority can arise either because participants in both groups try to avoid responsibility for onerous duties or both claim jurisdiction over activities that are beneficial to their own unit (Walton and Dutton, 1969). In a closely related manner, conflict may develop because participants are new in their jobs and their actions are therefore not predictable; new groups of young persons get into more difficulties than established units of older members.

Lack of Conflict-Settling Procedures

Tension is more likely to develop between groups if participants have little experience in settling strained relations or do not have agreed-upon methods for resolving disputes. It takes skill to prevent friction from flowering into animosity. If members of a board of education get into a disagreement with parents, and the superintendent of their system believes that conflict must be prevented at all cost because it damages the harmony that should always exist between board and community, the members will get little help from the professional educator, will probably have no plan for dealing with a conflict, and will have to settle the dispute on their own despite their lack of practice in doing so (Zeigler, Kehoe, and Reisman, 1985).

When police commissioners must deal with a technical issue (for example, whether a department should use the recombinant DNA procedure for identifying suspects, or the size of bullets that police officers should carry), members may be unsure how to decide such a matter if separate sets of experts press them in opposing directions and if there is no clear evidence about what might happen if one or another decision is made. Who should settle this kind of issue: the commissioners on their own, officials of the health department, members of the city council, invited experts, or some combination of these (Zander, 1979)?

Few Contacts

Another reason for bad relations between interdependent groups is physical separation so that they seldom see one another. If it is necessary to collaborate in order to accomplish assigned duties, it stands to reason that difficulty in doing so engenders tension. Those on each side think inattention by the others makes themselves look bad. Mere irritation can turn to anger if those in either party believe that members of the other body stay apart because they dislike the ones they are avoiding. Members in each unit assume the others are seldom available because they are hostile toward persons in their group. Thus, each becomes hostile toward their counterparts.

Being Disadvantaged

A different source of conflict arises when members in one group feel they are receiving fewer rewards than those in a rival unit. Perhaps members of the more advantaged body are given more pay for their effort, better working conditions, finer equipment, or less burdensome tasks. Guilt among the better treated and envy among the underprivileged also can cause unstable interpersonal relations.

Employees of a social agency may sense that those in other such organizations have more advantages. If members of their board of directors do not agree that the workers are disadvantaged, disagreement may develop between complainers and trustees. Members of a governing board, for their part, seldom believe they are deprived in comparison to employees because they usually have the power (if they wish to use it) to make things happen the way they like.

Enjoying a Contest

Intergroup conflict develops more easily if participants in either body welcome a dispute. Students of politics recognize that some politicians see a disagreement as a form of wit-matching that they enjoy for its own sake. Thus, they like to keep a contest going (Banfield and Wilson, 1963). A variation on this notion occurs among those who enjoy making powerful persons uncomfortable. Groups of students glow over their skill in stalling meetings of regents through the use of outrageous arguments, chants, songs, or a brass band. Such an indoor sport was common in the 1960s, and popular in the 1930s among students who said they were communists and wished to practice ways of wrecking meetings whose participants might make decisions of which the "reds" disapprove.

Facing a Crisis

Members of a decision-making unit may get along well among themselves and with those in other entities until a crisis occurs, such as a threat of financial loss, a strike, fire, a new restrictive regulation, or loss of an agency's license to operate. During such an emergency, tension may develop in their interactions with persons in a related organization due to their uncertainty about what should be done and a need for quick action.

Despite disagreement and anxiety among those involved in a crisis, the authors of a study of emergencies in boards of for-profit firms report that courtesy usually prevails during such bad times. But, they add, members' behavior is often so polite that resolution of the crisis is delayed because participants will not discuss delicate issues; thus, discussants never get to the bottom of things. These authors suggest that it may be necessary at times to deviate from the norms of courteous behavior in order to settle a conflict (Lorsch and MacIver, 1986).

Two other triggers of conflict between groups need no explanation. If members in one body try to gain power over those in another unit, and this move is resisted, a conflict is under way. Likewise, if those in one group seek to satisfy their own interests with little regard for the needs of others in a second group, bad relations tend to develop (Deutsch, 1990).

Causes of Worsening Conflict

Certain conditions make a dispute between groups hotter and harder to control.

Intergroup Resistance

As we saw earlier, resistance is an unfavorable emotional response among members to the style that change agents display while presenting their ideas and urging listeners to adopt those notions. Aspects of an influencer's style that arouse resistance among target persons include invalid or biased information, threats, self-serving greed, false accusations, anger, sarcasm, or ridicule of those being addressed. Listeners' reactions to those addressing them, whether characterized by fear, anger, greed, or defensiveness, clearly cannot calm a conflict. They are more likely to deepen it.

Retaliation

As most of us discovered in early years, people resist others' repulsive behavior, and their way of resisting often mirrors the others' actions. Janis (1989) put the idea colorfully in what he calls the "angry retaliation rule": "When you are thwarted, injured, or humiliated, don't let the bastards get away with it; do something to punish them in retaliation" (p. 191). Conflict is more likely when one party is perceived to be at fault for unpleasant circumstances and is openly blamed by those in a rival group.

When members of a county grand jury said those serving on the local water commission were using their expense accounts in wasteful ways, reported these matters to the press, described the extravagant and unnecessary trips some of the commissioners took and the fancy parties they held, the head of the commission retaliated by accusing jury members of sloppy investigating, favoritism toward commissioners who were not mentioned, and racial prejudice.

Members of a receiving group are more likely to retaliate if others' unpleasant style is unexpected or not explained and therefore appears to be deliberate. Some conditions facilitate retaliation: the target person suspects others' undesirable behavior will be repeated, persons in the environment encourage revengeful actions, no influential peacemakers are present to counsel and calm the rivals, or persons on both sides are unwilling to trust the others.

As a consequence of a two-sided retaliation, efforts to engage in conflict-resolving measures will be ignored; those on both sides will fail to cooperate with rivals, make no sensible search for a solution, use biased information, ignore the costs of retaliating, or derogate their rivals (Janis, 1989).

Acts of reciprocation are not always due to anger. When members of one party make rational and objective comments in a pleasant style, the ones addressed counter with comparable behavior (Patchen, 1993). My guess is that groups seeking a joint agreement in a situation where conflict can be common (as in a labor-management negotiation) typically try to reciprocate rivals' behavior with cooperative words and actions even if it takes a bit of self-control.

Escalation

When members of one party in a conflict resist a repulsive style used by those on the other side and retaliate by using the same behavior, an escalation often follows. Heat increases in the give and take because participants in the rival units retaliate with stronger words and body language than they receive. Those on each side try to outdo rivals in the vigor of their response.

An escalation more often develops under any or all of three circumstances: (1) Participants on each side believe that those in the other party intend to satisfy their own interests regardless of what happens to anyone else. Such a belief arouses members of opposing groups to use superior cunning, trickery, or force in dealing with adversaries and to abandon rules of fair play or courtesy in their determination to win. (2) Those in each entity see their own motives as more appropriate, proper, and wise than the motives of the other unit. Rivals' notions are viewed as wrong or evil. Rational analysis and discussion are abandoned for fear they will be taken as a sign of weakness. (3) Competitors excuse atrocious things they do toward others on the grounds that these acts are justified under the circumstances.

Polarization

If those on each side are convinced that their ideas are correct, the rival's are totally wrong, and neither party will move toward reconciling these notions, they are frozen in a state of disagreement — are *polarized*. As a result, progress toward resolving their dispute will be retarded. They argue in favor of their own beliefs and do not consider others' suggestions or even listen to them. Persons on each side can release the icy grasp on their separate views if they try out the ideas of opponents to see if they are useful or if they seek to learn what unstated needs those in the other party hope to settle by insisting on having their way (Fisher, Ury, and Patton, 1991).

Loyalty to Own Group

The stress of an intergroup dispute becomes greater when members are strongly committed to their own unit and as a result have little interest in the goals or plans of the other body. Part of the reason for this narrow-mindedness is that members pressure their colleagues to adhere to decisions made in their group. The greater the cohesiveness of the unit, the stronger these pressures and the less members are inclined to value the views favored in other teams (see Chapter Six). When the cohesiveness of groups generates stronger conflict, this cohesiveness is increased because the threat to the group, aroused by the dispute, brings members closer together. Thus, support for a group's standards worsens intergroup conflict, which in turn sharpens the need for greater defense of the group's way of life.

Importance of Issue

A conflict is stronger when an issue is more important to both sides. Athletic teams with little at stake may not play as well as they can, but teams competing for a championship exert extra effort and minimize their errors. What starts as a minor tiff may call more significant matters into play and the intensity of the conflict increases as these heavier topics are brought into the battle. Conflicts have a way of growing in size when each side feels it is important to win. When those involved in a conflict can see that a loss will interfere with their ability to achieve a valued goal, they dislike that contest and especially so when the goal is a measurable and attainable one, such as profit in a business firm.

Members' Dispositions

There are groups whose members more regularly see themselves as under attack or as being deprived, and thus they respond aggressively. Even when a rival group says it wants to cooperate, these members see the others' actions as untrustworthy, or leading to unfavorable consequences (Schopler and others, 1993). In such situations there are usually contrasting types of persons: one kind correctly comprehends the behavior of others, whether cooperative or competitive; the other kind regards all behavior of others toward their group to be competitive. Those of the first type are receptive when members of another group offer to help them, but they become aggressive when others are hostile. The suspicious types, by contrast, enter into a conflict eagerly, even when it is not appropriate because the others are trying to cooperate with them (Kelley and Stahelski, 1970).

In most faculties, churches, or large firms one often finds a set of critics who complain about the decisions made by executive bodies. They comment in angry and derogatory terms while refusing to listen to explanations that differ from their views. These bodies appeal to and recruit persons who prefer to distrust individuals in positions of authority.

Requirements of Culture

The severity of a quarrel between members of separate groups may increase if they live in a culture that admires displays of anger or stubbornness. In some Latin-American and Middle Eastern countries, as illustrations, it is considered manly to take offense quickly and respond aggressively to small affronts. In such places, those involved in a dispute are egged on by supporters to defend their honor and are disapproved if they do not. In areas of the United States where descendents of these cultures are gathered, one sees severe conflicts arise over exceedingly minor matters.

Even in subcultures of our country where everyone is native born, value may be placed on acting tough. In a rent strike at a city-owned housing project, the leaders tried to frighten officials into meeting their demands (Brill, 1971). They used rehearsed behavior to show that they were angry and powerful. They stared stonily at the mayor while refusing to answer his questions (silent stubbornness was perceived to be a way of displaying strength), exaggerated the number of persons taking part in the strike, used military terms when addressing one another in a public meeting, boasted publicly about the effectiveness of their hostile acts, and showed up at bargaining sessions wearing African tribal costumes.

Groups Composed of Non-Elite Persons

Students of social behavior observed years ago that individuals from lower-status socioeconomic neighborhoods in the United States are more inclined to use hostile behavior when trying to influence others or resolve a conflict. More recent studies show that the social class of group members affects their tendency to enter into a dispute with those in another body. As examples, elite persons in a group tend to avoid controversial topics and seldom allow their unit to get into a conflict with outsiders, because their peers would disapprove of their aggression. Boards with a majority of non-elite persons, in contrast, often get into disagreements with other bodies, interfere with moves by their chief officers, and take it upon themselves to represent the group's leader (without the latter's knowledge) when conferring with parties outside their organization (Middleton, 1983).

Governing boards composed of non-elite persons are more easily influenced by sources outside their unit. Where a group contains several non-elite subsets, each with its own advisers, members often get into a dispute over whose advisers are correct.

Authority That Does Not Restrain Hostile Behavior

During the 1960s, college students became experts at staging angry confrontations with school authorities. In many cases, a small band was able to draw uninvolved bystanders into active support of their views by behavior that led the police to handle their band roughly. Such altercations grew into serious disorders, damaging property and persons, as students recognized that faculty and deans were reluctant to punish them because these officials wanted to protect the students' rights to free speech. The absence of restraints and sanctions by superiors enabled dissension to become more intense.

Effects of Intergroup Breaches

Once a schism between groups begins, the characteristics of each entity change. Some of these modifications are good for the unit; others are not. When a rupture first arises, members with the most influence, whether legitimate or otherwise, take charge in their group. The greater the threat from the rival group, the more members welcome such lively leadership. At the same time, the speed of decision is hastened. Members talk more briefly, stick more closely to the point, avoid tangents more carefully, press harder for agreements, and emphasize actions to be taken rather than a need for similarity in opinions. Discussants play down differences among themselves in favor of finding common views. Members are more willing to go along with agreed-upon ideas instead of trying to have their own way.

Because their group is under pressure, members close ranks. They think well of their mates, express more confidence in one another than they had before the row began, and feel that they themselves and their ideas are being welcomed by colleagues. Any representative of a group who is to present its case in a meeting with persons from a rival body is carefully instructed by peers about what to say and is made to realize that a deviation from these instructions will be disapproved. As a result, the representative enters negotiations with a stance he does not have the right to change; he is a communicator of his group's resolutions rather than a solver of its intergroup problems.

Does a person in an intergroup conflict become more hostile toward a rival organization than when he is in a dispute with an individual? The evidence from a variety of settings suggests this is the case (Bodenhausen, Gaelick, and Wyer, 1978; Mummendey and Otten, 1993; Schopler and others, 1993). One reason may be that members give social support to one another's individual reactions such as fear, anger, or greed. Another reason may be that members of a group, caught up in a disagreement with those in a separate body, develop common views in the heat of the conflict and press one another to abide by these notions. Their group-developed ideas are based on their desire to help their unit win. Members typically do not trust those in an opposing organization. As a result, they demonstrate anger, resentment, and criticism more often than trust, admiration, understanding, or sympathy. They tell themselves that their behavior is appropriate and sensible, given their impossible relationship with those in the other body. Members, moreover, encourage one another to be as hostile as necessary to satisfy their wishes for their group and themselves. All of these effects appear to occur more often when a group disputes with a group than when a person disagrees with a person.

Useful Conflicts

Although conflicts can cause unfavorable consequences, some disputes do not create such reactions. Instead, participants may view contrasting opinions as a stimulant to creativity and an opportunity to seek new and better ideas both sides welcome. Thus, a conflict can prevent stagnant thinking and generate a "dither" that is beneficial to problem solving. Because of its refreshing quality, an intergroup dispute can be a means for airing problems so they receive the attention they deserve but have not been getting.

Differences between groups help each unit change itself. A set of persons using one approach to an issue discover how they are different from other groups, what is unique about their own body, and how they define their unit's identity. An altercation gives members a chance to test their group, to see how well it can meet a challenge; as a result, its cohesiveness increases, and useful group characteristics follow from an increase in the attractiveness of a unit among members. Whether the course of an intergroup conflict becomes wasteful or constructive depends in good part on how members go about resolving or controlling their conflict and on the similarity of objectives among conflicting parties. We turn to that issue in the next chapter.

Summary

A conflict exists when two parties disagree about what they should or should not do. A conflict is wasteful if the tension it generates prevents participants from thinking clearly or making sound decisions. It is useful if it awakens interest and curiosity, leading to creative efforts toward improving things and to the treatment of problems that have been unreasonably ignored.

A conflict is more likely to arise if members of a group and a rival unit want the same things and there is not enough for both, if members in each group block the other group's achievement of its goal, or if those on one side develop an emotional response to the manners of the others during discussion of their views.

A minor disagreement may be triggered into a more severe confrontation if there is ambiguity about division of responsibilities between groups, no procedures exist for resolving disputes, members of the separate units seldom have contacts with those in the other body, members of a group feel they receive fewer benefits than the rival body, participants enjoy a lively fight, or colleagues disagree with one another when an emergency arises.

A full-blown conflict may worsen if the disagreeing parties become polarized in their views, see the issues as important, develop two-sided resistance, attempt to retaliate for real or imagined harms, escalate their hostile actions, swear strong loyalty to their group, or are disposed to see themselves as under attack. The conflict may also worsen if the cultures of the separate sides encourage hostility, the groups are composed of persons from lower socioeconomic levels of society, or persons who have authority over the conflicting groups do not calm things down.

A conflict tends to centralize authority in a group and stimulate members to close ranks. A useful conflict opens members' eyes to the need for change and stimulates them to think about ways of introducing innovations.

Recommended Readings

Brickman, P. (ed.). *Social Conflict: Readings in Role Structures and Conflict Relationships.* Lexington, Mass.: Heath, 1974.
The book contains articles on the origins of social conflicts.

Deutsch, M. "Fifty Years of Conflict." In L. Festinger (ed.), *Retrospections in Social Psychology.* New York: Oxford University Press, 1980.
The author reviews his many studies of cooperation, competition, and conflict.

Schopler, J., and others. "Individual-Group Discontinuity: Further Evidence for Mediation by Fear and Greed." *Personality and Social Psychology Bulletin,* 1993, *19,* 419–431.
The authors report that intergroup interactions are dramatically more competitive than interactions between individuals. They believe this occurs because group members tend to support one another's self-interest.

Sherif, M., and others. *Intergroup Conflict and Cooperation: The Robber's Cave Experiment.* Norman, Okla.: University of Oklahoma Press, 1961.
An experimental study in which a sharp conflict was generated between two groups of boys in a summer camp and then resolved.

Weiner, B. "On Sin Versus Sickness: A Theory of Perceived Responsibility and Social Motivation." *American Psychologist,* 1993, *48,* 957–965.
This theory explains why persons help others, reject them, or aggress against them.

Zander, A. *Effective Social Action by Community Groups.* San Francisco: Jossey-Bass, 1990.
Considers how and why groups of activists get into conflicts with persons they are trying to influence.

12

RESOLVING CONFLICTS
BETWEEN GROUPS

If you observe a meeting where two groups seek to settle an issue on which they disagree, you will see participants in each body be careful not to antagonize their counterparts. Despite these preventive efforts, they may find themselves in a sharp dispute. Such a state of affairs creates discomfort for members, which motivates them to end the distress.

When a controversy exists between groups, it may be resolved in several ways: one body wins and the other loses, both win, or both lose. In the heat of a dispute, members of rival units often feel the only acceptable outcome is that their team win. Those who view a conflict in such terms typically are inclined to deepen a disagreement rather than resolve it. They turn to threats, ridicule, penalties, or other kinds of coercive behavior. They recruit allies, mislead opponents, ignore the other side's ideas, hire a lawyer, or do whatever else might ensure a victory for their side. Such behavior prevents rational problem solving and weakens the possibility of discovering a solution that pleases members of both parties.

In this chapter I describe several dispute-resolving procedures in which two groups cooperate with an eye toward attaining a solution that will benefit both. These methods are especially useful where participants hope to resolve a conflict in

201

ways that protect everyone's dignity. If those on either side refuse to work with rivals, no conflict-resolving process can work
outside of binding arbitration or a court of law. The latter two
methods tend, however, to arouse animosities that are seldom
relieved by an arbitrator's or jury's findings. Most of the processes proposed in this chapter try to reduce animosity while
helping participants resolve their disagreement. Before examining procedures for settling a dispute, we consider how members may prepare themselves to prevent an intergroup conflict.

Preparing for a Potentially Conflictful Meeting

Suppose a member knows that he and colleagues are to meet
in a decision-making conference with persons whose opinions
differ from his own and from those of his associates. In anticipat-
ing this session he asks himself what he might do to make the
meeting satisfying. He will be most content at the end of the
discussion, he knows, if the views of all participants are melded
into a useful, mutually agreeable outcome with a minimum of
irrational argument.

The results of the meeting may be more gratifying, he
recognizes, if he encourages several helpful conditions: (1) Participants listen carefully to proposals offered by those on the other
side, even though they do not accept all of them. (2) Some of
his own contributions are useful; discussants indicate that this
is the case. (3) His style of participation (firm, fair, friendly)
is imitated by others. (4) He does not push the discussion onto
a tangent in order to prevent rivals from succeeding. (5) He
and others are proud of the ideas the two units develop. The
point is, a participant can plan how to be helpful during discussions among members of two sides.

With such developments in mind, he prepares to do specific things, before (and during) the meeting, that might help
make the session effective: (1) He offers to join a few adversaries
beforehand to decide on ground rules concerning who will speak
and for how long, topics of discussion, what outcome is to be
sought, who will sit where, and principles of useful decorum.
(2) He tidies his thinking on the topics to be considered so he

can present his ideas clearly. (3) He appraises the advantages of his ideas and how he can defend them. (4) He plans to listen closely to others' comments. (5) He intends to evaluate their suggestions by using them, putting their ideas in his own words, and seeing if they work. (6) He will avoid behaviors that trigger resistance among listeners. Thus, he promises himself to steer away from

- Ridiculing those addressed. ("There you go again." "You always manage to do the wrong thing.")
- Making arbitrary demands. ("I want an answer now." "Here is what we insist you do.")
- Threatening listeners. ("We will take you to court so fast your head will spin." "I warn you, I never back away from a fight.")
- Using misinformation. ("All other clinics always make a profit. Why can't ours?")
- Employing hyperbole. ("You guys are extortionists." "Your plans are outrageous.")
- Making ad hominem remarks. ("You are stubborn people." "You could never see our side if you tried, which you will not.")
- Claiming innocence. ("It's not my fault that you are soreheads. I try to make a simple point and you blow up.")

In sum, an individual can plan to behave in ways that prevent discussion of an intergroup disagreement from being a waste of time and instead ensure its usefulness.

Planning Jointly to Inhibit Two-Sided Resistance

Before a touchy joint session, members of a group and their potential rivals may discuss how they can dampen emotional behavior during a meeting and enhance rational actions there. Examples of such decisions are found in writings on conflict resolution (Carver, 1990; Deutsch, 1973, 1990; Fisher, Ury, and Patton, 1991; Pruitt and Rubin, 1986; Ury, Brett, and Goldberg, 1989; Zander, 1990). Possible actions include the following:

1. Members of rival units agree they intend to work as prob-
    lem solvers. Toward this end they will suppress inclina-
    tions to be defensive, hostile, or fearful during the meet-
    ing and will try to understand what those in the other group
    say and why they say these things.

2. Each participant accepts as a given that his views may
    change during the discussion.

3. Conferees decide who will make the final decision, if one
    is needed, who is to have a say over what, and what rules
    will govern the choice of a final decision.

4. Members agree to use, if necessary, the help of a third
    party such as a referee, mediator, arbitrator, or rent-a-
    judge.

5. Discussants identify what those on each side must do to
    earn and retain the trust of the other party. For example,
    they might provide sound evidence for data they employ,
    bring in expert witnesses to support ideas that need bol-
    stering, or refer to past similarities in the beliefs, friend-
    ships, and motives among members on both sides.

6. They settle on the values that will guide them during the
    conference, such as fairness, accuracy, justice, equality,
    rationality.

7. Members in both parties spot similarities in the objectives
    of those in the two groups so that cooperativeness in their
    relations can be enhanced.

8. If each side has similar goals, they may observe that acts
    by one will move both toward shared objectives. Goal-
    directed actions of each tend to help others.

9. They recognize that they will be more likely to find a use-
    ful solution if they consider many alternatives rather than
    few.

10. Discussants demonstrate they are prepared to talk openly,
    and make concessions if necessary, to attain a sound and
    mutually satisfying solution.

11. They realize they may want to stop arguing in favor of
    the positions they prefer in order to identify why they sup-
    port these views and how the aims behind their prefer-
    ences might be met in other ways.

Settling a Conflict Between Groups

Imagine that a conflict develops between two bodies, despite preplanning of the kind just noted. How can they resolve this dispute?

An intergroup conflict becomes stronger as members support their group's position more loudly, reject rivals' views more vigorously, and express themselves more heatedly. Different degrees of disagreement demand different ways of resolving them. Thus, we will consider conflicts of several strengths, mild to severe, and several ways of dealing with each. These examples may help you develop procedures more suitable for your unique situation.

The first methods are useful in settling simple differences. The next few are appropriate for keener disputes. Still others are to be employed when efforts to resolve a conflict are under way but are not succeeding. And the last can be used when a disagreement is intractable, has become chronic. Some of these procedures need no help from a third party, as one among the discussants can provide the limited leadership needed. Others require the assistance of an understanding person, and still others demand direction by a trained individual. The fairness or bias of a third party is not a real issue in any of these methods because in all of them (except for binding arbitration) a third person helps both sides reach their own resolution, one that is acceptable to both; he does not tell them what they must do.

Lively Discussion but No Firm Disagreement

An individual or a set of persons ask members of a group to consider action on (1) help they need, (2) a problem that deserves the group's attention, or (3) an opportunity that could help the unit or its constituents. The two parties are not in a sharp dispute, but each brings a quite different perspective to the issue at hand and finds it hard to understand the other's views. Members of the approached group are interested enough to examine the matter with those who raise it. Examples: a group of parents ask the school board to introduce a course on saving the environment; the staff of a library system seeks funds from the city council to increase the number of books on creationism and race relations.

The procedure of *fact finding* is useful when members believe their major need is clarification of the central ideas (costs, concepts, contrasts) of a problem where a solution requires close collaboration with those in another unit. Representatives of the two bodies meet to reach a common comprehension of the situation under discussion, get the facts straight, or tell one another how they view the major issues. The topics may be complex, emotionally involving, or new to people on both sides. Such conferring can be preliminary to a decision, but it is not intended to settle the issue by itself.

Ordinarily the effect of such a discussion is calming for all at the table. A relaxed response is fostered if conferees come to the meeting with clear ideas about what they believe or know. Effective fact finding requires that participants be precise in expressing their views and in making sure they understand the ideas of others. The boundaries are open, and any topic is fair game. The only restrictions are those both parties set ahead of time in order to ensure that an orderly process is being followed.

Mild Intergroup Disagreement

A set of planners brings specific problems, proposals for action, or both before a group for the latter's comments; a disagreement develops about what should be done. Or an administrative committee discusses a change they might introduce, and word of this intention reaches interested bystanders, who object. Members of these groups believe that each side should have a say in reaching a solution. Examples: Should the hospital cafeteria be closed to the public during rush hours? Shall we lock buildings on the campus for two weeks during the winter in order to save energy? Should we create a community orchestra?

Intergroup Problem Solving. If the number of solutions is limited, discussants from each group may act as a unit and employ procedures described in Chapter Four for solving a problem. If a crisis develops, however, one of the procedures below may be more effective, because problem solving demands rational thinking, which, in the midst of a dispute, may be hard to maintain.

Evaluating Potential Solutions. Sometimes the nature of a problem is clearly defined, and the characteristics of a good solution are understood, but too many alternatives come up in a joint meeting or it is not clear why proponents of a given answer want that one rather than another. Choosing among the many options becomes the central issue, and a dispute arises over which potential answer seems most sensible. A procedure is needed to guide the process of selecting the best from among those available.

The method used in this kind of disagreement must be one that makes it possible for participants to discover why the others cling to their position — that is, to identify what the others hope to get out of it. This is so because if participants devote all their energies to giving arguments in favor of their own stand, they become more devoted to their initial point of view and find less value in ones advocated by others. An approach is needed that makes it possible for backers of a given position to become aware of what motives, fears, desires, or concerns they wish to satisfy and helps them to discover how those interests might be met by a different solution, one that most conferees will welcome. A conflict-resolving method in this instance must allow members to recognize that they could find satisfaction in an answer different from the one they are backing. The procedure to be used must be based, moreover, on the recognition that people who argue in favor of different answers do not necessarily have different motives behind their beliefs. Often, advocates of different solutions discover that the interests behind their separate stands are surprisingly similar. Where this is so, it should be possible to identify an outcome that fulfills this shared aim (Fisher, Ury, and Patton, 1991).

Choosing the best among a number of potential solutions can be facilitated by moving through a series of specified steps. Directing problem solvers through this sequence is easy; someone must simply move things along (Levi and Benjamin, 1976).

It begins once the problem has been clearly defined, participants are sure they understand it, and a variety of possible solutions have been proposed but not compared or evaluated.

Step One. All discussants are asked to describe in writing one or more solutions they prefer, ones that they feel sure those in the opposing party do not want. These statements, when collected, supply a set of alternatives worthy of discussion because they are, by definition, controversial: one party wants what the other does not. These differences of opinion stimulate interaction.

Step Two. Each of the desired outcomes is written on a blackboard or newsprint without identifying its author, and members choose the one they wish to discuss first. They are to base this judgment on which one seems most important (relevant and likely to work) for settling the issue at hand. The majority rules.

Step Three. Focusing on the outcome chosen above, persons on each side give their reasons orally for favoring or disliking it. They are asked to state these reasons in terms of the needs, desires, fears, or commitments they feel they or others can satisfy by accepting or rejecting this outcome. When taking this step, they have to place themselves in others' shoes in order to identify interests behind the stand those people are taking. Thus, they identify the motives of themselves and others and make these explicit aspects of the discussion.

Step Four. When a good number of pro and con reasons have been given, each participant privately rates, on a scale of + 10 to – 10, his or her degree of satisfaction (+) or dissatisfaction (–) with the solution under consideration.

Step Five. The discussants now select another potential outcome to consider as they did in Step Two. They state their reasons for or against this potential solution, as in Step Three, and rate their satisfaction or dissatisfaction with that alternative.

The above five steps are repeated three or four times. This usually is enough, because remaining options lose their appeal in light of the consideration given to those already discussed and rated. A final solution is then chosen, if it is not already obvious, in which the above-listed reasons and ratings of satisfaction are central information.

Note that this process separates the process of choosing a solution into its several components, so that comments can be cleanly concentrated on each facet of choice making in turn. While so doing, conferees have in mind what has been said about the value of each option and why. As a result, chances are good that the deciders will feel both sides have had an adequate discussion of relevant motives behind the choice they prefer.

Bargaining. When scarce resources or prized things are the central issues in a dispute, members may bargain to reduce their differences. They can bargain over work hours, work load, pay for services, space, vacation time, insurance benefits, areas of responsibility, or equipment. Participants on each side try to give up less than the other — to get a "bargain." Bargaining will work only if both units have control over something the other desires. Members of management want the energy of employees, and workers want payment for their labor. Neither side must be considerably more powerful than the other or have much more to offer during bargaining, because bribery or coercion, rather than bargaining, is then more likely to occur.

The purpose of bargaining is not always to get the best deal out of offers and counteroffers. It often is to reach a compromise in which each party proposes to give up something they know is useful to members on the other side. They try to make the sacrifice equal and satisfying to both groups. This can be an effective means for slowing or reversing the escalation of a conflict. But the sticky point in initiating a compromise is that it is risky to make the first offer because adversaries may consider this action to be a sign of weakness, which they can then exploit by refusing to make equal concessions of their own.

A number of tactics are used to encourage equal concessions by each side. The following list has been modified from one offered by Pruitt (1972).

1. Make a small unilateral concession with the statement that no further concession will be forthcoming until the adversary members concede something in return.
2. Propose an exchange of concessions (which is tantamount to making a unilateral move).

3. Show a readiness to make a concession if the opponent makes one as well.
4. Seek a private meeting with rivals if it will be easier to talk about compromises in private than in a public meeting.
5. Secretly offer an exchange of concessions through the good offices of an intermediary whose efforts can be disowned if the adversary is not interested.
6. Propose that a mediator who will help develop a mutually agreeable exchange of concessions be brought into the bargaining.

Offering concessions requires that members of each party search for proposals that will appeal to those on the other side. The usefulness of their suggestions will be enhanced for both units if members accurately describe their needs and motives to rivals so that participants can come up with gratifying offers. And the grants will be better received if members do not argue in support of their offer, because a hard sell suggests that the bargainer is trying to press the others rather than reach a mutually acceptable compromise.

Intergroup Conflict That Arouses Emotions

Suppose that members of one group must collaborate with those of another in order that both can do their jobs: architects cooperate with builders, artillerymen with infantry, or doctors with nurses. Imagine that one of these entities changes the way it does its job and that this shift is unacceptable to its collaborating unit. During protests over this unilateral change, those on each side become irritated, competitive, or otherwise involved in winning rather than working together to find a wise course of action. Despite the tension between them, discussants agree that this state of affairs is intolerable and that they would like to resolve it. As illustrations: the production department of a company announces that it will no longer try to fill salesmen's rush orders, the accounting department says that it is buying a different computer from the one serving the rest of the organization, the local yacht club pulls out of the annual waterfront fiesta. In each of these instances, response to the activists' moves is strong.

One difficulty with settling such a problem is that the feelings members have about persons in the adversary group interfere with efforts to resolve the initial concern; the conflicting units try to deal simultaneously with both problems (the initial conflict-causing act and the relations between the two units) and thus do not handle either one well. Take the case of the sailing club's defection from the waterfront fiesta. Those on the executive committee for the watery gala believe that the sailors resigned because they dislike members of the committee, feel the committee is doing a poor job, and want more say on the part they have during the event. Those on the governing board of the sailing club believe members of the executive committee think the sailors are lazy, want to tell the executives how to run their show, and want a better place in the program. These issues, concerning connections between the two groups, became more important than the initial problem as a result of discussions held by the conflicting bodies. Each of the two matters (pulling out and relations with the other unit) require separate attention. What may be needed is a procedure for identifying and relieving the feelings between members of the two bodies so that the club's defection can then be tackled as a separate problem.

Identifying Intergroup Feelings. Often, as I said, the substantive content of a dispute between a group and a set of its critics becomes a minor matter compared to the friction it causes between the two units. Members of groups that have decision-making responsibilities regularly recognize that their role makes them targets for outsiders who wish to blame someone for their own misfortune. Thus, the members decide to reduce discomfort in relations with those in another body, to identify and understand the origins of the stressful intergroup relations. Both sides agree to give this approach a try. They use a procedure modified from one proposed by Bennis (1969).

It begins with a joint meeting of the two groups, or subcommittees of them, in which they are told what they will be doing by a leader who is skilled in leading discussions. Each body then moves to a separate room where they take up three questions in turn, allowing thirty or forty-five minutes for each, and list their answers on separate sheets of newsprint. The questions are as follows:

1. What qualities best describe our group?
2. What qualities best describe the other group?
3. What qualities do we predict the other group will assign to us?

After the three lists are completed, the two units reassemble and act thereafter as one. Taking up one question at a time, a spokesperson for each group explains their answers and responds to questions. It is obvious at once that members of the two bodies differ in their perceptions of selves and others. Some of these views are wrong (on factual grounds), others are misperceptions or improper assumptions, and still others are surprisingly painful and correct. Most of the remaining talk turns to the origins of such contrasts and misunderstandings. The discussants find themselves calmly considering delicate matters they would have been unable to discuss previously without embarrassment, defensiveness, hesitation, or blaming. The procedure ends after this exploration of insights, as that usually satisfies participants: they feel informed and relieved. In some cases they move to the next logical issue: What can we do to improve relations between our groups? How shall we resolve the main issue, now that we better understand each other?

This procedure makes it possible for participants to discuss feelings and emotions as facts, as conditions that exist for reasons that can be understood and discussed objectively. Such discussion, moreover, has a tension-relieving effect — members feel they have blown off steam without indulging in repulsive behaviors that emotions often inspire disagreeing persons to use toward one another. The relations between the two groups are treated, and perhaps healed, independently of their agreement on the central issues in the conflict.

Intergroup Mediation. Members of a group and those with whom they are in a dispute involving relations between the two bodies may request the help of a mediator if they have tried to improve their connections but failed, are disturbed over this situation, or feel they cannot allow the conflict to continue. It is not always easy for those in disagreeing units to seek the help of an outsider, because many such bodies, I have observed, do not like to admit they are in a fight they cannot resolve, or do not wish to have discussions with persons they prefer to avoid. Before conflicting groups can seek such help, therefore, one party must have the courage to suggest to the other that they jointly need assistance and convince their opponents to go along with that idea.

A mediator is a skilled leader of a problem-solving discussion. He or she helps the two sides reach an agreement about how relations between the two will change in the future. The discussants, not the mediator, make these decisions, put them in writing, and promise to abide by them. Anything said in the session is confidential. Mediators are not necessarily highly trained; some are ordinary citizens who have been taught how to do this job and work at it part-time, for free. A mediator will not handle problems that need technical expertise, such as engineering, finances, or law. The procedure described here follows from one developed by members of a Quaker community (Beer, 1986). A mediator begins by explaining the process to be employed, offering encouragement to participants (who may be a bit uneasy), and describing a few ground rules. The following four steps are then taken:

Step One: Uninterrupted Time. The mediator asks representatives from each side to tell their story: what happened, why, what you did, what others did or did not do, and the like, without any interruption by listening opponents. Even though these accounts may be crafted to make the speakers appear in the best possible light, the listeners hear, usually for the first time, how the others view things. The mediator takes notes and encourages full revelations but does not try to get the facts straight at the moment.

Step Two: The Exchange. During this stage the guide asks disputants to respond to questions, accusations, and issues raised by those on the other side. Facts, intractable differences in opinions or feelings, and shared views and agreements are identified. Displays of anger or other emotions are checked by the mediator.

Step Three: Building an Agreement. By now the mediator can see the major issues at the heart of the disagreement. He describes them, asks disputants if these are the central matters, makes corrections where indicated, and leads disagreers into a discussion about what can be done to resolve each. The ensuing action plans are discussed in their smallest details while the helper repeatedly asks if the ideas are practical (will work and can be completed) as well as who will do what, and when. Often, both sides give up something to get important gains.

Step Four: Agreement. The agreement is put into writing so its exact nature can be recalled and used as a guide in the future, if need be, and persons on both sides sign it. This paper magically changes their relationship from being adversaries to being parties to an agreement, a most important transformation. Mediation move discussants from preoccupation with their dispute and their disaffection with each other to planning for the future, from distrust to willingness to "take a chance."

When members work with a mediator toward resolution of a conflict with another body, they are accepting a common goal, one that is bigger than either of their separate aims. This superordinate goal puts both sides in a cooperative relationship in which each is eager to help the other toward completion of their common task. Often, when groups are in a state of rivalry, mere contact between their units merely leads to more hostility. But if those same units collaborate on a common task, an important one, they get along well and forget their intergroup anger (Sherif and others, 1961).

Stalemate Requiring a Third-Party Adviser

It often happens that discussants on each side are unable to agree on a resolution yet believe they cannot ignore the desires of those with whom they disagree. Examples: the trustees of a private hospital refuse to give nurses an increase in wages, and the nurses then claim they are ill and cannot come to work; residents of a condominium community protest when the developer proposes to direct the flow of a pretty creek into an underground pipe; the owners of motorboats demand more berths for their crafts, but the governing board of the yacht club (dominated by owners of sailing vessels) refuses to give them more spaces. Participants in such disputes eventually may recognize that a suitable decision can be reached only by asking a neutral helper to provide suggestions. This adviser might be an arbitrator or a judge (rented or otherwise). The several procedures that follow are described more fully in a book on resolving conflicts by Ury, Brett, and Goldberg (1989).

Advisory Arbitration. In this procedure a professional arbitrator is hired who hears evidence presented by both sides and gives a non-binding opinion of the kind he would have rendered if this were a session where participants might promise to obey his ruling. After the arbitrator's advisory opinion, the participants can see who would have won if this were a binding arbitration. They may then plan their next steps: talk some more, try mediation, hire a binding arbitrator, go to court, enter into bargaining, or others. The costs are low in this approach, as the hearings are brief and the advisory ruling is given orally and informally.

Sometimes groups that got nowhere in intergroup mediation try this process in order to avoid the expense and formality of a regular arbitration hearing. Some courts demand the prior use of advisory arbitration in certain cases and will hear only those not resolved by such arbitration.

Mini-Trial. Another procedure to help opponents decide how to resolve their conflict is a mini-trial. In this method, lawyers representing each side (or colleagues playing the part of lawyers) present evidence and arguments before persons who are, or act as, judges. In some instances these persons may be three respected members of the organization or community, accepted by both sides, who have no part in the conflict. After hearing the two parties, the three "referees" publicly, in the presence of the rivals, discuss the problem and the evidence and make the appropriate ruling. They make their decision then and there. The disputers can then discuss whether the judges' suggested resolution is acceptable to them.

This procedure, it should be noted, puts the argument into the hands of three persons who are not emotionally involved, who hear both sides of the story, and who have the interests of both parties equally at heart. Their open discussion illustrates what a real judge might consider in making a "finding," and it uncovers new insights that the contenders may use if they wish to try again at settling the issue on their own.

Binding Arbitration. Here a neutral and professional arbitrator listens to evidence presented by both sides and issues a ruling that all have agreed to obey. In the 1930s, about 10 percent of contracts for collective bargaining required binding arbitration of disputes between union and management. Today, 95 percent have this requirement (St. Antoine, 1984). Boards elected by constituents (city councils or boards of religious congregations) often cannot enter into binding arbitration because they are forbidden by their charters to let anyone make a decision for them.

A binding arbitrator, in contrast to a mediator, is more concerned with the substance of the conflict than with the emotions aroused by it. At the outset, he or she asks participants to define the issue in terms both sides accept. Thereafter, the steps are not always the same, depending on the preferences of the arbitrator and of those taking part. The neutral person may set such requirements as a time limit, involvement by lawyers, the degree of adherence to rules of evidence, and how much say both parties have in reaching a final decision. Such an arbitrator takes an active role, asking questions until he is sure he understands the issue, has the data he needs to make a decision, and is confident both sides agree on these facts. The relevance of the evidence is important, but legal rules of procedure are not always used. Some sessions are more like conversations than jurisdictional hearings.

In certain cases it is easiest for an arbitrator to split the difference between opposing demands. If he or she does this often, those who use that arbitrator on their next case may take inflexible, widely differing stands and refuse to compromise, so that their difference cannot easily be separated by the arbitrator. If the decider is not able to find a fair ruling, he may ask each of the opposing bodies to make their best, most conciliatory final offer. He then chooses one or the other of these two "final offers" as his decision. The potential consequences of a request for such an offer may be so threatening to participants that they withdraw from arbitration before a judgment is made and try to settle the matter on their own or by another means (Pruitt and Rubin, 1986).

Persons who are involved in binding arbitration (or a court case), researchers have observed, are as much concerned about whether the decider has certain desirable attributes as they are about the content of the arbitrator's decision. The first of these attributes is the neutrality of the decision maker: he is perceived to be honest and to use appropriate facts when making his ruling. The second is trustworthiness: the arbitrator is perceived to be treating persons on both sides in a fair and reasonable way. The third is the status he assigns to participants: he does not degrade the standing of those in either of the rival groups or act as though he is superior to them. People engaged in binding arbitration, in sum, care about their relationship with the person who is making the decision they must adopt and about the procedures he uses. They are concerned about how that person functions and how he goes about making the ruling they are to obey. As is so often the case, they recognize that poor methods lead to poor results (Tyler, 1989).

Severe and Continuing Conflict

It can happen that parties in a dispute are unable to settle it and thus remain opponents for a long time. Members of each group are hostile toward the other and keep their distance, refusing to talk. Such a state of affairs, if carried on long enough, suggests that it will not fade away soon. But members in both parties may come to recognize that they have to improve their relations for the good of a larger organization or their own. No specific problem is at the heart of the matter beyond the enmity between the two bodies. Examples: an association dedicated to preventing greater growth of a community is opposed by one that favors increasing the town's size, but both bodies become aware that the city needs more income from taxes; unionized workers who have been locked out for years by the management of a company are now needed as employees because their skills are valuable for making a new product.

In such instances a procedure is desirable that allows separate sides to find ways of communicating comfortably and usefully. The frost between the two groups makes it unwise to bring the two together for a simple face-to-face discussion, as this has not worked in the past and would probably generate angry interchanges now. The Interface Conflict Resolving Model, proposed by Blake and Mouton (1984), is appropriate here. It requires members, or subsets who represent them, to move through a sequence of steps. Each phase takes a few hours, and the whole process may use three or four days. The steps are straightforward, and the discussants do all the work, so a director of this operation needs no special training. But the one in charge must be an experienced leader of discussion with a background in human relations. A group counselor or mediator could comfortably lead this procedure.

The main features of the method are as follows: The leader meets with representatives of the two groups (six to ten on a side), gives an overview of what is ahead, and sends each unit into a separate room.

Step One: The Optimal Relationship. Members of the two sets are asked to describe the qualities of an ideal relationship between their two groups. These are listed on sheets of newsprint. The properties might concern attitudes that underlie good relations between groups, common goals, standards of excellence, ways of cooperating, and the like.

Step Two: Consolidation. The two units assemble in one room. A spokesperson for each describes and explains the items on their list. The two bodies then work as a single entity to create a list of properties that would characterize an ideal relationship and which both sides accept.

Step Three: The Actual Relationship. The groups meet again in separate rooms and describe conditions that currently characterize the actual relationship between the two parties. If useful, they identify past events that shaped this state of affairs.

Step Four: Consolidation. As in Step Two, the groups work together again to create a joint description of the elements in the day-by-day relationship between the two groups, one that both sides accept as accurate.

Step Five: Planning for Change. Members of both parties, still meeting as one, now identify obvious gaps between the ideal and actual, decide what changes are needed to reduce these differences, and plan how these transformations can be achieved.

Step Six: Progress Review. In six months or so, the two parties meet to examine their success in resolving past hostilities and to plan their next steps.

This approach has several beneficial characteristics. The participants attempt to visualize an ideal situation at the outset. This gives them a task that is not embarrassing to discuss while freeing their imaginations to identify what the qualities of good intergroup relations are or could be. They begin to see how things could be improved. The gap between ideal and real is a strong stimulant to wishing for a closer fit between the best and actual. Each group learns, in a noncontroversial setting, how others think about relations between the two bodies and where the similarities and differences lie in their views. The director of this procedure has no say in the ideas created; he does not tell them what to think or what their thoughts imply. He mainly moves participants from one step to another and presses for decisions where necessary. This process sets up a way of working among participants that makes it possible for them to deal with touchy subjects objectively; feelings are treated as facts. Unlike previous methods in this chapter, the procedure brings up important topics that are usually avoided, such as those relating to group values, legitimate vested interests, fair and unfair status differences, prestige, rivalry, or reasons for distrust.

Summary

A person who plans to take part in a meeting of two groups for discussion of a tender topic can plan how to help keep the session free of wasteful conflict. Suggestions on what such an individual might do were listed earlier. Members of both sides may, moreover, agree ahead of time on things they will do during the session to dampen emotional behavior and enhance rational work by the two groups. Examples of preventive agreements they might make were also listed.

Different degrees of intergroup conflict require different methods of resolution. Examples are as follows:

- If the discussion is lively but no firm disagreement exists, members may engage in fact finding or intergroup problem solving.
- If there is mild disagreement, participants may wish to use intergroup problem solving, a procedure for evaluating potential solutions in which they follow preplanned steps in order to find the best among a number of alternative answers, or intergroup bargaining.
- If emotions are aroused by the conflict, persons on both sides may join in identifying their intergroup feelings or in working toward a resolution with a mediator.
- If those in an intergroup conflict are stalled and believe they must have the help of a third party, they may work with a mediator, ask an arbitrator to give them an advisory (nonbinding) decision, ask an arbitrator to make a decision that members promise (ahead of time) to obey, or develop a mock trial using a neighbor or a rented judge as the decision maker.
- If an intergroup conflict is severe and continuing, and members of each party cannot meet face-to-face without becoming hostile, those involved in the disagreement may employ the Interface Conflict Resolving Model, which helps them communicate about crucial aspects of their relationship with minimal emotional interference and guides them in developing resolutions for their dispute.

Recommended Readings

Beer, J. *Peacemaking in Your Neighborhood: Reflections on an Experiment in Community Relations.* Philadelphia: New Society, 1986. This is a report of a program in which ordinary citizens were trained to be mediators for anyone in their community who needed such help. Provides advice on how to mediate.

Blake, R. R., and Mouton, J. S. *Solving Costly Organizational Conflicts: Achieving Intergroup Trust, Cooperation, and Teamwork.* San Francisco: Jossey-Bass, 1984.
The authors serve as consultants to parties frozen in a chronic and bitter conflict. The book tells how they help the two sides communicate and resolve a deep dispute.

Fisher, R., Ury, W. L., and Patton, B. *Getting to Yes: Negotiating Agreement Without Giving In.* Boston: Houghton Mifflin, 1991.
An interesting how-to manual on ways discussants can avoid arguments and settle them if they get too hot.

Pruitt, D., and Rubin, J. *Social Conflict: Escalation, Stalemate, and Settlement.* New York: Random House, 1986.
Explains the origins of conflicts and describes a variety of tactics for dealing with them.

Ury, W. L., Brett, J. M., and Goldberg, S. B. *Getting Disputes Resolved: Designing Systems to Cut the Costs of Conflict.* San Francisco: Jossey-Bass, 1989.
A variety of procedures for settling conflicts in all kinds of settings is presented.

Zack, A. (ed.). *Arbitration in Practice.* Ithaca, N.Y.: Cornell University Press, 1984.
Contains articles providing practical advice for lawyers who have an interest in the arbitration of disputes.

13

CONCLUSION:
EVALUATING AND IMPROVING
GROUP OPERATIONS

Members of the governing board for the Methodist church were often bored during meetings. A major reason for this disinterest was the behavior of the secretary. He brought the board's mail to its gatherings, opened letters at the conference table, tore tough envelopes apart, and mumbled to himself over their contents. During one such demonstration, a woman asked, "Wouldn't it be better if you opened those elsewhere? We can't hear over that commotion." The secretary responded, "Nobody except the reverend ever says much, and he talks loud enough. I don't see what difference this makes."

The chairlady, emboldened by this exchange, remarked, "It's true; few of us talk a lot. But I must ask, are there times when anyone wants to speak and can't get an opening to do so?" This query changed the tone of the meeting. Several trustees said there is too little give and take. Usually, they added, the minister introduces each topic or describes an action the board ought to take and in the same breath suggests how he thinks the board should vote on the matter. His ideas are sensible, based on much experience in running a church, so board members do little more than nod assent. Each trustee feels colleagues would disapprove if he or she offered ideas different from those proposed by the pastor.

The minister was surprised by these statements. He had sometimes wondered why members offered few ideas of their own, but he had not noticed that he held the floor during most of a meeting. He knew that some trustees headed organizations bigger than the church and that the board seldom gained the benefit of the members' wisdom. So he offered to change his behavior. When he posed a problem hereafter, he said, he would not short-circuit discussion by describing his preferred solution. He would make sure that members of the board had an opportunity to raise issues and offer other answers. He would, in short, help members have a share in the leadership of meetings. The secretary, swept along by these comments, said he would no longer open his mail during meetings, and the chairlady promised to help the minister stick to the revisions in his role. Meetings of the group became more lively thereafter. As everyone felt free to speak, their boredom vanished, and the minister liked meetings more, even though he said less.

The changes in this board were not planned; they happened because members accidentally fell into evaluating its procedures. Members of many other groups decide how they will review their unit's performance, and they invent ways to better its operations. An example of a preplanned process for group evaluation occurred in a small group of clerks that kept track of membership data for a national association and prepared periodic reports describing changes in the membership within separate regions, the income of regions, their budgets, costs of operating parts of the society, and the influence of the association on local problems.

The members of this crew had trouble working together because its assignment was divided in ways that required several of them to deal with uninteresting numbers while others worked with data that were useful and welcomed by regional officers of the association. The persons who did the latter work had prestige within the organization because their reports were appealing to readers.

The supervisor recognized something had to be done to reduce tension within the team. He booked a room away from the workplace and asked the staff to meet there for an all-day planning session — the first time they had done such a thing. He began the day by asking a few questions, inviting participants to spend thirty minutes or so on each. Examples: How well do you think this team is performing? How could its operations be improved? How well are you doing your job? In what ways might you do better? How well do the seven of you get along? What changes might generate more harmony among you? By the end of the day, the members had identified things they felt were wrong in their ways of working and had found methods that would improve these matters. The boss suggested they meet again in six months to see if the group's climate had improved. He noted, "A day of talk like this really works. We discovered things that needed improvement. We'll have a new feeling in our office now, I believe. Thanks for being so honest and fair."

The members of both these groups, as is the case in most bodies, want their unit to do well. When it succeeds, they want it to do better. Raising aspirations for the quality of its performance is an accepted view in our society: a group should improve as time goes by, regardless of its purpose (Zander, 1971, 1985).

Most members are used to evaluating their own actions or having others do so in school, sports, work, or community. Yet members of groups I know well seldom evaluate how well their entity is doing. Although they want their unit to improve, they are not eager to appraise others' behavior or describe such appraisals publicly. In the absence of reliable data to the contrary, moreover, most members think their group is doing fine and say so when asked. (No news is good news.) It is useful for a group to evaluate its actions in a planned way so that important issues will be reliably weighed. In this chapter we examine examples of how group processes can be evaluated. Most of the instances I offer are simple and informal. Members may create their own methods for appraising their particular operations, in light of suggestions offered here.

Evaluation and Feedback

Responsible members of a group judge the quality of its actions by observing how close the body comes to meeting its criteria of success — whether it is reaching goals or revealing characteristics that members want for the unit. If the group does not have desired results, the evaluators change the group's goal (to a more difficult or easier level), its procedures, or both. When a group's efforts fall short, for example, members tend to lower its goal or dope out ways of improving its performance. If the group's performance exceeds its goal, they prefer to raise its level of aspiration but leave its way of work unchanged.

Members who evaluate their group's performance and then decide to change its objectives, methods, or both, are engaged in a *feedback cycle*. In such a system, members set criteria of success for a given activity. Then they perform the required actions, determine the effects of such moves on the group or its environment, compare the level of the group's performance with the established criteria, decide what they should do in light of this comparison, set new goals or procedures to be followed, and move through this cycle again. The essential point is that no group can sensibly appraise and improve its operations unless it takes the steps in such a cycle. The meaning of a group's performance is not simply something in the attainment itself but in the relationship between its results and what members want their group to accomplish (Zander, 1971).

Evaluating Efficiency and Effectiveness

In some groups, especially those employing resources in their activities (such as funds, energy, labor, time, space), members want to know how much its actions cost, because there is a limit to the availability of the resources it needs. *Efficiency* is defined as the amount of resources expended by a unit for a given level of attainment. Three different kinds of efficiency may interest group members, according to Deniston, Rosenstock, and Getting (1986). In each of these three, an *action* by a group is any organized effort that employs specific assets to perform particular operations aimed at attainment of designated objectives. In one approach for denoting the efficiency of a group, members determine the cost per objective. This is attained by dividing the total number of objectives accomplished by the total amount of resources spent. In another method, members determine the cost of each action toward gaining an objective. Here they divide the number of actions performed by the number of resources expended. Or they examine the amount of gain per action, by dividing the number of objectives attained by the number of actions performed.

The *effectiveness* of a group is described by how well it has accomplished its objectives. Members may be interested in one or all of three measures of effectiveness. In one, the score attained by the group (on some objective measure) is divided by the score the body would have accomplished in the absence of the given action. A board of a United Fund, as an example, may reach the goal of its financial campaign because it is given one very large and unasked-for gift, not because its solicitors have done their work well. Therefore, attainment of the goal in this case is not a true measure of how well the the solicitors performed.

In a second evaluation of group effectiveness, members divide the number of actions performed by the number that were supposed to have been performed. A set of workers who try hard but do not complete as many moves as desired is not as effective as one that completes all the steps expected of them. A third ratio determines the total amount of resources expended divided by the amount of resources that were supposed to have been used. A body that reaches its goal at more expense than intended is not as effective as it ought to be. From these several approaches for measuring group efficiency and effectiveness we see that an action may be less suitable than desired for several reasons: assumptions about the links between objectives, actions, and resources are not valid; actions are not performed as intended; resources are not used as planned; or attainment of the goal is too uncertain to be measured accurately. Clearly, members of a group who work through ratios like these develop an improved understanding of the quality of their unit's procedures along with reasons for, and costs of, their success or failure.

The Peter F. Drucker Foundation (1993) provides advice for evaluating the effectiveness of a nonprofit organization. Drucker describes the importance of evaluating one's group, and he offers a workbook containing questions that members answer privately about major features of a group's life before they meet to compare and discuss their separate appraisals. This evaluation procedure also helps members plan what they believe their body must do in order for it to be effective. When making appraisals, members respond to questions under five main topics: What is our group's mission? Who depends on our group's actions? What do these constituents want or expect of us? What have been our results? What is our plan for the future?

To illustrate questions a respondent is to answer, the following are queries listed under the topic, What is our mission? (p. 5).

> What, as you see it, is the mission (purpose) of this group?
> Why does this group exist?
> What are we trying to achieve?
> What specific results is this body seeking?
> What are the group's major strengths?
> What has it done well?
> What are the group's weaknesses?
> How should the group's statement of mission be improved?
> What results relevant to our purpose did this body fail to achieve this year?
> Why were these failed?

The author cites questions members of a group might ask themselves if their unit is the kind that tries to educate or treat individual participants: "Looking backward, what did this organization contribute to you? What is still important to you? What should we do better? What should we stop doing?" (p. 40).

Members of groups that hold face-to-face meetings may prefer to deal with more specific questions when evaluating how well their body is doing. Napier and Gershenfeld have proposed a set of queries with which to evaluate members' participation in group meetings (1993, p. 451ff.). Do participants

> "Create a positive atmosphere?
> Support and encourage participation?
> Listen and respond to varying opinions?

Clarify statements or ask clarifying questions?
Share opinions, feelings, ideas, and suggestions honestly
and clearly?
Help others stay on agenda topics?
Identify and utilize resources within the group?
Observe the group process and evaluate progress?
Comment on the quality of interpersonal processes when
helpful?
Encourage others into taking group-building roles?"

In a group that holds regular meetings, members find it useful to take a few moments after each session to rate, anonymously, the qualities of the unit that members may wish to maintain or improve. A questionnaire to be used for this purpose, called a *post-meeting reaction,* is usually brief and uncomplicated. The ratings are summarized and reported to members at that time or at the next session, and the results are discussed ("How can we improve our meetings?").

In a common approach to a post-meeting evaluation, a respondent is instructed to "place a check mark on a line at the point that best describes how you feel about the nature of this meeting." Each line contains five degrees of response. At one end, representing the lowest level (1), a word or phrase describes a small or unfavorable amount of the quality being rated. At the other end (5), a word or phrase denotes the best or most favorable level of that quality. For example, a scale might provide a rating from "Very passive (1)" to "Very active (2)." Respondents provide their own meanings for rating levels of 2, 3, or 4. Typical end points for scales describing qualities of a meeting include the following:

Conflicted	Harmonious
Unsatisfying	Satisfying
Confusing	Clarifying
Dominated by a few	Most people participated
Boring	Interesting
Leadership was not helpful.	Leadership was helpful.
We were rushed.	Time available was adequate.

Most agenda topics were trivial.	Our time was well spent.
We are inefficient in our discussions.	We are efficient.

The averages of such ratings by all participants are not as important as the discussion on why a given quality is rated low or high and what, if anything, needs to be done.

Another means of gaining extra awareness is to use observers who sit at one side to watch events during the group's actions, record these, and report them to members for their consideration. Or members may use several small discussion groups that consider how well their entity is doing and why. Each of these small bodies considers a different aspect of the group's operations. (These two methods were discussed in Chapter Four.) The comments by observers or discussants are not evaluations. They are descriptions of events that seemed to be high points in the interactions among members and that influenced the nature of following events. Members ask themselves whether it is useful to encourage or discourage such behaviors hereafter. If observers or small-group discussants do their job well, the rest of the group is eager to discuss the contents of their reports, either because they disagree with them or want them to be explained, or because they want to show how useful moves could be fostered in the future.

Identifying and Implementing
Changes in Group Procedures

A prime problem for members of a group is to decide, after data from an evaluation are in hand, what members should modify in their group. They may find it useful to answer questions like the following: What broad aspects of our group ought to be changed? Why are these changes necessary? What specific modifications might be introduced? How can these modifications be implemented? Who will do what? When will it happen? The views of members on such issues point them toward needed moves and ways of introducing them. The group may also be assessed in terms of the four characteristics of a strong group (from Chapter One), and members may then define actions that will bolster any of the qualities that ought to be strengthened. Planners often find that modifications in their group demand changes in the style of collaboration among members or in their membership skills. Such modifications are often hard to discuss because they touch on personal characteristics of members and arouse uneasiness in those who become targets of the group's discussion. We return to such matters soon.

Improving the efficiency or effectiveness of a group is a less touchy issue, because these characteristics are typically based on objective data that seldom require evaluation of members' personal characteristics. Evaluators identify which parts of their group's activities contribute to the unit's efficiency or effectiveness. Once these have been determined, needed changes in practice can be introduced.

Determining how to improve a group's meetings can be difficult if an unwanted quality is due to unskilled or thoughtless behavior of members and these actions have to be openly discussed in order to decide what changes will help the group. Examples of undesirable qualities in interaction among members are infrequent or inhibited communication, lack of harmony in interpersonal relations, omission of required processes when making group decisions, failing to use resources available within the group, or infrequent sharing of leadership by members.

What kinds of moves might members make when an evaluation of their meetings indicates that a change is needed to improve them? In the case of a lack of open communication, decision makers may decide to take any of the following actions to enliven the flow of talk:

- Make sure members know one another's duties, talents, and interests so that they can ask one another for, or offer, suitable information to colleagues.
- Help members be comfortable with one another by providing opportunities for them to associate freely at meetings and at special, friendship-bolstering occasions.
- Demonstrate to a member that his ideas have been useful to colleagues.

- Make differences of opinion visible to members so they will want to develop a common view and talk with one another to do so.
- Promote common goals and cooperative relations among members so they will wish to help one another.
- Remind higher-status persons that their greater power may unwittingly make them a threat to others. Powerful persons need to take the initiative in making members comfortable.
- Assure members that officers of their association are not rigid, have changed their minds in the past, and can be influenced by the rest of the group.

If there is a lack of harmony among members, they may employ suggestions offered in Chapters Seven and Twelve on ways to reduce conflict, or they may examine causes for conflicts, described in Chapter Eleven, to make sure that these are not present in their group.

If decision making by their group's membership is slow or clumsy, members can appraise their way of solving problems to be sure they are employing each of the processes, described in Chapter Four, that a sound decision-making procedure must contain and to be sure they get rid of conditions that inhibit good procedures when making decisions.

Improving the Skill of Group Members

In order that changes in a group's operations can be put into place and performed well, members often have to learn what colleagues now expect of them and how to do these things. Ordinarily, if a group is attractive to a member, that person is willing to make suggested changes in his behavior so that the group will continue to be a source of satisfaction for him. If the group is unimportant to a member, he is less interested in making sure he performs capably for it. It follows that efforts to improve the way of life in a group and to make necessary changes in the roles of members will be more successful if participants who are to make changes want to remain within that unit.

Most members ask themselves if they are doing as well as they might in their group. They judge the quality of their actions by comparing them with the behaviors of colleagues. If they do less well than others (have fewer good ideas, are less often influential, develop fewer friends, are given fewer responsibilities), their desire to be like their model persons will be aroused. This desire is stronger if they judge the others to be similar to themselves; it is weaker if they see the others as too different. Often a member senses that colleagues would welcome a change in his behavior. He realizes, as illustrations, that he receives from others unusually sharp questions, frequent disapprovals or disagreements, few suggestions, or obvious inattention, all of which suggest that fellow members are not happy with the way he behaves in meetings. Such self-detected cues are powerful sources of influence if the persons to whom they are directed are eager to remain as members of that unit.

As a result of such evidence a member may recognize on his own that he should try to change his way of acting — that he ought to construct a new style for himself. He might decide, as instances, to talk more, listen more closely to things others say, question unclear suggestions by others, commend useful comments by colleagues, volunteer more often for duties useful to the group, or be more patient when things go slowly. Because his plan is a private one and he is in charge of creating this new role, he makes changes in behavior (or tries to do so) without announcing them to others. He watches for cues from others, however, to see if things he is trying to institute are recognized and appreciated by them. Do his new and different actions make a difference in the eyes of others? The member learns how to improve his behavior by becoming aware of the things he does when in the group, developing sensitivity to interpersonal behavior among colleagues, and understanding the consequences of his own behavior and that of others.

To learn how to learn in such a situation, a member often needs to examine his feelings and motives and to compare them to the apparent feelings and motives of others. Why does he want to change his membership behavior? Is it to get more approval? To become more powerful? To get out of doing work? To keep busy? Are these motives ones that suit the group's goals or those of other members? Will colleagues approve of his reasons for trying to change his role? Does it matter if they disapprove?

Most moves a member makes to improve his performance are probably self-directed, because a person dislikes to tell others that he questions the quality of his own actions in that group or that he plans to change his style of membership behavior. While self-directed attempts to improve one's value are better than ignoring the quality of one's actions, they are subject to distortion by the person who is trying to change his style. The changes in oneself, the cues one recognizes in the behavior of others, or the ways one interprets these cues can be misunderstood by a member if he has little sensitivity to the actions of associates. Thus, it often is better if a person who wishes to transform himself makes this desire known to at least a few others in the group and asks them to tell him how they react to his behavior while he is attempting to improve. Do they see any changes at all? Are these ones he intended to develop? Do the observers approve of these actions? If not, what other modifications might he try? Here, a member invites others to serve as his tutors.

In some units, after members have evaluated their group's qualities or its meetings, the appraisers recognize that changes they need to introduce in the group will require different behaviors from many members. All then agree to help each other develop the desired transformations. Toward this end, they jointly decide how each person should change, based on what the group needs from each. A member then attempts, over a period of time, to make the transformations asked of him or her. Next, those in the group discuss each person in turn and tell each what is working well, what is not, and what else needs attention.

Clearly, members can become uncomfortable when their behavior is the focus of a group's discussion or when they are to comment on a colleague's actions. In order to make public feedback encouraging, rather than inhibiting, for a target person, members have to provide an atmosphere that bolsters the learner's confidence in such information. First, members provide a nurturing environment in which a target person is assured that his behavior will not be derogated by colleagues. Second, they make sure they understand what kind of change each member intends to develop so that they know what to watch for. Third, members provide advice, models, methods, and comments that are useful for each (Bradford, Gibb, and Benne, 1964; Bunker, 1974).

Finally, it is noteworthy that a group becomes more committed to a member as he better fulfills what is needed from him by others. As each member modifies his or her style in ways that best suit that body, the participants value each other more, and the group grows in strength and ability to function well (Moreland and Levine, 1992).

Summary

Members of most groups want their group to do well and improve as time passes, but few review their group's activities and evaluate how well the unit has been doing so they can identify where the group could be improved.

Actions by a group may be less effective than desired because they were not performed as intended, resources were not used as planned, or the goal was so ambiguous that attainment of it could not be measured. Efficiency of a group's action is measured by determining the amount of resources expended by the group for a given level of achievement.

Groups use different procedures for evaluating their activities. Among them are the following:

- Members privately complete rating scales and evaluations in which they respond to questions under such headings as: What is our group's mission? Who depends on the actions of this group? What do these constituents expect of us? What have been our results? What is our plan for the future? They compare their separate responses and plan, on the basis of them, how their group might be improved.
- Members complete standardized questions after each meeting, or a number of meetings, concerning events in that ses-

sion or set of sessions. These comments are summarized and discussed at a subsequent gathering.

- Members provide ratings on a set of scales that ask about the climate in a given meeting. The results are summarized and discussed at a later session.
- Leaders of the group ask observers to sit at one side and observe the processes in the meeting and any occurrences that determine the flow of discussion. The observers' comments are reported and discussed at the end of that meeting.
- Small groups are appointed to discuss happenings in their group that may help or hinder it in the future. Each group is given a different question to consider. The reports of these groups are discussed at a meeting for that purpose.

When members of a group agree their unit needs to be improved, they develop new practices and put these in place. Where improvement of a group's processes requires changes in the behavior of members, the next steps may be difficult. Members may either try to improve their style of member behavior on their own, seek the advice of a few colleagues, or ask for a group discussion of changes each should try to develop in order to be more useful members.

Recommended Readings

Drucker, P. F. "The Five Most Important Questions You Will Ever Ask About Your Nonprofit Organization." In Peter F. Drucker Foundation for Nonprofit Management, *The Drucker Foundation Self-Assessment Tool for Nonprofit Organizations.* San Francisco: Jossey-Bass, 1993.
The author explains why and how members should evaluate the operations of their group or organization and provides worksheets for members to use for answering Drucker's five most important questions.

Moreland, R., and Levine, J. "Socialization in Small Groups: Temporal Changes in Individual-Group Relations." In L. Berkowitz (ed.), *Advances in Experimental Social Psychology.* Vol. 15. Orlando, Fla.: Academic Press, 1980.

This article describes how groups teach a member, over a period of time, to become more suited for membership.

Mueller, R. *Board Score: How to Judge Board Worthiness.* Lexington, Mass.: Lexington Books, 1982.
This writer has written books on ways of improving boards for profit-making organizations. In this volume he offers a set of questions and a way of scoring them so that members can give their board a grade on its performance.

Pfeiffer, J., and Jones, J. *Structured Experiences for Human Relations Training.* La Jolla, Calif.: University Associates, 1973.
This small book contains several dozen exercises and questionnaires members of groups may use to improve their understanding of how their group operates and how members relate to one another.

Rossum, C. *How to Assess Your Nonprofit Organization with Peter Drucker's Five Most Important Questions.* San Francisco: Jossey-Bass, 1993.
This volume shows readers how to use the material provided by Drucker for rating one's nonprofit organization.

REFERENCES

Adler, T. "Bad Mix: Combat Stress. Decisions." *Monitor,* Mar. 1993, p. 1.

Back, K., and others. "The Methodology of Studying Rumor Transmission." *Human Relations,* 1950, *3,* 307–312.

Bales, R. "How People Interact in Conferences." *Scientific American,* 1955, *192,* 31–35.

Banfield, E., and Wilson, J. *City Politics.* New York: Cambridge University Press, 1963.

Beer, J. *Peacemaking in Your Neighborhood: Reflections on an Experiment in Community Relations.* Philadelphia: New Society, 1986.

Bennis, W. *Organization Development: Its Nature, Origins, and Prospects.* Reading, Mass.: Addison-Wesley, 1969.

Blake, R. R., and Mouton, J. S. *Solving Costly Organizational Conflicts: Achieving Intergroup Trust, Cooperation, and Teamwork.* San Francisco: Jossey-Bass, 1984.

Bodenhausen, G., Gaelick, L., and Wyer, R. "Affective and Cognitive Factors in Intragroup and Intergroup Communication." In C. Hendrick (ed.), *Group Processes and Intergroup Relations.* Newbury Park, Calif.: Sage, 1978.

Bradford, L., Gibb, J., and Benne, K. *T-Group Theory and Laboratory Method.* New York: Wiley, 1964.

237

Brehm, S., and Brehm, J. *Psychological Reactance: A Theory of Freedom and Control.* San Diego, Calif.: Academic Press, 1981.

Brill, H. *Why Organizations Fail.* Berkeley: University of California Press, 1971.

Bunker, D. "Social Process Awareness Training: An NTL Approach." In D. Milman and G. Goldman (eds.), *Group Process Today: Evaluation and Perspective.* Springfield, Ill.: Charles C. Thomas, 1974.

Camadena, M. "Brainstorming Groups—Ambiguity Tolerance, Communication Apprehension, Task Attraction and Individual Productivity." *Small Group Research,* 1984, *15,* 251–264.

Cartwright, D. "Some Principles of Mass Persuasion: Selected Findings of Research on the Sale of United States War Bonds." *Human Relations,* 1949, *2,* 253–267.

Cartwright, D. (ed.). *Studies in Social Power.* Ann Arbor: Institute for Social Research, University of Michigan, 1959.

Cartwright, D., and Zander, A. (eds.). *Group Dynamics Research and Theory.* New York: HarperCollins, 1968.

Carver, J. *Boards That Make a Difference: A New Design for Leadership in Nonprofit and Public Organizations.* San Francisco: Jossey-Bass, 1990.

Christopher, W. *The Achieving Enterprise.* New York: American Management Association, 1974.

Cohen, A. "Upward Communication in Experimentally Created Hierarchies." *Human Relations,* 1958, *11,* 41–53.

Connolly, T., Routhieux, R., and Schneider, S. "On the Effectiveness of Group Brainstorming." *Small Group Research,* 1993, *24,* 490–503.

Craig, A. "Functional and Dysfunctional Aspects of Government Bureaucracy." In E. Vogel (ed.), *Modern Japanese Organization and Decision Making.* Tokyo: Tuttle, 1975.

Crowe, B., Bochner, S., and Clark, A. "The Effects of Subordinates' Behavior on Managerial Style." *Human Relations,* 1972, *25,* 215–237.

Delbeq, A., Van de Ven, A., and Gustafson, D. *Group Techniques for Program Planning.* Glenview, Ill.: Scott, Foresman, 1975.

Deniston, O., Rosenstock, I., and Getting, V. "Evaluation of

Program Effectiveness." *Public Health Reports,* 1986, *83,* 323–335, 603–910.

Deutsch, M. "The Effects of Cooperation and Competition upon Group Process." *Human Relations,* 1949, *2,* 129–152, 199–231.

Deutsch, M. *The Resolution of Conflict.* New Haven, Conn.: Yale University Press, 1973.

Deutsch, M. "Cooperation, Conflict, and Justice." In S. Whelan, E. Pepitone, and V. Abt (eds.), *Advances in Field Theory.* Newbury Park, Calif.: Sage, 1990.

Driskell, J., and Salas, E. "Group Decision-Making Under Stress." *Journal of Applied Psychology,* 1991, *76,* 463–478.

Drucker, P. F. "The Five Most Important Questions You Will Ever Ask About Your Nonprofit Organization." In Peter F. Drucker Foundation for Nonprofit Management, *The Drucker Foundation Self-Assessment Tool for Nonprofit Organizations.* San Francisco: Jossey-Bass, 1993.

Emerson, R. "Mount Everest: A Case Study of Communication Feedback and Sustained Goal Striving." *Sociometry,* 1966, *29,* 213–227.

Falbo, T. "Multidimensional Scaling of Power Strategies." *Journal of Personality and Social Psychology,* 1977, *35,* 537–547.

Festinger, L. "Informal Social Communication." *Psychological Review,* 1950, *57,* 271–282.

Festinger, L. *A Theory of Cognitive Dissonance.* New York: HarperCollins, 1957.

Festinger, L., Pepitone, A., and Newcomb, T. "Some Consequences of Deindividuation in a Group." *Journal of Abnormal and Social Psychology,* 1952, *47,* 382–389.

Fiedler, F. *A Theory of Leadership Effectiveness.* New York: McGraw-Hill, 1967.

Fisher, R., Ury, W. L., and Patton, B. *Getting to Yes: Negotiating Agreement Without Giving In.* Boston: Houghton Mifflin, 1991.

Fiske, S. "Controlling Other People: The Impact of Power on Stereotyping." *American Psychologist,* 1993, *48,* 621–628.

Forsyth, D. *An Introduction to Group Dynamics.* Pacific Grove, Calif.: Brooks/Cole, 1983.

Forward, J. "Group Achievement Motivation and Individual

Motives to Achieve Success and Avoid Failure." *Journal of Personality,* 1969, *37,* 297–309.

French, J., and Raven, B. "The Bases of Social Power." In D. Cartwright (ed.), *Studies in Social Power.* Ann Arbor: Institute for Social Research, University of Michigan, 1959.

Galanter, M. *Cults: Faith, Healing, and Coercion.* New York: Oxford University Press, 1989.

Goffman, I. "On Cooling the Mark Out." *Psychiatry,* 1952, *15,* 451–463.

Goldman, M., and Greason, C. "Inducing Compliance by a Two-Door-in-the-Face Procedure and a Self-Determination Request." *Journal of Social Psychology,* 1981, *114,* 229–235.

Goodstadt, B., and Kipnis, D. "Situational Influences on the Use of Power." *Journal of Applied Psychology,* 1970, *54,* 201–207.

Guzzo, R., and Waters, J. "The Expression of Affect and the Performance of Decision Making Groups." *Journal of Applied Psychology,* 1982, *67,* 67–74.

Hall, J., and Williams, M. "A Comparison of Decision-Making Performances in Established and Ad Hoc Groups." *Journal of Personality and Social Psychology,* 1966, *3,* 214–222.

Hawkinshire, F., and Ligget, J. "Lewin's Paradigm of Planned Change." In S. Whelan, E. Pepitone, and V. Abt (eds.), *Advances in Field Theory.* Newbury Park, Calif.: Sage, 1990.

Hollander, E. "Conformity, Status, and Idiosyncrasy Credit." *Psychological Review,* 1958, *65,* 117–127.

Hollander, E., and Offerman, L. "Power and Leadership in Organizations." *American Psychologist,* 1990, *45,* 179–189.

Holsti, E. "Crisis, Stress, and Decision Making." *International Social Science Journal,* 1971, *23,* 53–67.

Horwitz, M., and Berkowitz, N. "Interpersonal and Intergroup Methods of Managing Social Conflict." In S. Whelan, E. Pepitone, and V. Abt (eds.), *Advances in Field Theory.* Newbury Park, Calif.: Sage, 1990.

Hurwitz, J., Zander, A., and Hymovitch, B. "Some Effects of Power on the Relations Among Group Members." In D. Cartwright and A. Zander (eds.), *Group Dynamics Research and Theory.* New York: HarperCollins, 1968.

Janis, I. *Victims of Groupthink.* Boston: Houghton Mifflin, 1972.

Janis, I. *Crucial Decisions: Leadership in Policymaking and Crisis Management.* New York: Free Press, 1989.

Janis, I., and Mann, L. *Decision Making.* New York: Free Press, 1977.

Jones, E. *Ingratiation: A Social Psychological Analysis.* New York: Appleton-Century-Crofts, 1964.

Kahn, R., and Katz, D. "Leadership Practices in Relation to Productivity and Morale." In D. Cartwright and A. Zander (eds.), *Group Dynamics Research and Theory.* New York: HarperCollins, 1960.

Kahn, R., and others. *Organizational Stress: Studies in Role Conflict and Ambiguity.* New York: Wiley, 1964.

Kanter, R. *Commitment and Community: Communes and Utopias in Perspective.* Cambridge, Mass.: Harvard University Press, 1972.

Kelley, H. "Communication in Experimentally Created Hierarchies." *Human Relations,* 1951, *4,* 39–56.

Kelley, H., and Stahelski, A. "Social Interaction Bases of Cooperators' and Competitors' Beliefs About Others." *Journal of Personality and Social Psychology,* 1970, *16,* 66–91.

Kerr, N. "Motivation Losses in Small Groups: A Social Dilemma Analysis." *Journal of Personality and Social Psychology,* 1983, *45,* 819–828.

Kipnis, D. *The Powerholders.* Chicago: University of Chicago Press, 1976.

Kipnis, D., and Consentino, J. "Use of Leadership Powers in Industry." *Journal of Applied Psychology,* 1962, *46,* 291–295.

Kipnis, D., and Lane, W. "Self Confidence and Leadership." *Journal of Applied Psychology,* 1962, *46,* 291–295.

Kipnis, D., Schmidt, A., and Wilkinson, L. "Intraorganizational Influence Tactics: Explorations in Getting One's Way." *Journal of Applied Psychology,* 1980, *65,* 440–452.

Kramer, R. "The Effects of Resource Scarcity on Group Conflict and Cooperation." In E. Lawler and others (eds.), *Advances in Group Processes: A Research Annual.* Greenwich, Conn.: JAI Press, 1990.

Larson, C., and LaFasto, F. *Teamwork: What Must Go Right, What Can Go Wrong.* Newbury Park, Calif.: Sage, 1989.

Lebra, T. *Japanese Patterns of Behavior.* Honolulu: University of Hawaii Press, 1979.

Lederman, L. "Suffering in Silence: The Effects of Fear of Talking on Small Group Participation." *Group and Organizational Studies,* 1982, *7,* 279–284.

Levi, A., and Benjamin, A. "Jews and Arabs Rehearse Geneva: A Model of Conflict Resolution." *Human Relations,* 1976, *29,* 1035–1044.

Likert, R. *New Patterns of Management.* New York: McGraw-Hill, 1959.

Likert, R., and Likert, J. *New Ways of Managing Conflict.* New York: McGraw-Hill, 1976.

Lippitt, R., Watson, J., and Westley, B. *The Dynamics of Planned Change.* Orlando, Fla.: Harcourt Brace Jovanovich, 1958.

Lippitt, R., and others. "The Dynamics of Power." In D. Cartwright and A. Zander (eds.), *Group Dynamics Research and Theory.* New York: HarperCollins, 1968.

Littlepage, G., Nixon, C., and Gibson, C. "Influence Strategies Used in Meetings." *Journal of Social Behavior and Personality,* 1992, *7,* 529–538.

Locke, E., and Latham, G. *A Theory of Goal Setting and Task Performance.* Englewood Cliffs, N.J.: Prentice-Hall, 1990.

Lohmann, R. A. *The Commons: New Perspectives on Nonprofit Organizations and Voluntary Action.* San Francisco: Jossey-Bass, 1992.

Lorsch, J., and MacIver, E. *Pawns or Potentates: The Reality of America's Corporate Boards.* Cambridge, Mass.: Harvard University Press, 1986.

McGregor, D. *The Human Side of Enterprise.* New York: McGraw-Hill, 1959.

Medow, H., and Zander, A. "Aspirations for Group Chosen by Central and Peripheral Members." *Journal of Personality and Social Psychology,* 1965, *1,* 224–228.

Messé, L., Kerr, N., and Satler, D. "But Some Animals Are More Equal Than Others: The Supervisor as a Privileged Status." In S. Worchel, W. Wood, and J. Simpson (eds.), *Group Process and Productivity.* Newbury Park, Calif.: Sage, 1992.

Middleton, M. *The Place and Power of Nonprofit Boards of Directors.* New Haven, Conn.: Institution for Policy Studies, Yale University, 1983.

Mohr, L. "The Concept of Organizational Goal." *American Political Science Review,* 1973, *62,* 470–481.

Moore, C. *Group Techniques for Idea Building.* Newbury Park, Calif.: Sage, 1987.

Moreland, R., and Levine, J. "Socialization in Small Groups: Temporal Changes in Individual-Group Relations." In L. Berkowitz (ed.), *Advances in Experimental Social Psychology.* Vol. 15. Orlando, Fla.: Academic Press, 1980.

Moreland, R., and Levine, J. "Problem Identification in Groups." In S. Worchel, W. Wood, and J. Simpson (eds.), *Group Processes and Productivity.* Newbury Park, Calif.: Sage, 1992.

Morris, C., and Hackman, J. "Behavioral Correlates of Perceived Leadership." *Journal of Personality and Social Psychology,* 1960, *13,* 350–361.

Mullen, B., and Baumeister, R. "Group Effects of Self-Attention and Performance — Social Loafing, Social Facilitation and Social Impairment." In C. Hendrick (ed.), *Group Processes and Intergroup Relations.* Newbury Park, Calif.: Sage, 1987.

Mummendey, A., and Otten, S. "Aggression: Interaction Between Individuals and Groups." In R. Felson and J. Tedeschi (eds.), *Aggression and Violence, Social Interactionist Perspectives.* Washington, D.C.: American Psychological Association, 1993.

Nagasandaram, M., and Dennis, A. "When a Group Is Not a Group: The Cognitive Foundation of Group Idea Generation." *Small Group Research,* 1993, *24,* 453–489.

Napier, R., and Gershenfeld, M. *Groups, Theory and Experience.* Boston: Houghton Mifflin, 1993.

Nemeth, C. "Minority Dissent as a Stimulant to Group Performance." In S. Worchel, W. Wood, and J. Simpson (eds.), *Group Process and Productivity.* Newbury Park, Calif.: Sage, 1992.

Nemiroff, P., and King, D. "Group Decision Making Performance as Influenced by Consensus and Self-Orientation." *Human Relations,* 1975, *28,* 1–21.

O'Connor, K., Gruenfeld, D., and McGrath, J. "The Experience and Effects of Conflict in Continuing Work Groups." *Small Group Research,* 1993, *24,* 362–382.

Orwell, G. *Animal Farm.* Orlando, Fla.: Harcourt Brace Jovanovich, 1946.

Osborn, F. *Applied Imagination.* New York: Charles Scribner's Sons, 1937.

Patchen, M. "Reciprocity of Coercion and Cooperation Between Individuals and Nations." In R. Felson and J. Tedeschi (eds.), *Aggression and Violence, Social Interactionist Perspectives.* Washington, D.C.: American Psychological Association, 1993.

Pavitt, C. "What (Little) We Know About Formal Group Discussion Procedures." *Small Group Research,* 1993, *24,* 217–235.

Pruitt, D. "Methods for Resolving Differences of Interest: A Theoretical Analysis." *Journal of Social Issues,* 1972, *28,* 133–154.

Pruitt, D., and Rubin, J. *Social Conflict: Escalation, Stalemate, and Settlement.* New York: Random House, 1986.

Pruitt, D., and others. "Aggression as a Struggle Tactic in Social Conflict." In R. Felson and J. Tedeschi (eds.), *Aggression and Violence, Social Interactionist Perspectives.* Washington, D.C.: American Psychological Association, 1993.

Raven, B. "A Power/Interaction Model of Interpersonal Influence: French and Raven Thirty Years Later." *Journal of Social Behavior and Personality,* 1992, *7,* 217–244.

Rohlen, T. "The Company Work Group." In E. Vogel (ed.), *Modern Japanese Organization and Decision Making.* Tokyo: Tuttle, 1975.

Rosenfeld, H., and Zander, A. "The Influence of Teachers on the Aspirations of Students." *Journal of Educational Psychology,* 1961, *52,* 1–11.

Rossum, C. *How to Assess Your Nonprofit Organization with Peter Drucker's Five Most Important Questions.* San Francisco: Jossey-Bass, 1993.

Rothman, J., Erlich, J., and Teresa, J. *Promoting Innovation and Change in Organizations and Communities.* New York: Wiley, 1976.

St. Antoine, T. "Arbitration and the Law." In A. Zack (ed.),

Arbitration in Practice. Ithaca, N.Y.: Cornell University Press, 1984.

Savard, C., and Roger, R. "A Self-Efficacy and Subjective Utility Theory Analysis of the Selection and Use of Influence Strategies." *Journal of Social Behavior and Personality,* 1992, *7,* 273–292.

Schacter, S. "Deviation, Rejection, and Communication." *Journal of Abnormal and Social Psychology,* 1951, *46,* 190–207.

Schnurman, M. "Kissing-Up to the Boss May Smack of Insincerity, But It Works." *Contra Costa Times,* September 26, 1993, p. 8C.

Schopler, J., and others. "Individual-Group Discontinuity: Further Evidence for Mediation by Fear and Greed." *Personality and Social Psychology Bulletin,* 1993, *19,* 419–431.

Scott, W. *Values and Organizations.* Skokie, Ill.: Rand McNally, 1965.

Shaw, M. E. *Group Dynamics: The Psychology of Small Group Behavior.* New York: McGraw-Hill, 1981.

Sherif, M., and others. *Intergroup Conflict and Cooperation: The Robber's Cave Experiment.* Norman, Okla.: University of Oklahoma Press, 1961.

Stasser, G. "Pooling of Unshared Information During Group Discussions." In S. Worchel, W. Wood, and J. Simpson (eds.), *Group Process and Productivity.* Newbury Park, Calif.: Sage, 1992.

Tannenbaum, R. *Control in Organizations.* New York: McGraw-Hill, 1968.

'tHart, P. *Groupthink in Government: A Study of Small Groups and Policy Failure.* Lisse, The Netherlands: Swets and Zeitlinger, 1990.

Thomas, E., and Zander, A. "The Relationship of Goal Structure to Motivation Under Extreme Conditions." *Journal of Individual Psychology,* 1959, *15,* 121–127.

Turner, M. "Group Effectiveness Under Threat." *Journal of Social Behavior and Personality,* 1992, *7,* 511–528.

Tyler, T. "The Psychology of Procedural Justice: A Test of the Group-Value Model." *Journal of Personality and Social Psychology,* 1989, *57,* 1–9.

Ury, W. L., Brett, J. M., and Goldberg, S. B. *Getting Disputes Resolved: Designing Systems to Cut the Costs of Conflict.* San Francisco: Jossey-Bass, 1989.

Vogel, E. (ed.). *Modern Japanese Organization and Decision Making.* Tokyo: Tuttle, 1975.

Vogel, E. *Japan as Number One, Lessons for America.* Tokyo: Tuttle, 1979.

Vroom, V., and Yetton, P. *Leadership and Decision Making.* Pittsburgh: University of Pittsburgh Press, 1973.

Walster, E., Berscheid, E., and Walster, G. "The Exploited: Justice or Justification?" In J. Macauley and L. Berkowitz (eds.), *Altruism and Coping Behavior.* San Diego, Calif.: Academic Press, 1971.

Walton, R., and Dutton, J. "Organizational Context and Interdepartmental Conflict." *Administrative Science Quarterly,* 1969, *14,* 522–543.

Weicker, A. "Behavior Settings Reconsidered: Temporal Stages, Resources, Internal Dynamics, Context." In D. Stokols and A. Altman (eds.), *Handbook of Environmental Psychology.* New York: Wiley, 1987.

Wheelan, S., and McKeage, R. "Developmental Patterns in Small and Large Groups." *Small Group Research,* 1993, *24,* 60–83.

Whyte, W. *The Organization Man.* New York: Doubleday, 1957.

Wiggins, J., Dill, F., and Schwartz, R. "On Status-Liability." *Sociometry,* 1965, *28,* 197–209.

Witteman, H. "Group Members' Satisfaction: A Conflict-Related Account." *Small Group Research,* 1991, *22,* 24–58.

Zajonc, R. "The Process of Cognitive Tuning in Communication." *Journal of Abnormal and Social Psychology,* 1960, *61,* 159–167.

Zander, A. *Motives and Goals in Groups.* San Diego, Calif.: Academic Press, 1971.

Zander, A. *Groups at Work.* San Francisco: Jossey-Bass, 1977a.

Zander, A. "Recruiting and Removing Members." In A. Zander, *Groups at Work.* San Francisco: Jossey-Bass, 1977b.

Zander, A. "The Discussion of Recombinant DNA at the University of Michigan." In D. Jackson and S. Stich (eds.), *The*

Recombinant DNA Debate. Englewood Cliffs, N.J.: Prentice-Hall, 1979.

Zander, A. "The Value of Belonging to a Group in Japan." *Small Group Behavior,* 1983, *14,* 3–14.

Zander, A. *The Purposes of Groups and Organizations.* San Francisco: Jossey-Bass, 1985.

Zander, A. *Effective Social Action by Community Groups.* San Francisco: Jossey-Bass, 1990.

Zander, A. *Making Boards Effective: The Dynamics of Nonprofit Governing Boards.* San Francisco: Jossey-Bass, 1993.

Zander, A., Cohen, A., and Stotland, E. "Power and the Relations Among Professions." In D. Cartwright (ed.), *Studies in Social Power.* Ann Arbor: Institute for Social Research, University of Michigan, 1959.

Zander, A., Forward, J., and Albert, R. "Adaptation of Board Members to Repeated Success or Failure by Their Organization." *Organizational Behavior and Human Performance,* 1969, *4,* 56–76.

Zander, A., and Newcomb, T., Jr. "Group Levels of Aspiration in United Fund Campaigns." *Journal of Personality and Social Psychology,* 1976, *6,* 157–162.

Zander, A., and Quinn, R. "The Social Environment and Mental Health: A Review of Past Research at the Institute for Social Research." *Journal of Social Issues,* 1962, *18,* 48–67.

Zander, A., and Wolfe, D. "Administrative Rewards and Coordination Among Committee Members." *Administrative Science Quarterly,* 1964, *9,* 50–69.

Zeigler, H., Kehoe, E., and Reisman, J. *City Managers and School Superintendents: Response to Community Conflict.* New York: Praeger, 1985.

INDEX